BASIC AND APPLIED PERSPECTIVES ON LEARNING, COGNITION, AND DEVELOPMENT

The Minnesota Symposia on Child Psychology

Volume 28

BASIC AND APPLIED PERSPECTIVES ON LEARNING, COGNITION, AND DEVELOPMENT

The Minnesota Symposia on Child Psychology

Volume 28

edited by

CHARLES A. NELSON

University of Minnesota

Routledge

Taylor & Francis Group

LONDON AND NEW YORK

First published 1995 by Lawrence Erlbaum Associates, Inc.

Published 2018 by Routledge
2 Park Square, Milton Park, Abingdon, Oxon, OX14 4RN
52 Vanderbilt Avenue, New York, NY 10017

First issued in paperback 2018

Routledge is an imprint of the Taylor & Francis Group, an informa business

Library of Congress Cataloging-in-Publication Data

Basic and applied perspectives on learning, cognition, and development / edited by Charles A. Nelson.
p. cm. — (Minnesota symposium on child psychology ; v. 28)
Includes bibliographical references and index.
ISBN 0-8058-1833-2 (alk. paper)
1. Cognition in children. 2. Connectionism. 3. Learning, Psychology of. 4. Language acquisition. 5. Mathematics—Psychological aspects. I. Nelson, Charles A. (Charles Alexander) II. Series: Minnesota symposia on child psychology (Series) ; v. 28.
BF723.C5B28 1995
153.1′5—dc20 95-24726
CIP

ISBN 13: 978-1-138-98116-4 (pbk)
ISBN 13: 978-0-8058-1833-8 (hbk)

Contents

Preface vii

1. **Self-Organizing Processes in Learning to Learn Words: Development is not Induction** 1
Linda B. Smith

2. **Connectionism and Language Learning** 33
Brian MacWhinney and Franklin Chang

3. **Systems Learning Symbol Systems: Commentary on MacWhinney and Smith** 59
Karen Freeman and Gedeon Deák

4. **Inventing Arithmetic: Making Children's Intuition Work in School** 75
Lauren B. Resnick

5. **Learning Mathematics From Classroom Instruction: Cross-Cultural and Experimental Perspectives** 103
James W. Stigler and Clea Fernandez

6. **Mathematics Achievement of American Students: First in the World by the Year 2000?** 131
Harold W. Stevenson

7. Research and Reform for U.S. Mathematics Education: What Counts? A Commentary on Stevenson, Stigler and Fernandez, and Resnick **151**
Kathleen E. Kremer, Emma K. Adam, and Shane R. Jimerson

8. An Evolutionary Approach to Cognition and Learning **175**
William R. Charlesworth

9. The Evolution of Mind and Culture: A Commentary on Charlesworth **219**
James E. Turnure

Author Index **233**
Subject Index **241**

Preface

This volume represents the papers presented at the 28th Minnesota Symposium on Child Psychology, held in October 1993, at the University of Minnesota, Minneapolis. As has been true since the inception of the Minnesota Symposia series, the faculty of the Institute of Child Development invited an internationally renowned group of investigators to present their work and to consider problems of mutual concern.

The current volume is primarily concerned with basic and applied aspects of cognitive development. As students of this field are well aware, although our current views of cognitive development owe a great deal to Jean Piaget, this field has undergone profound change in the years since Piaget's death. This can be witnessed both by the influence connectionist and dynamical systems models have exerted on theories of cognition and language, and by how basic work in cognitive development has begun to influence those who work in applied (e.g., educational) settings. This volume brings together an eclectic group of distinguished experts who represent the full spectrum of basic to applied aspects of cognitive development.

The volume opens with chapters on cognition (by Linda Smith) and language (by Brian MacWhinney and Franklin Chang) that represent the current zeitgeist in cognitive science—dynamical systems and connectionist views of cognition. Smith considers the problem of learning biases, paying particular attention to shape bias. She argues that novel word interpretations are derived from self-organizing attentional processes that create learning biases as learning unfolds. MacWhinney and Chang describe their work with connectionist approaches to language learning. Using German as an example, the authors provide powerful models of lexical learning, inflectional morphology, and role assignment. Overall, MacWhinney and Chang provide a compelling approach to language learning. Karen Freeman and Gedeon Deák then provide a wonderful commentary on the first two chapters. Although Dęák and Freeman applaud Smith, and MacWhinney and Chang, for their experimental rigor and innovative approaches to studying language acquisition, they raise the issue of whether these approaches (connectionist and dynamical systems) are psychologically plausible. It is left to the reader to decide the issue.

After these introductory chapters, the next section of the book turns to more applied issues. Although the focus of the chapters by Lauren Resnick, James Stigler and Clea Fernandez, and Harold Stevenson primarily deal with arithmetic learning, the research programs described in these chapters have profound implications for virtually all aspects of education and learning. Resnick, for example, presents a wonderful exposition of "invented arithmetic." Drawing on her own extensive research program, she argues that even young children possess the cognitive sophistication to engage in thinking that reflects true mathematical reasoning. Resnick's chapter is complemented by that of Stigler and Fernandez. These authors primarily deal with how children learn mathematics from classroom instruction. What is refreshing about this work is that it bridges the gap between experimental work in cognitive development (e.g., children's learning) and curriculum instruction. In addition, it accomplishes this feat in a cross-cultural context, paying particular attention to American and Japanese educational systems. The last chapter in this section is by Harold Stevenson. Stevenson, too, deals primarily with mathematics education, and presents a comprehensive review of his own research program. The theme of this chapter is concerned with differences in how Americans educate their children, relative to educators in Asia and to some degree, Europe. Also touched on are differences in the expectations children and parents in these cultures have of the educational system. A commentary on these three chapters is then provided by Kathleen Kremer, Emma Adam, and Shane Jimerson.

The final chapter in the book is by William Charlesworth. Charlesworth attempts to view cognitive development from the perspectives of ethology and evolutionary biology, and in so doing provides a theoretical perspective that is novel and in some ways, prescient: for example, how can our views of cognition incorporate recent work in biology? A commentary on this last chapter is then provided by James Turnure.

Collectively, the chapters presented in this volume represent a continuing attempt by this editor to bring seemingly disparate fields together under one "roof" to provide a coherent picture of child development. In the present case, my goal was to begin a dialogue with those who study children's learning in experimental settings with those who study children's learning in more naturalistic settings, and who have an eye towards the application of basic research.

The Minnesota Symposium has a long and cherished history here at the Institute of Child Development. Many people are responsible for assisting me in making the symposium itself, and the resulting volume, a success. First and foremost, of course, I owe my thanks to the presenters and contributors. Second, the graduate students at the Institute of Child Development deserve thanks for attending to many of the administrative details of the symposium. Third, I owe my eternal gratitude to my secretary LuJean Huffman-Nordberg, without whom neither the symposium itself nor the volume would exist. Finally, I would like to acknowledge the financial support for the symposium from the Institute of Child Development (Richard Weinberg, Director), the College of Education (Robert Bruininks, Dean), the Center for Research in Learning, Perception, and Cognition (Albert Yonas, Director), the Center for Applied Research in Educational Improvement (Geoffrey Maruyama, director), and lastly, the NIH-supported (5-T32-HD07279) Biobehavioral Training Grant in Developmental Disabilities (Megan Gunnar, Robert Blum, and Charles A. Nelson, directors).

Charles A. Nelson

1 Self-Organizing Processes in Learning to Learn Words: Development is not Induction

Linda B. Smith
Indiana University

Young children are so adept at learning words that they often learn an object name from hearing a single object named. For example, a 2-year-old who sees a tractor for the first time and is told that it is a *tractor* is likely, from that moment forward, to recognize and name a variety of other tractors. How is it that young children do this? How do they know which of the object's properties are relevant to what it is called? In this chapter, I propose the answer lies, in part, in the self-organizing processes of attention—processes that fuse past experience and immediate context to create learning biases on-line.

This proposal turns upside-down some usual ideas about what makes a learner smart. Children are characteristically viewed as smart word learners because word learning is directed, constrained, and characterized by many regularities. The account offered here suggests that the directed, constrained, and stable properties of children's early word learning are the developmental product of processes that are undirected, open, and variable.

The plan of the chapter is as follows: First, I consider the problem of learning biases—the indeterminacy of experience, the induction problem, and the current disputes about biased learning in children. Second, I present in some detail empirical findings on the developmental and contextual fluidity of the "shape bias," one of the biases evident in early word learning. This evidence shows that children's novel word interpretations change continuously, that they become increasingly context dependent, and that they are influenced by a variety of factors from syntax to the twinkling of glitter. Third, I offer an account of these data in terms of self-organizing attentional processes that create learning biases *in the moment* of learning. Finally, I consider more generally how "constrained" development may be the emergent property of a complex dynamic system. These ideas in their broad form have a long history in developmental psychology; nonetheless, they still hold profound promise for understanding and encouraging learning.

BIASED LEARNING

Indeterminacy

In introducing a series of papers by eminent developmentalists, Gelman (1990) pointed to attention as a key theoretical problem. She asked "how it is that our young attend to inputs that will support the development of concepts they share with their elders" (p. 3). The problem of selecting the right information for learning from the environment is ubiquitous in cognitive science because of the indeterminacy of environmental information. There is an infinite number of objectively correct descriptions consistent with any stimulus domain—of English sentences, of visual scenes, of speech, of objects. This fact means that unbiased experience is insufficient to single out a particular interpretation of the world.

Quine's (1960) riddle concerning the indeterminacy of translation illustrates the problem nicely for the task of word learning: Imagine that you are in a new land with a foreign language. After some time in this land and merely from hearing natives use the language, you acquire words and phrases and ultimately achieve some fluency. But how do you do this? And given that you do, how do you know that what you have taken a word to mean in this language is what the native speaker means it to mean? When a rabbit hops by and the native says "rabbit," is he saying "hopping," "white," "furry," "long ears," "rabbit," "rabbit parts," all of these, or some of these? Critically, you would not be able to acquire the same word meanings as the native if you and the native did not construe the world in the same way. Since people do learn words, the conclusion from this riddle is that people interpret experience in only some ways and not others; that is, learning is biased.

There are not only philosophical arguments for biased learning. There is also evidence that children are highly biased word learners. They interpret novel count nouns as referring to categories of similar objects and not to an individual object (Katz, Baker, & Macnamara, 1974); they interpret novel words as referring to objects that have not been named (Markman, 1989); they interpret novel words as referring to taxonomically and not thematically related objects (Markman, 1991; Waxman & Kosowski, 1990); and they interpret novel count nouns as referring to objects that are similar in shape (Landau, Smith, & Jones, 1988).

The *fact* that children's early word learning is biased is incontestible. The *idea* of biased learning, however, has been contested.

The Induction Problem

The controversy revolves around the conceptualization of learning biases as "solutions to the induction problem." The induction problem results from a highly abstract conceptualization of learning coupled with the indeterminacy of experience. This conceptualization treats knowledge as a set of beliefs and learning as a process of induction—as hypothesis generation and confirmation. For example, Osherson, Stob, and Weinstein (1986) described learning as consisting of:

> 1. a learner,
> 2. a thing to be learned,
> 3. an environment in which the thing to be learned is exhibited to the learner,
> 4. the hypotheses that occur to the learner about the thing to be learned on the basis of the environment.
>
> Learning is said to be successful in a given environment if the learner's hypothesis about the thing to be learned eventually becomes stable and accurate (p.7).

The problem with learning construed in this way is that it is well understood to be nearly impossible (see, for example, Fodor, 1987; Piatelli-Palmarini, 1989). Given the indeterminacy of environmental input, no single induction will be uniquely determined by any set of experiences (Goodman, 1955). For example, the continued experience of hearing rabbits called *rabbit* is consistent with the induction that *rabbit* means rabbit, with the induction that *rabbit* means rabbit parts, and with the induction that *rabbit* means rabbit up until February 2020. This then is the induction problem: *If* learning consists of hypothesis generation and confirmation, then learning is not possible. This induction problem can be solved, however, if limits are placed on the kinds of hypotheses that can be entertained, *if* some hypotheses are not allowed.

Learning Biases as Constraints

The findings on children's biased word learning are often interpreted in these terms—as "constraints on hypotheses" that "solve the induction problem," "limit the hypothesis space," and "rule out" alternatives (see Markman, 1989; 1992; Woodward & Markman, 1991). In this view, the reason word learning is fast and lexical development is orderly is because learning and development are proscribed by internal constraints. Word learning is smart in this view because children know before they start what word meanings are possible. Biased learning thus takes on considerable importance in the philosophical frame of the induction problem. Children's word learning biases are seen as foundational and as universal properties of mind; they are why the lexical categories of language are structured as they are *and not some other way*. It is this interpretation of biased learning that has proven contentious among developmentalists.

Much of the debate has centered on whether this *idea* of constraints implies innate and fixed word learning principles. Constraints that solve the induction problem have been interpreted as "hard-wired" because by this view of learning, *no* learning can occur unless the hypothesis space is limited—unless some hypotheses are explicitly ruled out. Thus constraints can not themselves be learned unless there are constraints on constraints (see Fodor, 1987, for explicit discussions of this implication). Many developmentalists object to the idea of fixed constraints because the evidence on children's word learning suggests that it is neither rigid, innate, nor unaffected by input (see Kuczaj, 1990; Merriman & Bowman, 1989; Nelson, 1988; MacWhinney, 1991). Others (Markman, 1992; Woodward & Markman, 1991), however, have argued that these critics overinterpret the implications of constraints. In this view, children's word learning biases can solve the induction problem without being caused by hard-and-fast rules. Rather, there may be default assumptions about the meanings of words, assumptions that guide learning but that can be overridden with strong counter examples. Moreover, although constraints can not themselves be learned (and still solve the induction problem), they may develop according to some maturational plan that depends on input.

What Do Developmentalists Want?

In a thoughtful review of the disputes surrounding biased word learning, Siegler (1992) pointed to what may be the core cause of developmentalists' discomfort with the idea of constraints. He asked what it was that developmentalists want from a theory of development. The treatment of learning biases as constraints on induction shifts biased learning from a phenomenon to be explained to a solution to a philosophical perplexity. The empirical focus becomes not the processes that enable children to interpret words in context but whether children's biased learning has the properties needed to "solve the induction problem." The present thesis is that the induction problem is (or should be) irrelevant to developmentalists. Learning is not necessarily hypothesis testing. Development is not induction. Learning in living organisms is of far greater complexity than philosophical discussion admits.

I turn now to empirical studies that support this conclusion. The evidence on the development of a shape bias in learning nouns suggests a profoundly different vision of children's biased word learning than does the induction problem. Learning biases are revealed as the exquisite transient products of a history of undirected complex processes. The results provide a more deeply *developmental* rather than philosophical solution to indeterminacy.

THE ORIGINS OF THE SHAPE BIAS

The importance of shape in early word learning was first noticed by Clark (1973) in her analyses of diary records of children's early word use. She observed that young children's noun overextensions occurred when the known referent was similar in shape to the new object (see also Anglin, 1977; Bowerman, 1977). More recently, Barbara Landau, Susan Jones, and I used artificial word learning tasks to study the role of shape in children's learning of names for concrete things. In these tasks, we present children with a novel object, name it, and then ask what other objects have the same name. For example in our first study (Landau, Smith, & Jones, 1988), we presented children with the exemplar shown in Fig. 1.1 and named it, "This is a dax." We then showed children the test objects also illustrated in Fig. 1.1 and asked about each test object, "Is this a dax?" Children systematically extended the new "name" to test objects that were the same shape as the exemplar but refused to call different shaped (but same texture or size) test objects by the name.

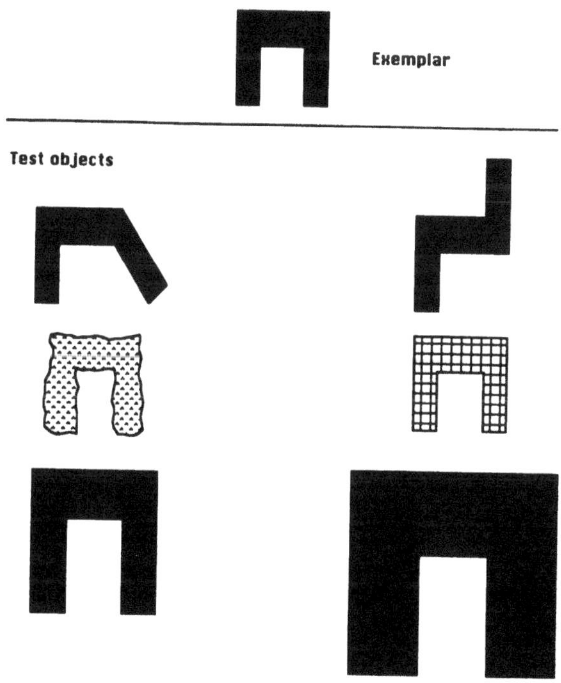

FIG. 1.1. Sample stimuli from Landau, Smith, and Jones (1988). All stimuli were three-dimensional objects made of wood, wire or sponge.

Critically, this shape bias was evident only in a word learning task. In a second similarity judgment task, children were shown the exemplar and test objects but only asked about each test object whether it was *like* the exemplar. In this nonnaming task, children did not attend exclusively to shape. Instead, they attended to all the dimensions—shape, texture, and size—and judged objects to be alike if they differed by a small amount on any dimension and judged the objects to be different if they differed by a large amount on any dimension. This finding of a shape bias that is specific to children's generalization of object names has been replicated a number of times in several laboratories (e.g., Imai, Gentner, & Uchida, 1993; Smith, Jones, & Landau, 1991; Soja, 1992).

The shape bias has all the properties one would expect of a word-learning constraint that "solves the induction problem." It limits the hypothesis space: Children do not interpret a noun as referring to any kind of category but to categories of similarly shaped objects. It is early: children as young as 2 years-of-age have been shown to generalize newly learned nouns by shape. It is lexically specific: Children do not just always attend to shape regardless of the task but do so specifically when naming objects. Finally, it is helpful: Many common nouns refer to categories of similarly shaped objects (Biederman, 1987; Rosch, 1978), so a shape bias guides initial hypotheses in a likely right direction.

A Learned Shape Bias

A first question to ask about the shape bias concerns its developmental origins. Where does the shape bias come from? One possibility is that the shape bias preexists word learning—that it is either innate or derives from category knowledge acquired prelingually before children learn words. Another possibility is that the shape bias emerges in the course of early word learning. Children do not acquire their very *first* words rapidly (e.g., Bloom, Lifter, & Broughton, 1985; Dromi, 1987; Goldfield & Resnick, 1990). Rather, fast word learning occurs after children have already learned some initial words. In light of this developmental pattern, Markman (1992) hypothesized that children might learn their first words by "brute force" but that "word-learning constraints should be available to babies by the time they are capable of fast word learning" (p. 60). What process might make word learning constraints "available?"

We hypothesized that the shape bias might be a learned generalization from language input, that children learn to attend to shape by learning some initial set of words—a set that includes names for many shape-based categories. We sought evidence for this idea in a longitudinal study of seven children from 15 to 20 months-of-age (Jones, Smith, Landau, & Gershkoff-Stowe, 1992; Smith, Jones, Landau, & Gershkoff-Stowe, 1994). Parents kept diary records of all new words spoken by their child. At the beginning of the study, the children had very few words in their productive vocabulary (the children with the fewest words had less than 5). At the end of the study, each child had over 150 words and for each child more than half of these named concrete objects. Thus, if the shape bias is learned from learning words, children should not show a shape bias at the beginning of the study but should show one at the end—after they had learned a number of object names.

We tested this prediction by having the children come into the laboratory every 3 weeks to participate in a novel word-learning task. The stimuli used in that task are shown in Fig. 1.2. They include an exemplar object made of wood and three test objects that matched the exemplar in either color, shape, or texture. The word learning task was organized into four stages: (a) The exemplar and test objects were placed on the table and the child was allowed to play with them; (b) the experimenter picked up the exemplar and said, "This is a dax. Look this is a dax"; (c) the experimenter, still holding the exemplar, held out her other hand, palm up and said, "Give me a dax. Give me another dax"; (d) all objects handed over were placed back on the table and children were allowed to play with them. Children were tested with the same stimulus objects and novel name each week.

We calculated the mean number of times per session that children selected (pointed to, handed over, or named "dax") the test object that matched the exemplar in shape, in color, or in texture as a function of the number of object names in the child's productive vocabulary. Objects' names were defined as nouns that named concrete objects and included common names, proper names (e.g., mommy), and onomatopoeia used referentially (e.g., choo-choo).

The results are shown in Fig. 1.3. As is apparent, shape choices did not predominate early in the study but did by the end. More specifically, children began to systematically extend the novel word "dax" to the same shape test object *after* they had 50 object names (and about 80 total words) in their productive vocabulary. This point (50 object names) in the word learning trajectory is

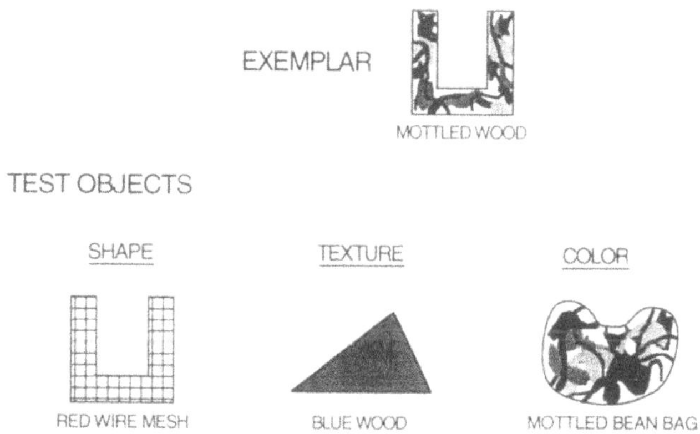

FIG. 1.2. Stimuli used in the longitudinal study of the development of the shape bias.

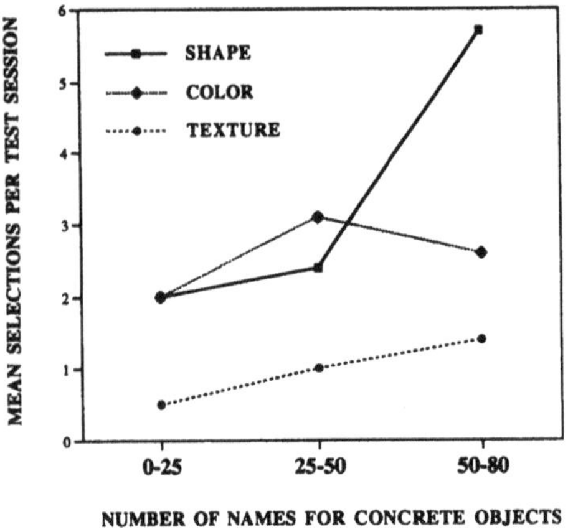

FIG. 1.3. Mean number of selections of test objects that matched the exemplar in shape, color, or texture as a function of the mean number of object names in the child's productive vocabulary.

after the spurt in noun acquisitions known as the "naming explosion" as defined by Gopnik and Meltzoff (1987; see also Dromi, 1987; Gershkoff-Stowe & Smith, 1995). The developmental timing of the shape bias thus suggests that it may be the consequence of word learning—the consequence of learning some number of names for shape-based categories.

Talking and Attending

Two subsequent experiments showed the emergence of the shape bias to be linked to the transient developmental phenomenon of lexical overextensions (Smith, Jones, Landau, & Gershkoff-Stowe, 1994). Our original plan in these experiments was to test the hypothesis that the shape bias was lexically specific—from its very beginning. We reasoned that even very young children should attend to shape only in naming tasks and not in other tasks if the shape bias is learned from learning words. To test this prediction, we presented different groups of 18- and 24-month-olds with either a novel word interpretation task or a similarity judgment task. We found no shape bias for 18-month-olds in either task—just as expected if these children had not learned enough shape-based lexical categories to show a robust shape bias. Contrary to expectations, however, we found a strong shape bias for 24-month-olds in *both* the similarity and naming tasks. Is the shape bias, then, not specific to *naming* early in development?

Children's spontaneous naming behavior in the experiment suggests that the shape bias is specific to the activity of naming. Although we had assigned half the 24-month-olds to a nonnaming Similarity task, these 24-month-olds had assigned themselves to the naming task. On the basis of these children's behavior, we suspect that there may be no such thing as a nonnaming task for a 2-year-old. Specifically, the 2-year-olds in the Similarity task repeatedly tried to name the objects —offering English names for our laboratory creations. Fig. 1.4 shows some examples of the names offered by the children. Although they are not easily predicted *a priori*, in retrospect the offered names appear to be based on aspects of shape. These results suggest that young children's overextensions in the early course of language learning may be intimately related to the development of the shape bias. And like the shape bias, these overextensions may arise because children have learned that names for common objects often refer to objects of similar shape.

We pursued the co-occurrence of spontaneous naming, the overgeneralization of English names to novel objects, and attention to shape in a second experiment. We used only the similarity judgment task. On each of four trials, we presented children with a set of novel (laboratory created) objects. The children were allowed to interact freely with the objects. Then we picked up one object and asked the child to give us one "like it." We never named any object but we recorded all attempts by the children to name these objects with recognizable English names and their judgments of "likeness." The children were 18-, 20-, 24-, 30- and 36-months-of-age. The results are shown in Fig. 1.5. As is apparent, there is both a rise and fall in spontaneous attempts to name these objects with English words and a rise and fall in attending to shape when making similarity judgments. Spontaneous naming, overgeneralization of English nouns and attention to shape change together.

These results show that both behaviorally and developmentally, the behavior of naming and attending to shape co-occur. However, overgeneralized naming and the attention to shape that it recruits, decline with age. From other experiments, we know that 36-month-olds focus on shape when naming objects (e.g., Landau et al., 1988). But in this experiment, 36-month-olds did not focus on shape when making similarity judgments and they did not spontaneously name objects. Instead, 36-month-olds attended to a variety of object attributes and they said such things as "Did you make this?" "Is this clay?" Apparently, 36-month-

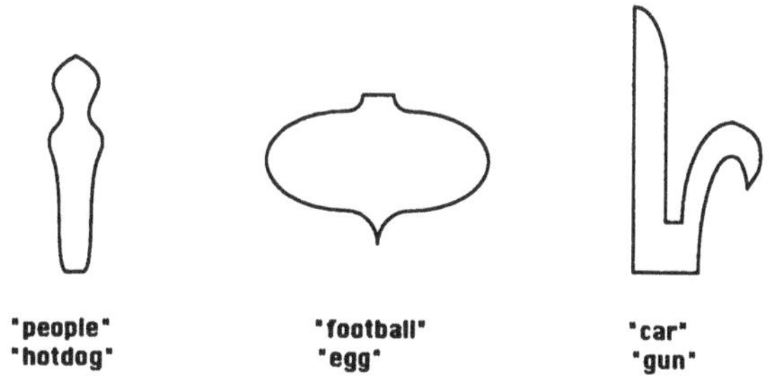

FIG. 1.4. Examples of overgeneralizations of English words offered by the 24-month-olds in the non-naming similarity judgment task. All stimuli were 3-dimensional objects.

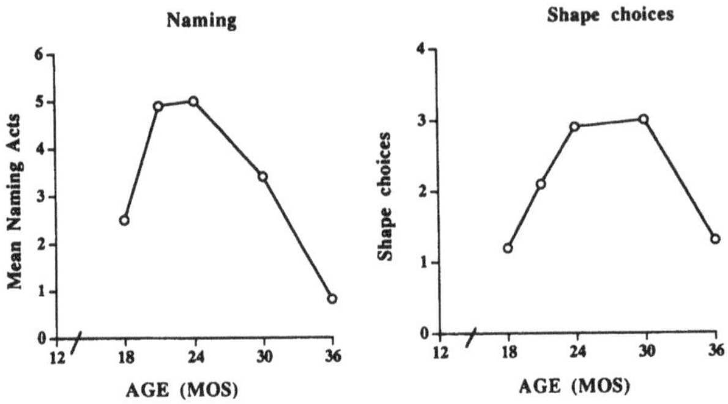

FIG. 1.5. Mean number of English names offered for novel objects in a Similarity judgment task as a function of age and mean number of same-shape choices in that same Similarity judgment task as a function of age.

olds know too much to be only interested in naming and they know too much to only attend to shape.

Why do spontaneous naming and attention to shape emerge together? It seems likely that both behaviors originate in the initial learning of some object names. This learning gives rise to the self-generated activity of naming and this activity recruits attention to shape. Why do spontaneous overextensions and attention to shape in nonnaming tasks decline? Perhaps because the activity of naming invites new learning. By attending to shape, by *offering* names for novel objects, children put themselves in a new learning environment from which they may learn even more how objects are named and about different kinds of tasks.

Unconstrained Learning

The results of these experiments suggest that the shape bias is a product of word learning. A *learned* constraint is a problem if the theoretical purpose of constraints is to "solve the induction problem." The shape bias, once acquired, might "solve" the induction problem for learning nouns by limiting children's hypotheses to ones about (or consistent with) similarity in shape. But a *learned* constraint presents a new induction problem—the problem of how the shape bias itself is induced from experience. One possible solution to this new induction problem is that the shape bias is somehow innately specified but made available (triggered) by initial word learning. However, we do not need to postulate unknown innate mechanisms nor unknown triggering devices. There are well-known and specifiable learning mechanisms through which a shape bias can be easily learned.

To demonstrate this fact, Michael Gasser and I asked a connectionist network—a relatively unconstrained general-purpose learning device—to learn a shape bias (for related simulations, see Gasser & Smith, 1991, 1995; Smith 1993). We used the three layer network illustrated in Fig. 1.6. The objects to be named by the network were presented as patterns of activation on the input layer. Objects were specified in terms of distributed representations on four dimensions. One of these input dimensions was arbitrarily deemed *shape*. The names for objects were represented by patterns of activation on the output layer. The "hidden" layer between input and output represents the internal representations that emerge in response to an object as it is named. As in all connectionist networks, what the network knows resides in the connection weights between layers and the network learns by changing these connection weights in response to experience. We used the common learning algorithm called back propagation in which connection weights are adjusted as a consequence of the degree of difference (the error) between the output of the network and the correct response (the target).

We taught the network names for categories of objects—some of which were organized by similarity in shape and some of which were not. We did not present the network with only shape-based categories because not all early nouns refer to objects similar in shape. The first words of children include names for similarly shaped objects (e.g., *dog*, *cat*, and *cup)* but also names for "objects" with no set shape (e.g., *milk* and *light)*. We specifically taught the network 18 "good shape" categories: All instances of a category were highly similar to each other in shape. We also taught the network 18 "bad shape" categories: All instances of a category were highly similar to each other only on one dimension other than shape. Thus, across the 36 trained categories, shape was important for half of the categories, and each of the other three dimensions was important for one-sixth of the categories.

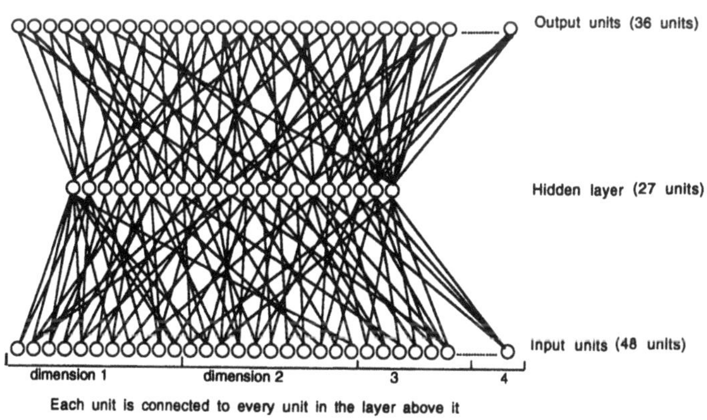

FIG. 1.6. The three-layer network used to simulate the learning of a shape bias. Each dimension at the input level is comprised of 12 units.

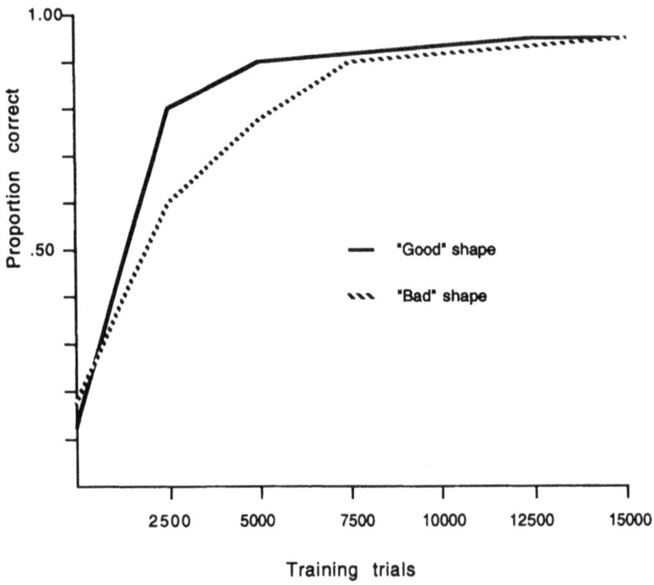

FIG. 1.7. Mean proportion correct naming by the network of trained categories well-organized by shape ("Good" shape) and poorly organized by shape ("Bad" shape) as a function of training trials.

Figure 1.7 shows that the network learned both the good shape and bad shape categories and learned the good shape ones more rapidly than the bad shape ones.[1] The key question, however, is whether the network developed a shape bias. Given a *novel* object from a *novel* category, does the network attend to shape? We addressed this question by examining the pattern of activation on the hidden layer in response to novel objects. If the network learned to emphasize shape, then the pattern of activation on this layer should be based principally on the input shape. In other words, same shaped novel objects should give rise to more similar internal representations than different shaped objects.

Figure 1.8 shows the dissimilarity of patterns of activation on the hidden layer for novel objects that were the same *only* in shape and for novel objects that were the same *only* on some other dimension and thus different in shape. As is apparent in Fig. 1.8, as the network learned the 36 trained categories, it developed a generalized shape bias—"perceiving" novel objects that were different in

[1]The number of training trials required to teach the network these categories, and necessary for the development of a shape bias, might seem high. However, such a conclusion is probably not warranted. We have as yet no metric that relates training trials for a network with the experiences of a child. For example, the naming of a single object once might correspond to 1000 network training trials. Thus, the only predictions that can be made and evaluated are ordinal ones.

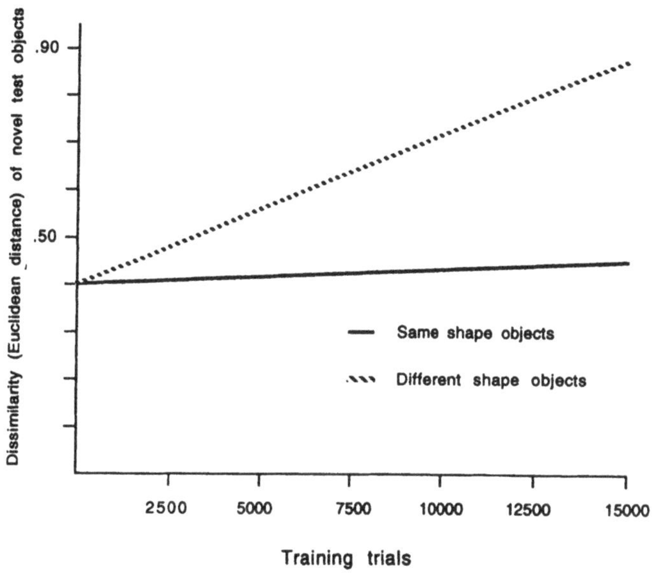

FIG. 1.8. Mean dissimilarity of the patterns of activation on the hidden layer for pairs of novel objects that were the same in shape only or that were the same only on some other dimension and different in shape as a function of training trials.

shape to be much more dissimilar than objects that were the same in shape. In sum, a shape bias can be learned.

This simulation of a learned shape bias is *not*, of course, a serious model of how children learn words nor a serious model of the shape bias. It is far too simple in too many ways. The results of the simulation are also not a contribution to connectionist theorizing; a shape bias is trivially easy for an associative network to learn. But this is precisely the point. Word-learning biases can originate in *relatively* unbiased learners. I emphasize the "relatively" because this network did have biases (or constraints on outcome)—its input was organized along four dimensions and it learned by a particular learning rule. But these are not specific constraints on possible hypotheses about word meanings. They are rather the general characteristics of a general purpose learner —and these general characteristics when placed in a *particular* environment yield a shape bias.

Development, however, does not stop here with the emergence of a shape bias. Rather the processes that made this initial bias will make other biases. Further, a small bias in a general purpose learner is a potent force on the direction of future development—encouraging the formation of other biases and creating new opportunities for learning. Thus a learned shape bias may be just the start of a self-propelling developmental process.

CONTEXTUAL INSTABILITIES

If the shape bias is learned by associations between attending and naming, other biases that reflect other regularities about lexical categories should also be learned as well. We examined this prediction in a series of experiments designed to challenge the shape bias. We sought contexts in which children might systematically attend to properties other than shape.

Eyes and Sneakers

In our first experiment in this series (Jones, Smith, & Landau, 1991), we examined the property of eyes. We asked whether the presence of eyes drew attention to texture in the task of naming an object. We reasoned that for many eyed objects, texture—whether the object was furry, or scalely, or feathered—was highly relevant to its lexical categorization. Consistent with this idea, Massey and Gelman (1988) showed that young children pay particular attention to texture when making judgments about which kinds of eyed objects (statues versus living things) can move on their own.

Accordingly, we examined 36-month-olds' interpretation of a novel word when it named an object with eyes versus when it named one without eyes. The exemplars and test objects for the two stimulus conditions are shown in Fig. 1.9. In both conditions, the experimenter named the exemplar (e.g., "This is a dax.") and asked about each test object whether it had the same name as the exemplar (e.g., "Is this a dax?"). The complete experiment included multiple exemplars and multiple queries about each kind of test object. The key results are summarized in the figure; next to each test object is the proportion of times children agreed that the novel noun named that test object. As is apparent, when the objects were eyeless, the children extended the name to same shape objects. But when the objects had eyes, the children extended the name only to the same-shaped and same-textured test object. Additional experiments showed that the presence of eyes affected children's attention only in a naming task; in a similarity judgment task, children did not systematically attend to any particular dimensions regardless of whether the objects had eyes or not. These results show that by the time children are 3 years old, after they have learned many kinds of words, there is more than merely a shape bias. There is also a shape + texture bias, at least in the context of naming objects with eyes.

Eyes, of course, are not just any object property. Eyes appear to be developmentally special in that infants show heightened looking to eyes and to objects with eyes (e.g., Fantz, 1963). Thus, one might hypothesize that young children are specially prepared by evolution to learn how objects with eyes are named. Certainly, the salience of eyes should enhance children's learning about the properties associated with them. However, we have preliminary evidence to suggest that the power to modulate the shape bias is not unique to "special" properties.

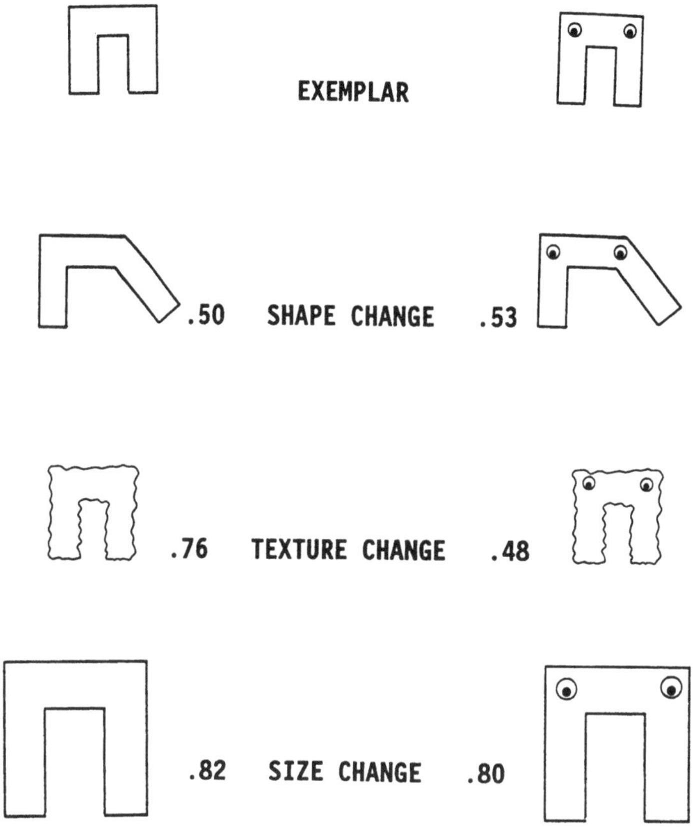

FIG. 1.9. Sample stimuli from Jones, Smith, and Landau (1991) and the proportion of times 3-year-old children extended the name of the exemplar to each of three kinds of test objects.

The new evidence derives from a replication of the original Eyes study. However, in this study, we removed the eyes from one stimulus set and added sneakers (Jones & Smith, 1994). The resulting stimuli are shown in Fig. 1.10. The mean proportion of times 36-month-olds extended the novel name to each test object or said that each test object was "like" the exemplar is also given in the figure. As is apparent, in the naming task only, children attended to shape and texture when the stimuli had sneakers, just as they attended to shape and texture when the stimuli had eyes. It is unlikely that children are specially prepared to learn how sneakered things are named. Rather, it seems that children will learn and make use of any regularity when naming an object. In this way, children's smart interpretations of novel words seem to derive from a system that is open to influence.

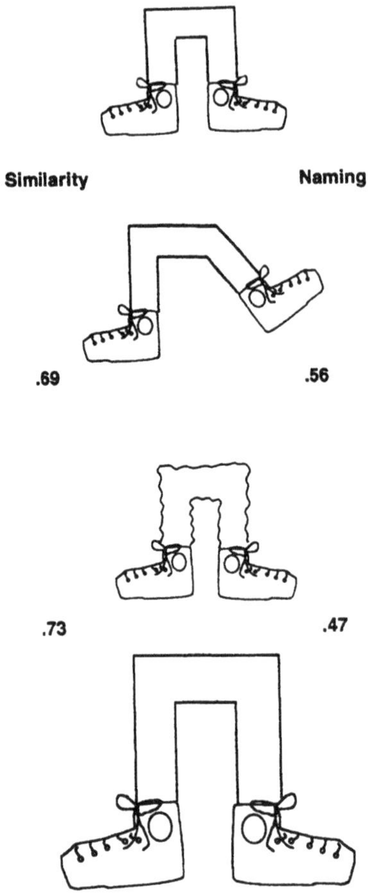

FIG. 1.10. Sample stimuli from a replication of Jones et al. (1991) that put sneakers rather than eyes on the stimuli and the mean proportion of times that 3-year-old children judged the test object to be "like" the exemplar in the Similarity judgment task and judged the text object to have the same name as the exemplar in the Naming task.

Syntactic Frame and Glitter

Children's naming behavior is not just open to the effects of learning, it is also open to influence by local in-task forces on attention. Indeed, children's interpretation of *some* novel words qualitatively reorganizes with changes in illumination. The relevant study (Smith, Jones, & Landau, 1992) investigated 36-month-olds' shifting attention to color and shape when asked to interpret a novel word presented in the syntactic frame of a count noun, *is a dax*, or in the syntactic frame of an adjective, *is a dax one*. The stimuli, shown in Fig. 1.11, varied in shape and color, and the colors were realized by putting glitter in paint. These stimuli were presented (between subjects) either under ordinary illumination or

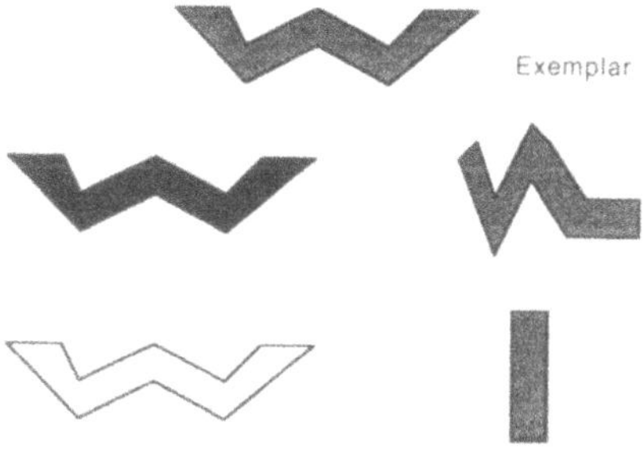

FIG. 1.11. Stimuli used in Smith, Jones, and Landau (1992). The colors of the exemplar and test objects were realized with glitter.

in a darkened chamber with a spotlight. The effect of the spotlight was to make the glitter sparkle.

The results are shown in Fig. 1.12. The spotlight had little effect when the novel word was a noun but controlled attention when the novel word was an adjective. Children understood the novel noun as referring to same shaped objects under both ordinary and spotlighted illumination. But, children understood the novel adjective as referring to same shaped objects under ordinary illumination and as referring to the sparkling color when presented under the spotlight. In other words, attention to shape in the context of a novel noun withstands the challenge of glitter but attention to shape in the context of a novel adjective does not.

These results show that knowledge of language and local idiosyncratic forces on attention combine nonlinearly to organize 36-months-olds' attention in the service of interpreting a novel word. An attentional system that coherently combines past learning and current context is one that *creates learning biases online*—modulating the wisdom inherent in the stabilities of language by the clever recognition that the highly salient property in the here-and-now may be the one talked about.

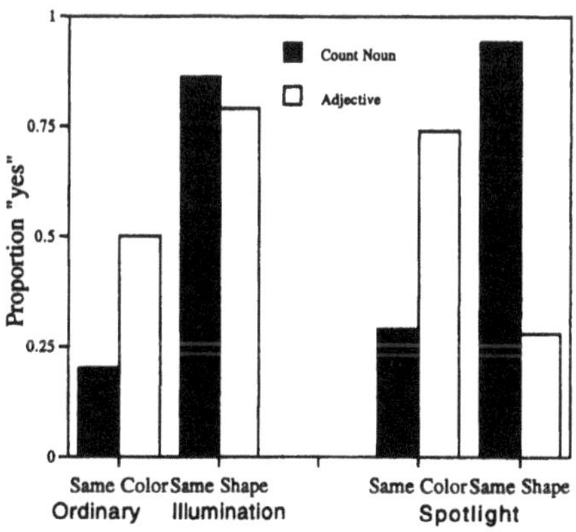

FIG. 1.12. Mean proportion of times the novel word in either a count noun or adjectival frame was extended to test objects that matched the exemplar in either color only or shape only under ordinary illumination or under a spotlight.

Unstable Biases

The context dependency of 36-month-olds' novel word interpretations is considerable. What object properties 36-month-olds attend to depends on: the task—whether the child is asked to interpret a novel word or make a similarity judgment; the properties of the objects—whether they have eyes or sneakers or are eyeless or sneakerless; the syntactic frame—whether the novel word is presented in the frame of a count noun or an adjective; the local details of the communicative and perceptual context—whether, for example, the objects are spotlighted or not.

This context dependency undermines the utility of learning biases as "solutions to the induction problem." What set of assumptions about word meanings can tell a child to:

> Attend to shape if there is a novel noun unless the objects have eyes or sneakers, then attend to shape and texture.
>
> If there is a novel adjective, attend to shape unless some other property is very salient, then attend to that.

The contextual specificity of children's novel word interpretations suggests that they cannot be explained by principles that reside only in the child. Children's attention to object properties in word learning tasks is both stable and contingent, both highly organized and open to influence. The instabilities seem to great to be explained by some set of word learning principles. Yet, they also seem too systematic and central to the phenomena of biased learning to be left unexplained.

Developmental Instabilities

Critically, context effects in 36-month-olds are not the only instabilities in need of explanation. There is also the fact of development. Many of the experiments on the context-sensitivity of 36-month-olds' novel word interpretations included groups of children both younger and older than 36 months (see Jones & Smith, 1993, for a review). Jones and Smith (1993) summarized and integrated the results of these many experiments with the theoretical curves in Fig. 1.13. On the *y* axis is the strength of children's preference for shape over other dimensions. The points at 36 months summarize the results just reviewed on the context-dependencies at this age. At 36 months, children systematically attend to shape when generalizing a novel noun to eyeless objects: they attend to shape but slightly less so given those same stimuli but when the novel word is presented in an adjectival frame; they attend to shape, but not exclusively, when generalizing a novel noun to objects with eyes; they do not attend to shape more than other dimensions in similarity judgment tasks, and they do not attend to shape given a novel adjective and highly salient, glittery, colors.

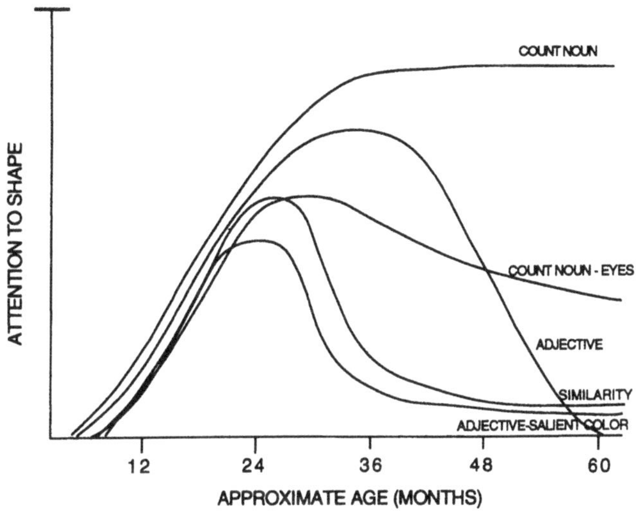

FIG. 1.13. Theoretical developmental trajectories summarizing findings across experiments: The degree to which attention is directed exclusively to shape as a function of age and task contexts.

The functions through these points summarize the developmental results: that the shape bias emerges between 18 and 24 months and appears initially both in tasks that the experimenter defines as a naming task and ones the experimenter defines as a nonnaming similarity judgment tasks (Smith et al., 1994); that the effect of eyes on children's novel word interpretations increases with development (Jones et al., 1991); and that attention to shape in the context of a novel adjective rises early in development and then falls such that by the time children are 5 years old, an adjectival frame pushes attention away from shape (Landau, Smith, & Jones, 1992).

These curves depict a shape bias that emerges with development and changes continuously—becoming increasingly differentiated and increasingly specific to context. In these data, there is no evidence for an enduring constraint on word learning. There is only a shape bias at *some moment in developmental time in some specific task context*. These data suggest that biased learning in children is smart because it is adaptive and fluid, not because it is prescient.

SELF-ORGANIZING ATTENTION

In this section, I explore how adaptive learning biases may be created on-line out of a history of experiences and the details of the moment. I specifically propose that biases are the transient products of attentional processes that fuse past experience and immediate input into a single coherent and highly organized behavior. The proposal is summarized in Fig. 1.14. Adaptively smart and continually evolving novel word interpretations derive from: (a) the multiple forces that organize attention in task, (b) the nonlinearities in attentional process, and (c) the consequences of each act of naming on the system as a whole.

Multiple Forces on Attention

At the core of this proposal is the view of attention as an open process. Everyday experience, confirmed by a century of research (see, Allport, 1989; James, 1890), shows attention to be attracted by intensity, movement, change, and novelty—stimulus properties that universally engage. Considerable research also shows attention to be open to influence from learning (e.g., Medin, Altom, Edelson, & Freko, 1982). Infants, children, adults all learn and use contextual cues that predict the relevance of other properties (e.g., Reber, 1989; Younger, 1990). Indeed, the evidence suggests that people will implicitly learn almost any predictive contextual cue (see especially Lewicki, Hill, & Sasak, 1989). Our findings about children's novel word interpretations fit squarely with everything that is known about attentional learning.

The openness of attention is a key part of what makes it smart. Learned associations cause attention weights to shift to reflect the utility of particular dimensions in similar contexts and thus attention incorporates the stable mappings between language and categories (see Medin & Schaffer, 1978; Nosofsky, 1984; Smith, 1993). Direct stimulus effects keep attention fresh and timely so that it incorporates the singularities of the here-and-now. Because the focus of attention emerges in the moment from the mix of these multiple forces, it is creative. Such a system does not need to know ahead of time anything specific

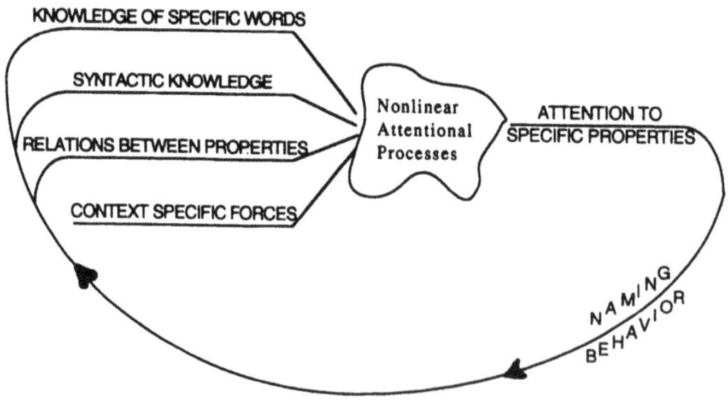

FIG. 1.14. A self-organizing attentional system.

about what adjectives mean in the context of glitter. A novel learning bias can emerge from the novel combination of the local peculiarities with past learning.

Importantly, children's attention may *not* be open to *all* possible kinds of influences. Rather, attentional processes may be best thought of as perceptual in the sense of being influenced *only* by *well-learned associations* between cues and attending and by *direct stimulus effects*. This possibility is suggested by two extensive series of experiments investigating children's use of conceptual information about objects in generalizing newly learned names (Landau, Jones & Smith, 1995; Smith, Jones, & Landau, 1994). The major result across these studies was that 2-and 3-year-olds' novel word interpretations were sharply organized by syntax and the intensity of specific properties, but unmoved by our telling (or showing) children what an object could do or its intended function. These results suggest that children's attention may be tightly organized only by automatic and nonreflective processes—a possibility that fits the fact of young children's generally nonselective attention in nonnaming tasks (e.g., Smith, 1989). Thus, the task of interpreting a novel word may rapidly organize selective attention precisely because this task brings with it many well-learned associations that automatically shift attention weights.

A Nonlinear Attentional System

Multiple, potentially competing, forces can yield coherent attentional biases only if these forces interact nonlinearly—only if the various pulls and pushes on attention are effectively compressed into well-organized attentional patterns. There is clear evidence for nonlinearities in children's attention in the task of interpreting a novel word. Children's attention leaps from ignoring-texture to attending-to-texture with the addition of eyes, from attending-to-shape to attending-to-color with the addition of a spotlight (given an adjectival frame). Yet children's attention also does not move from shape in the context of a count noun even when challenged by spotlighted glitter. These results show that the attentional system does more than just sum across the various pushes and pulls; the attentional system combines forces nonlinearly.

Two possible nonlinearities are all-or-none attention to individual dimensions and a winner-take-all resolution of competing forces on attention. All-or-none attention to individual dimensions has been suggested by modeling of children's attention to dimensions in nonnaming categorization tasks (Smith, 1989). Such a mechanism would mean that if associations among syntactic frame and object properties exceed some threshold, the attentional mechanism would attend completely to shape. A winner-take-all process is suggested by the different effect of a spotlight on the interpretation of a novel noun and a novel adjective. By one description of these results, the noun syntactic frame "beat" the spotlight for control of attention but the spotlight beat the adjective context. The next empirical step in this line of research is to determine the precise nature of these nonlinearities and the processes that create them.

Learning to Learn

In the present account, children's novel word interpretations continually evolve because word learning is both the in-task product of this nonlinear attentional system and an agent of change. In this way, "dumb" nonspecific cognitive processes create a self-organizing developmental trajectory that *seems* directed. I illustrate these ideas by first reconsidering children's emerging understanding of nouns and adjectives and then by considering Soja and colleagues (Soja, 1992; Soja, Carey, & Spelke, 1991) data on children's emerging understanding of mass and count nouns.

Nouns and Adjectives. Our evidence (Smith et al., 1992) as well as others (e.g., Gelman & Markman, 1985; Taylor & Gelman, 1988) suggests that by the time children are 3 years old, they interpret novel adjectives differently from novel nouns—at least in some contexts. An early behavioral difference between nouns and adjectives can be explained, however, without positing any specific knowledge about the semantics of nouns and adjectives. To see this, assume that young children, say 2-year-olds, have learned only that the syntactic frame of a count noun, "that's a ______," in the context of a rigid object is associated with the behavior of attending to shape. From all that is known about associative learning, one would expect a generalization gradient around this original learning: Children's attention to shape should decrease in word learning situations as those situations become increasingly dissimilar to the context of original learning. More specifically, the pull of shape should be less if we make the syntactic frame less similar to that of a count noun. Thus the simple idea of a generalization gradient predicts that the strength of the pull to shape will be weaker in the context of a novel adjective than a novel noun. In this way, "knowing" only about nouns could account for the differential effect of a spotlight on interpreting novel words in noun versus adjective frames.

My purpose in raising this possibility, however, is not to "explain away" children's apparent knowledge about adjectives. Rather, this possibility is interesting because it shows what might be the first developmental step to an understanding of the different semantic force of nouns and adjectives. If children are less likely to attend to shape in the context of an adjective—whatever the reason for this decreased likelihood—then they are more likely to learn differently about adjectives than nouns. Put another way, *because* the generalized association to shape is weaker and more easily challenged in the context of a novel adjective than a novel noun, children are *biased* to learn differently about adjectives and nouns. This early bias, which falls out of an association between count noun syntax and attention to shape will start the development process in the right direction just as well as specific knowledge about adjectives. A simple generalization gradient will create an opportunity for learning specialized and distinctive knowledge about adjectives—learning that may culminate in the sophisticated use of lexical contrast (e.g., Au & Laframboise, 1990; Au & Markman, 1987).

Mass and Count Nouns. Soja and colleagues' (Soja, 1992; Soja, Carey, & Spelke, 1991) results on young children's interpretation of novel words in count and mass noun contexts also illustrates how directed development might emerge from the limited associations that arise from learning the names for a few concrete objects. Such objects—for which shape similarity is crucial for naming—are also rigid. Thus, the early learned association may be between the syntax of a count noun, rigidity, and attention to shape. Soja (1992) examined 24- and 30-month-old children's interpretation of a novel count noun (e.g., *this is a mell*) and their interpretation of a novel mass noun (e.g., *this is some mell*) in the two stimulus contexts. The structure of a trial in each stimulus context is illustrated in Fig. 1.15. The stimuli for the object trials were rigid, made of hardened clay or plastic or wood and the stimuli for the substance trials were nonrigid, made of hair gel, hand cream, and foam. Critical test objects matched the exemplar either in shape or in substance. In Soja's task, children were asked on each trial to choose which of the two test objects had the same name as the exemplar. Soja found that children's choices were modulated by both the syntactic frame and the rigidity of the stimulus. Shape choices were more frequent given rigid objects

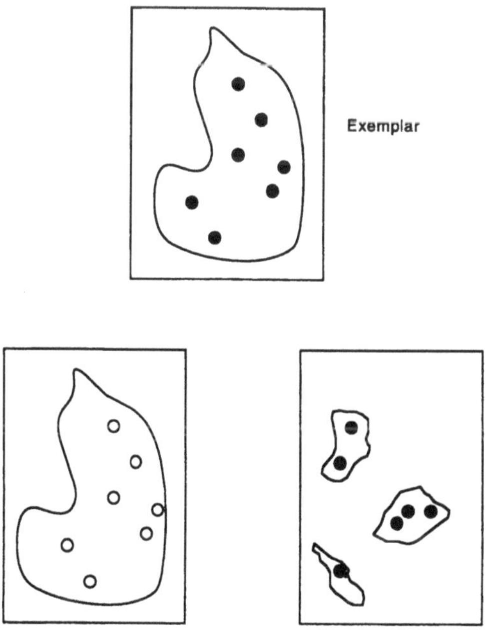

FIG. 1.15. Sample stimuli from Soja (1992). On object trials, the exemplar and test objects were made of rigid substances such as wood. On substance trials, the exemplar and test objects were made of nonrigid substances such as foam.

and a count noun. Substance choices were more frequent given a nonrigid substance and a mass noun. Soja concluded that children possessed knowledge both about count-mass syntax and the perceptual properties critical to distinguishing objects and substances.

Soja's data, however, can also be explained by positing only a strong association between a count-noun syntactic frame, rigidity, and attention to shape. Figure 1.16 shows a redrawing of Soja's data; proportion of shape choices are shown as a function of the hypothesized similarity of each kind of test trial to the hypothesized original learning—a count-noun naming a shape based category of rigid objects. As is apparent, children's shape choices appear to reflect a generalization gradient, decreasing as similarity from the prototypical naming context decreases. But this generalization gradient means there is a bias to learn differently about how rigid and nonrigid objects are named and about the differences between mass and count nouns. Again, knowing about one kind of novel word creates —by its very existence—biases for learning about other kinds of words.

Notice also in Fig. 1.16 that the generalization gradient is steeper for older than for younger children. The older children do not just choose shape less often (and at near chance levels) on substance trials as do younger children but given a nonrigid substance in the context of a novel mass noun, they systematically extend the name to the same substance. What was initially a novel-word learning context not tightly controlled by previous learning has perhaps become a distinct context giving rise to distinct attentional biases.

Context, Predictability, and Explanation

Gelman (1990) asked: "How is it that our young attend to inputs that will support the development of concepts they share with their elders?" The complex system

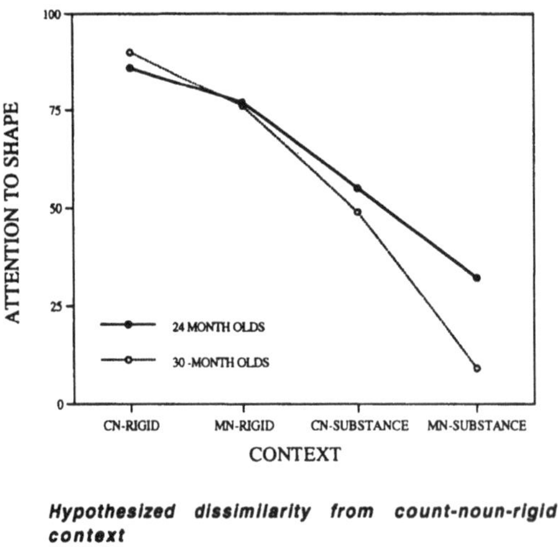

FIG. 1.16. Mean percentage choice of the test object that matched the exemplar in shape in Soja (1992) as a function of the hypothesized dissimilarity of the testing condition from the context of original learning. Chance equals 50%. Redrawn from data reported in Soja (1992).

pictured in Fig. 1.14 is one answer to this question. The very nature of attentional processes—their openness to learning, to immediate input, and their nonlinearity—create self-adjusting learning biases. Children know what inputs to attend to because they have an attentional system that is always in motion, always learning, always adapting. The evidence on the shape bias that provides the basis for this proposal is, of course, evidence about just one of several well-documented learning biases. However, other forms of biased word learning may also be the products of self-organizing attentional processes. Attention seems a particularly good to place to look for mechanistic explanations of the "taxonomic assumption," the "mutual exclusivity principle" (see Markman, 1992 for a similar suggestion), and children's use of gaze (e.g., Baldwin & Markman, 1989).

Sometimes models such as this one that emphasize learning and context are criticized as being incapable of prediction and thus untestable. The assumption behind these criticisms is that fluid and changeable cognition is necessarily unpredictable. The data and the model show the weakness of this criticism and the route to prediction and explanation. Children's attention in novel word interpretations tasks exhibits both stability across some contexts and variability across others. The model offers a way to explain—and predict—both of these. The model posits that attention is *determined* by long-term associations, direct stimulus effects, and nonlinear attentional processes. To the degree we can specify these, we can predict performance. To the degree we can manipulate these, we can empirically test the model.

Beyond the specific claims of the model is the more general lesson to be learned from the data and our conceptualization of them. The lesson is that learning *by its very nature* creates new opportunities for learning and for development. Learning one thing changes the likelihood of what else will be learned. Each newly created bias creates new opportunities for learning and new biases.

A SELF-ORGANIZING DEVELOPMENTAL LANDSCAPE

A useful metaphor for thinking about how the activity of a system creates and recreates learning biases is a dynamic version of Waddington's (1957) epigenetic landscape. Waddington's original landscape is a three-dimensional surface like that shown in Fig. 1.17. The developing organism is represented by the ball. The hills and valleys represent the ease with which developmental outcome is influenced by genetic and experiential factors. At some points, a small environmental perturbation can send the developing individual down one path or another. At other points, the course of development is tightly restricted, canalized.

A key problem with this static representation of epigenesis is that it fixes all possible outcomes at the start of development. Given this representation, it is easy to think of experience as a "trigger" that selects a particular prespecified

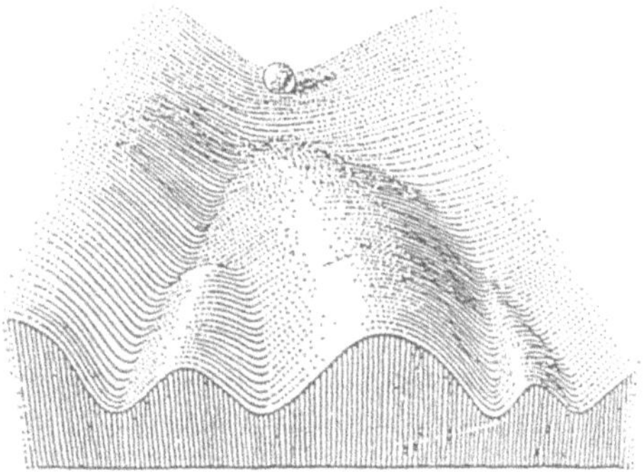

FIG. 1.17. Waddington's epigenetic landscape. Redrawn from Waddington (1957).

outcome but that does not actually make outcomes. Some theorists have explicitly accepted this prespecified view of development (and argued that learning does not exist in any real sense, for example, Fodor, 1987; Piatelli-Palmarini, 1989). Waddington, however, viewed his fixed landscape as an inadequate representation precisely because it fixed all developmental outcomes at the start. In his last book, Waddington (1977) offered a dynamic version of the epigenetic landscape.

Muchisky, Gershkoff-Stowe, Cole, and Thelen (1994) used Fig. 1.18 to portray Waddington's dynamic landscape. The idea is that as the organism develops,

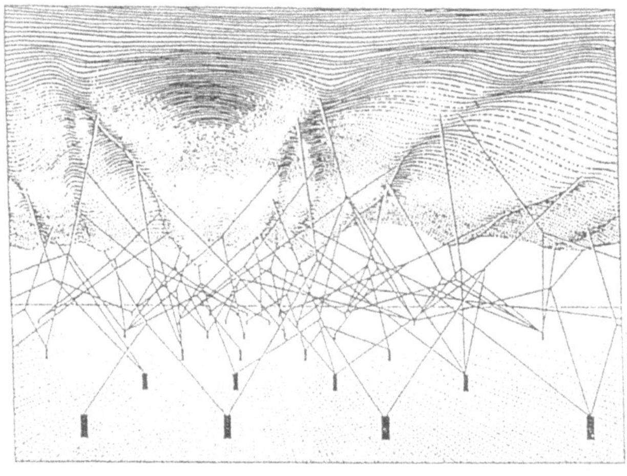

FIG. 1.18. A dynamic epigenetic landscape from Muchisky et al. (1994). The developmental landscape is connected to—affecting and affected by—an underscape of processes.

as the ball rolls down the valley, its experiences directly affect the underscape or processes that *make the landscape*. They and Waddington use the metaphor of strings connecting the two scapes; as the ball hits a particular location, it changes the pull on the landscape from the underscape below—and thus the local tension. The altered local tension changes the tension of strings that pull the future landscape in complexly connected ways—changing the potential for development. The vision is of an epigenetic landscape that is always changing—creating and recreating future paths and opportunities. Development in this view does not begin with a fixed set of biases proscribing what can and cannot be. Rather developmental process continually creates biases. There are no fixed set of outcomes, only possibility.

The data on children's changing novel word interpretations fit this vision. A small bias acquired from a statistical regularity between the names for things and shape similarity creates by its very existence other biases. In this way, development invents biases that increasingly fit the language being learned and the world. We begin to understand how children learning different languages might have word learning biases that specifically fit the language they are learning—a possibility for which there is growing evidence (e.g., Bavin, Ng, Brimmell, & Gabriel, 1993; Gopnik & Choi, 1990).

The idea of dynamic biases created in the history of many interacting forces, the idea that learning creates new opportunities for learning, the idea of self-organizing developmental processes, are not new. They are the classic ideas of *development*—of Piaget (1952), of Werner (1957), of Bertanfly (1933), ideas that persistently emerge in attempts to specify the mechanisms of developmental change (see Bates, 1979; Gibson, 1988; Oyama, 1985; Siegler, 1989; Thelen, 1989; Tucker & Hirsh-Pasek, 1993).

DEVELOPMENT IS NOT INDUCTION

Children learn words rapidly, often from hearing a word used once in context to label an object. By some estimates, children learn over nine words a day between the time they are 2 and 5 years-old (Templin, 1957). When one stands back and looks at young children's word learning, it appears so rapid and so highly organized that it is easy to believe that word learning is directed by processes that know in advance the possible meanings of words. But when we look close up at the processes that actually enable young children to interpret a novel word in context, we see that they are highly contingent, variable, and open. The very quickness, the very smartness, of word learning appears born in this elegant sensitivity to context.

How do we reconcile these empirical truths about developmental process with the logical truth of the induction problem—that if learning consists of hypothesis formulation and confirmation, then there must be severe constraints on the hypotheses that can be formed? We reconcile it by taking the induction problem for what it is, an abstraction that is true only as an abstraction. Learning is hypothesis testing only in its most abstract sense and constraints on learning also exist only as an abstraction across much more complex and messier processes. "Constraints" are distributed across many psychological processes and experiences and are emergent in the complex history that is development. This idea has precedence in ethology (e.g., Fentress, 1978; Gottlieb, 1971; Lehrman, 1970). Constrained development appears an emergent property of self-organizing and undirected processes. Examples from nipple-seeking in rat pups and the development of bird song illustrate the point.

Nipple-Seeking in Rat Pups. Rat pups are born able to find their mother's nipples at birth. They move over her body in the direction of the nipples until they find one and attach. Smell is critical to this search. Anosmic rat pups do not search for nipples and can die of starvation. Further, if the mother's nipple is washed with a new smell, rat pups cannot locate the nipple (Alberts, 1981). How do rat pups know the smell of their mother's nipple? The research shows that the critical smell is amniotic fluid, that the preference is learned in utero, and that it can be altered dramatically by altering the smell of the amniotic environment (Pederson & Blass, 1981). After giving birth, mother rats lick their newly born pups and their own nipples and thus place the familiar smell where the rat pup needs to go. Nipple-seeking in rat pups is thus organized by a consortium of general purpose learning mechanisms, developmental timing, and restricted environments. Globally, learning is constrained; but locally and mechanistically that constraint is the emergent product of a history of more open events.

Song in Cowbirds. The development of song in the cowbird presents a similar picture of complexities of developmental process. Male cowbirds develop several songs, each with a stereotyped vocal pattern. Females do not sing but use the males' songs to pick a mate (West, King, & Duff, 1990). Males raised in isolation and who have heard no other male sing still develop a song. The songs of isolates are sometimes labeled *innate* or the *default* song (e.g., Marler, 1982). West et al. (1990) question the utility of this characterization given that isolation is not a neutral environment and that isolates are too socially impaired to measure the effectiveness of the putative default song in courting females. Further, their research shows that the key factor in learning a potent song is social rearing, and in particular, rearing with female cowbirds. Male cowbirds raised from the egg with no contact with other males and thus with no opportunities to hear a cowbird song develop effective courting songs if raised with female cowbirds. These songs are "supernormal"; they are more effective releasers of copulatory postures by females than the songs of normally reared males. West and King have shown that males learn these supernormal songs by monitoring female reaction to their singing. Females raise their wings in response to certain segments and this wing-raising appears to reinforce those segments in the male singer. Males raised in normal social groups watch both male and female reactions to their songs; these normally reared males develop less potent courting songs because segments that females like (and raise their wings too) elicit aggressive gestures from other males. Indeed, males raised only with females and whose songs work so well in mating invite deadly attacks from other males when released into a social group. Again, we see how learning and the behavior it engenders creates new opportunities for learning. And, as Alberts and Decsy (1990) conclude, we see how "nature can regulate apparent complexity with the simplest of underlying mechanism [but] sometimes relies on intricacy of mechanism to [make] a seemingly simple result" (p. 577).

The development of birdsong, like nipple-seeking in newborn rats, like the shape bias in children's word learning, is an example of learning that could be easily pointed to as *constrained* or *prepared*. But the significance of these words dissipates in the full complexity of the processes that actually make development happen. Small biases create new opportunities for learning that build seamlessly on one another. When one looks back in time on the developmental trajectory as a whole, one sees order and a global directedness—but that directedness is made one open, variable, contingent step at a time.

ACKNOWLEDGMENT

This research was supported by PHS grant, RO1 HD 28675.

REFERENCES

Alberts, J. R. (1981). Ontogeny of olfaction: Reciprocal roles of sensation and behavior in the development of perception. In R. N. Aslin, J. R. Alberts, & M. R. Petersen (Eds.), *Development of perception: Psychobiological perspectives* (Vol I, pp. 321–351). New York: Academic Press.

Alberts, J. R. & Decsy, G. J. (1990). Terms of endearment. *Developmental Psychobiology 23*, 569–584.

Allport, A. (1989). Visual attention. In M. I. Posner (Ed.), *Foundations of cognitive science* (pp. 631–682). Cambridge, MA: MIT Press.

Anglin, J. M. (1977). *Word, object and conceptual development*. New York: W. W. Norton.

Au, T. K., & Laframboise, D. E. (1990). Acquiring color names via linguistic contrast: The influence of contrasting terms. *Child Development, 61*, 1808–1823.

Au, T. K., & Markman, E. M. (1987). Acquiring word meaning via linguistic contrast. *Cognitive Development 2*, 217–236.

Baldwin, D. A., & Markman, E. M. (1989). Mapping out word-object relations: A first step. *Child Development, 60*, 381–398.

Bates, E. (1979). *The emergence of symbols: Cognition and communication in infancy.* New York: Academic Press.

Bavin, E. L., Ng, B. C., Brimmell, T., & Gabriel, B. (1993). *Is there really a shape bias?* Unpublished data, LaTrobe University.

Bertanfly, L. von (1933). *Modern theories of development*. Oxford: Oxford University Press.

Biederman, I. (1987). Recognition by components: A theory of human image understanding, *Psychological Review*, *94*, 115–147.

Bloom, L., Lifter, K., & Broughton, J. (1985). The convergence of early cognition and language in the second year of life: Problems in conceptualization and measurement. In M. Barrett (Ed.), *Children's single-word speech* (pp. 149–180). New York: Wiley.

Bowerman, M. (1977). The acquisition of word meaning: An investigation of some current conflicts. In N. Waterson & C. Snow (Eds.), *Proceedings of the Third International Child Language Symposium*. New York: Wiley.

Clark, E. V. (1973). What's in a word: On the child's acquisition of semantics in his first language. In T. E. Moore (Ed.), *Cognitive development and the acquisition of language*. New York: Academic Press.

Dromi, E. (1987). *Early lexical development*. New York: Cambridge University Press.

Fantz, R. L. (1963). Pattern vision in newborn infants. *Science*, *140*, 296–297.

Fentress, J. C. (1978). *Mus muscicus*: The developmental orchestration of selected movement patterns in mice. In G. M. Burghardt & M. Bekoff (Eds.), *The development of behavior: Comparative and evolutionary aspects* (pp. 321–342). New York: Garland STPM.

Fodor, J. A. (1987). *Psychosemantics*. Cambridge, MA: Bradford Books/MIT Press.

Gasser, M., & Smith, L. B. (1991). The development of a notion of sameness: A connectionist model. In *Proceedings of the 13th Annual Conference of the Cognitive Science Society* (pp. 719–723). Hillsdale, NJ: Lawrence Erlbaum Associates.

Gasser, M. & Smith, L. B. (1995). *Learning nouns and adjective meanings: A connectionist account*. Manuscript submitted for publication.

Gelman, R. (1990). First principles organize attention to and learning about relevant data: Number and the animate-inanimate distinction as examples. *Cognitive Science*, *14*, 79–106.

Gelman, S. A., & Markman, E. M. (1985). Implicit contrast in adjectives vs. nouns: Implications for word-learning in preschoolers. *Journal of Child Language*, *12*, 125–143.

Gershkoff-Stowe, L., & Smith, L. B. (1995). *Naming errors during the "naming explosion": A study of early changes in lexical processing*. Under review.

Gibson, E. J. (1988). Exploratory behavior in the development of perceiving, acting, and the acquiring of knowledge. *Annual Review of Psychology*, *39*, 1–41.

Goldfield, B. A., & Resnick, J. S. (1990). Early lexical acquisition: Rate, content, and the vocabulary spurt. *Journal of Child Language*, *17*, 115–130.

Goodman, N. (1955). *Fact, fiction, and forecast*. Cambridge, MA: Harvard University Press.

Gopnik, A., & Choi, S. (1990). Do linguistic differences lead to cognitive differences? A cross linguistic study of semantic and cognitive development. *First Language*, *10*, 199–215.

Gopnik, A., & Meltzoff, A. N. (1987). The development of categorization in the second year and its relation to other cognitive and linguistic developments. *Child Development*, *58*, 1523–1531.

Gottlieb, G. (1971). *Development of species identification in birds*. Chicago: University of Chicago Press.

Imai, M., Gentner, D., & Uchida, N. (1993). *Children's theories of word meaning: The role of shape similarity in early acquisition*. Unpublished manuscript.

James, W. (1890). *Principles of Psychology*. New York: Henry Holt.

Jones, S. S., & Smith, L. B. (1993). The place of perceptions in children's concepts. *Cognitive Development*, *8*, 113–140.

Jones, S., & Smith, L. (1994). *Sneakers and eyes modulate the shape bias*. Unpublished data.

Jones, S., Smith, L., & Landau, B. (1991). Object properties and knowledge in early lexical learning. *Child Development*, *62*, 499–516.

Jones, S., Smith, L., Landau, B., & Gershkoff-Stowe, L. (1992, October). *The origins of the shape bias*. Paper presented at the Boston Child Language conference.

Katz, N., Baker, E., & Macnamara, J. (1974). What's in a name? A study of how children learn common and proper names. *Child Development*, *45*, 469–473.

Kuczaj, S. A. (1990). Constraining constraint theories. *Cognitive Development, 5*, 341–344.

Landau, B., Smith, L. B., & Jones, S. S. (1992). Syntactic context and the shape bias in children's and adult's lexical learning. *Journal of Memory and Language, 31*, 807–825.

Landau, B., Smith, L. B., & Jones, S. (1995). *Object shape, object function, and object name.* Manuscript submitted for publication.

Landau, K. B., Smith, L. B., & Jones, S. S. (1988). The importance of shape in early lexical learning. *Cognitive Development, 3*, 299–321.

Lehrman, D. S. (1970). Semantic and conceptual issues in the nature-nurture problem. In L. B. Aronson, E. Tobach, D. S. Lehrman, & J. S. Rosenblatt (Eds.), *Development and the evolution of behavior* (pp. 17–52). San Francisco: Freeman.

Lewicki, P., Hill, T., & Sasak, I. (1989). Self-perpetuating development of encoding biases. *Journal of Experimental Psychology: General, 118*, 323–338.

MacWhinney, B. (1991). A reply to Woodward and Markham. *Developmental Review, 11*, 192–194.

Markman, E. M. (1989). *Categorization and naming in children: Problems of induction.* Cambridge, MA: MIT Press, Bradford Books.

Markman, E. M. (1991). The whole object, taxonomic, and mutual exclusivity assumptions as initial constraints on word meanings. In J. P. Byrnes & S. A. Gelman (Eds.), *Perspectives on language and cognition: Interrelations in development* (pp-72–106). Cambridge, England: Cambridge University Press.

Markman, E. M. (1992). Constraints on word learning: Speculations about their nature, origins, and domain specificity. In M. Gunnar & M. Maratsos (Eds.), *Modularity and constraints in language and cognition: The Minnesota Symposia of Child Psychology, 25*, 59–101.

Marler, P. (1982). Some ethological implications for neuroethology: The ontogeny of birdsong. In J. P. Ewert, R. R. Capranica, & D. J. Ingle (Eds.), *Advances in vertebrae neuroethology* (pp. 21–52). New York: Plenum.

Massey, C., & Gelman, R. (1988). Preschoolers' ability to decide whether pictured unfamiliar objects can move themselves. *Developmental Psychology, 24*, 307–317.

Medin, D. L., Altom, M. W., Edelson, S. M., & Freko, D. (1982). Correlated symptoms and simulated medical classifications, *Journal of Experimental Psychology: Learning, Memory, and Cognition, 8*, 37–50.

Medin, D., & Schaffer, M (1978). Context theory of classification learning. *Psychological Review, 85*, 207–238.

Merriman, W. E., & Bowman, L. L. (1989). The mutual exclusivity bias in children's word learning. *Monographs of the Society for Research in Child Development, 54* (3–4, Serial No. 220).

Muchisky, M., Gershkoff-Stowe, L., Cole, E., & Thelen, E. (in press). The epigenetic landscape revisited: A dynamic interpretation. *Advances in Infancy Research.*

Nelson, K. (1988). Constraints on word learning? *Cognitive Development, 3*, 221–246.

Nosofsky, R. M. (1984). Choice, similarity and the context of classification. *Journal of Experimental Psychology: Learning, Memory & Cognition, 10*, 104–114.

Osherson, D. N., Stob, M., & Weinstein, S. (1986). *Systems that learn.* Cambridge, MA: MIT Press.

Oyama, S. (1985). *The ontogeny of information: Developmental systems and evolution.* Cambridge, England: Cambridge University Press.

Pedersen, P. E., & Blass, E. M. (1981). Olfactory control over suckling in albino rats. In R. N. Aslin, J. R. Alberts, & M. R. Petersen (Eds.), *Development of Perception: Psychobiological perspectives* (Vol I, pp. 359–382). New York: Academic Press.

Piaget, J. (1952). *The origins of intelligence.* New York: Norton.

Piatelli-Palmarini, M. (1989). Evolution, selection and cognition: From "learning" to parameter setting in biology and the study of language. *Cognition, 31*, 1–44.

Quine, W. V. (1960). *Word and object.* Cambridge, MA: MIT Press.

Reber, A. (1989). Implicit learning and tacit knowledge, *Journal of Experimental Psychology: General*, *118*, 219–236.

Rosch, E. (1978). Principles of categorization. In E. Rosch & B. Lloyd (Eds.), *Cognition and categorization* (pp. 28–46). Hillsdale, NJ: Lawrence Erlbaum Associates.

Siegler, R. S. (1989). Mechanisms of cognitive development. *Annual Review of Psychology*, *40*, 353–380.

Siegler, R. S. (1992). What do developmental psychologists really want? In M. Gunnar & M. Maratsos (Eds.), *Modularity and constraints in language and cognition: the Minnesota Symposia of Child Psychology*, *25*, 221–232.

Smith, L.B. (1989). A model of perceptual classification in children and adults. *Psychological Review*, *96*, 125–144.

Smith, L. B. (1993). The concept of same. *Advances in child development and behavior*, *24*, 216–253.

Smith, L. B., Jones, S. S., & Landau, B. (1992). Count nouns, adjectives, and perceptual properties in children's novel word interpretations. *Developmental Psychology, 28*, 273–289.

Smith, L. B., Jones, S., & Landau, B. (1994). *Naming in young children: An encapsulated attentional mechanism.* Manuscript submitted for publication.

Smith, L. B., Jones, S., Landau, B., & Gershkoff-Stowe, L. (1994). *Word learning and the origins of the shape bias.* In preparation.

Smith, L. B., & Thelen, E. (1993). Can dynamic systems theory be usefully applied in areas other than motor development? In L. B. Smith & E. Thelen (Eds.), *A dynamic systems approach to development: Applications* (pp. 151–170). Cambridge, MA: MIT Press.

Soja, N. (1992). Inferences about the meanings of nouns: The relationship between perception and syntax. *Cognitive Development*, *7*, 29–46.

Soja, N., Carey, S., & Spelke, E. (1991). Ontological categories guide young children's inductions of word meanings: Object terms and substance terms. *Cognition*, *38*, 179–211.

Taylor, M., & Gelman, S. A. (1988). Adjectives and nouns: Children's strategies for learning new words. *Child Development*, *59*, 411–419.

Templin, M. C. (1957). *Certain language skills in children.* Minneapolis: University of Minnesota Press.

Thelen, E. (1989). Self-organization in developmental processes: Can systems approaches work? In M.R. Gunnar & E. Thelen (Eds.), *Systems and developmental: The Minnesota Symposium on Child Psychology, Vol. 22* (pp. 77–118). Hillsdale, NJ: Lawrence Erlbaum Associates.

Tucker, M., & Hirsh-Pasek, K. (1993). Systems and language: Implications for acquisition. In L. B. Smith, & E. Thelen, (Eds.), *A dynamical systems approach to development: Applications.* Cambridge, MA: MIT Press.

Waddington, C. H. (1957). *The strategy of the genes.* New York: Allen & Unwin.

Waddington, C. H. (1977). *Tools for thought: How to understand and apply the latest scientific techniques of problem solving.* New York: Basic Books.

Waxman, S. R., & Kosowski, T. D. (1990). Nouns mark category relations: Toddler's and preschoolers' word-learning biases. *Child Development*, *61*, 1461–1473.

Werner, H. (1957). The concept of development from a comparative and organismic point of view. In D. B. Harris (Ed.), *The concept of development* (pp. 125–148). Minneapolis: University of Minnesota Press.

West, M. J., King, A. P., & Duff, M. A. (1990). Communicating about communicating: When innate is not enough. *Developmental Psychobiology*, *23*, 585–598.

Woodward, A. L., & Markman, E. M. (1991). Constraints on learning as default assumptions: Comments on Merriman and Bowman's "The mutual exclusivity bias in children's word learning." *Developmental Review*, *14*, 57–77.

Younger, B. (1990). Infants' detection of correlations among feature categories. *Child Development*, *61*, 614–621.

2 Connectionism and Language Learning

Brian MacWhinney
Franklin Chang
Carnegie Mellon University

SYMBOLS AND CONNECTIONS

Linguistic behavior is governed by a rigid set of social conventions. If we wake up one morning and decide to deliberately throw all these conventions to the wind, we will soon be talking gibberish, and no one would understand us. Indeed, even our best friends might think we had gone quite insane. In everyday language, we could say that we had decided to "break the rules" of English grammar. Of course, force of habit inclines us against striking off on this iconoclastic course. Having spent so many years of our lives cooperatively following the rules, it is easier to continue to follow them than to wander off into new territory. This view of linguistic rules as social conventions and habits is grounded firmly on everyday experience and common sense. I think it is a view that virtually everyone accepts.

During the 1960s and 1970s, scientists took this common sense idea of a linguistic rule and reworked it into a basic principle underlying artificial intelligence (AI), Chomskyan theoretical linguistics, and cognitive psychology. By viewing the brain as a computer, they began to think of the mind as a system for transforming symbolic strings according to well-specified rules. The vision of human language as a system of formal rules was an important ingredient underlying two decades of work in linguistics and cognitive science. This work led to the emergence of complex and impressive systems of rules and symbols that I have called the "Big Mean Rules" (MacWhinney, 1994).

In recent years, the biological and epistemological underpinnings of these great symbolic systems have become increasingly shaky and vulnerable. Two basic observational problems faced by all of these analyses are the fact that no developmental psychologist ever observed a child learning a rule and no neuroscientist ever traced the neural substrate of either a rule or a symbol. Similarly, attempts in the 1970s to demonstrate the psychological reality of rules in adults (Fodor, Bever, & Garrett, 1974; Jaeger, 1984; Linell, 1979; Ohala, 1974a, 1974b, 1974c; Trammell, 1978) yielded uniformly disappointing results.

Given these doubts and empirical failures, it made sense for researchers to begin to explore alternatives to symbols and rules. In the late 1980s, work in connectionist modeling (Rumelhart & McClelland, 1986a) began to challenge the necessity of rules and categories, focusing attention instead on models based on simple, observable cues and connections between these cues. These new models correct a fundamental, fatal flaw inherent to symbolic models. This is the problem of excessive descriptive power.

The great power of AI systems derives from the computational architecture of the Von Neumann serial computer and the application of this architecture to human cognition by Simon, Newell, and their followers (Klahr & Kotovsky, 1991; Newell & Simon, 1972). This architecture provided unlimited symbol passing, full generativity, and unlimited scalability based on the system of data paths, memory addresses, and processing cycles that could be formalized in the logic of production systems. A modeler could take a few symbols, concatenate them into rules and, magically, the computer could conjure up a working model of mental processing. These models were at the same time both too powerful and too weak. They were too powerful in that they allowed one to model the learning of things that could never in reality be learned. At the same time, they were too weak in that they failed to generalize properly across language types and patterns. Moreover, attempts to identify a uniquely correct model without adding further constraints were shown to be impossible in principle (Anderson, 1978). Neural nets (Grossberg, 1987; Hopfield, 1982; Kohonen, 1982) limit this descriptive power by imposing two stringent limitations on computational models: a prohibition against *symbol passing* and an insistence on *self-organization*.

Neural networks require that the computations involved in the models echo the connectionist architecture of the brain. The basic constraint involved here is the prohibition against symbol passing. Neuroscience has shown that the brain cannot use memory addresses to bind variables; there is no neural mechanism that can assign an absolute "address" to a particular neuron (Squire, 1987). Neurons do not send Morse code, symbols do not run down synapses, and brain waves do not pass phrase structures. Unlike the computer, the brain has no general scheme for register assignment, data pathing, or memory addressing. Moreover, the individual components of the neural system do not have the reliability of the electrical components of a standard digital computer (von Neumann, 1956). In general, the brain provides no obvious support for the symbol-passing architecture that provides the power underlying the von Neumann machine. Instead, computation in the brain appears to rely ultimately on the formation of redundant connections between individual neurons.

By itself, the requirement that computation be performed locally without symbol passing or homunculi is not enough to fully constrain descriptive power. One could still hand-wire a connectionist system to perform a specific function or to model a particular behavior. By detailed weight setting and the use of gating and polling neurons, virtually any function can be wired into a neural net (Hertz, Krogh, & Palmer, 1991). An early example of a fully hand-wired connectionist architecture was Lamb's stratificational grammar (Lamb, 1966). More recently, we have seen hand-wired connectionist models in areas such as speech errors (Dell, 1986; MacWhinney & Anderson, 1986; Stemberger, 1985), ambiguity resolution (Cottrell, 1985), and lexical activation (Marslen-Wilson, 1987) The "implementational" approach to hand-wiring spares the modeler the tedium of hand-wiring by running the wiring procedure off symbolic templates. For example, Touretzky (1990) has shown that there are techniques for bottling the full power of a LISP-based production system architecture into a neural net. These demonstrations are important because they show how difficult it is to control excessive modeling power.

In order fully to constrain descriptive power, modelers must match the constraint against symbol passing with the requirement that networks be *self-organizing*. This is to say, that models cannot be hand-wired and the connections between units must be developed on the basis of automatic learning procedures. It is this property of neural nets that makes them particularly interesting to the developmental psychologist and which also poses the greatest challenge to detailed modeling work. When the prohibition against symbol passing is combined with the demand for self-organization, the class of potential models of language learning becomes extremely limited. In fact, there is currently no detailed model of language acquisition that can satisfy these two criteria. Is this evidence that the criteria are too strict? I think not. Rather it is evidence that we can use these criteria to constrain our search for a truly plausible model of language acquisition. More importantly, it appears that those models which come closest to satisfying these criteria are also the same models that display further interesting and important properties, such as category leakage (McClelland & Kawamoto, 1986), graceful degradation (Harley & MacAndrew, 1992; Hinton & Shallice, 1991; Marchman, 1992), and property emergence (MacWhinney, Leinbach, Taraban, & McDonald, 1989; Gupta & Mozer, 1993).

When these twin constraints are taken seriously, along with the standard conditions that must be imposed on any formal model (MacWhinney, 1978b), building successful models becomes a tough job. When we add a third constraint—the need to demonstrate scalability—building powerful connectionist models becomes a nearly impossible task. Some modelers try to make headway against these odds by ignoring the scalability constraint and confronting only the first two constraints. This leads them to building models of very small pieces of the language acquisition puzzle. For example, some networks are constrained to well-defined topics such as the acquisition of the English past tense (Cottrell &

Plunkett, 1991) or German gender (MacWhinney et al., 1989). Other models have focused on small slices across larger problems such as question answering (St. John, 1992) or word recognition (McClelland & Elman, 1986). Some of these toy models may use only a few dozen sentences or a few dozen words. When one attempts to add additional words or sentences to these models, their performance often begins to degenerate. These problems with inadequate scalability are particularly serious in the study of language acquisition, since there is evidence that the move from a vocabulary of 500 words to a vocabulary of 700 words is a smooth accretional transition for the language-learning child. If connectionist models are to provide serious alternatives to symbolic models, it is crucial that they directly address each of these three issues: scalability, symbol passing, and self-organization. Any attempt to ignore one of these constraints detracts from the cognitive relevance of the modeling enterprise.

GRAND PRETENTIONS, MODEST REALITY

Like the symbolic paradigm before it, the connectionist paradigm hopes to provide a general model of human cognition. Because it has staked out such a wide territory, the connectionist paradigm is committed to providing an account of all of the core issues in language acquisition, including grammatical development, lexical learning, phonological development, second language learning, and the processing of language by the brain. Despite these grand pretensions, the reality of connectionist modeling is more sober and modest. In fact, much of the work to date has focused on the learning of narrow aspects of inflectional morphology in languages like English and German. Although limited, work in this area has taught us a great deal. This chapter sketches out the achievements of connectionist models in this well-researched area and then examines how we can move from these preliminary achievements to a fuller, more explanatory, unified approach to all of the core issues facing language acquisition theory.

Let us begin by reviewing some recent connectionist models of the learning of inflectional morphology. The first study of this topic was a model of English past tense marking presented by Rumelhart and McClelland (1987, 1986b). A more fully elaborated version of this model was developed by MacWhinney and Leinbach (1991). The task of these models was to convert the stem of an English verb into another inflected form, such as the past tense. For example, given a stem such as "eat," the model could produce "eats," "eating," "ate," or "eaten."

Like all connectionist models, this model based its performance on the development of the weights on the connections between a large collection of "units." The pattern of inputs and the connections between units was designed to implement the pattern of an autosegmental grid that has been developed in phonological theory (Goldsmith, 1976; Nespor & Vogel, 1986). The idea is that each vowel or consonant sound is a bundle of features that sits inside a slot within the framework or grid of the syllable. Words, in turn, are formed from combinations of syllables in a metrical grid. The MacWhinney–Leinbach model used 12 consonantal slots and 6 vowel slots and allowed for words of up to three syllables. The actual segments of the stem were filled into this grid in either a left-justified or a right-justified fashion. For example, the word "bet" would fill out the grid in this way:

```
 left-justified:     bCC  EV  tCC  VV  CCC  VV  CCC
right-justified:     CCC  VV  CCC  VV  CCb  VE  CCt
```

Each of the slots was in turn composed of a group of feature units. Since each of these feature units was bound to its particular slot, we can think of each unit as a slot/feature unit. For example, the first consonantal slot in the left-justified representation for "bet" would have active units for the labial, consonantal, and voiced features required for the sound /b/. Each of the consonantal slots had ten units and each of the vowel slots had eight units. The architecture of the network is given in Fig. 2.1. The complete training corpus used 6,949 different verb forms, derived from the 2,161 highest frequency verbs in English (Francis & Kučera, 1982). Of these 2,161 verbs, 118 were irregulars and 2,043 were regulars. The frequency with which a given form was included in the training epochs was determined by its frequency in the Francis and Kučera (1982) word frequency list. The highest frequency verbs were included most often. Learning in the model was controlled by the back propagation algorithm (Rumelhart, Hinton, & Williams, 1986).

The network did an excellent job learning its input corpus, producing the correct output forms for 97% of the forms. At the end of 24,000 epochs of training, the only forms that it was still missing were low-frequency irregulars such as "bled" or "underwent." Generalization testing showed that most new

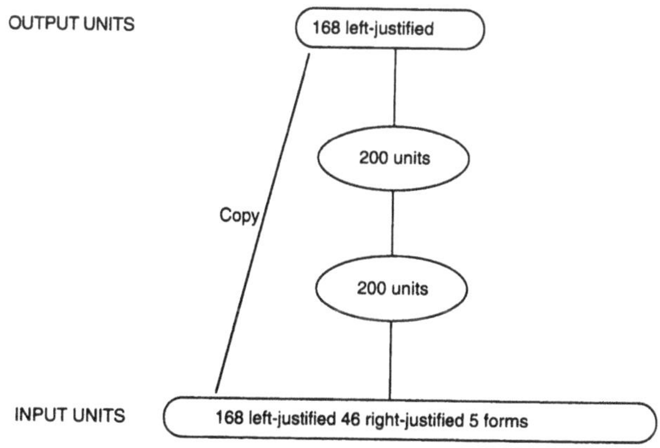

FIG. 2.1. Architecture of the model for English.

verbs were produced in the regular past, but that a few forms were treated as irregulars. Additional generalization testing is reported in MacWhinney (1993) and Ling and Marinov (1993).

English is a relatively poor language, at least in regard to its system of inflectional morphology. It has virtually no marking of case or gender. Nouns have only a single basic suffix for plurality and virtually the same suffix for the possessive. Although there are a few irregular past tense verbs, even the system of verbal morphology is fairly simple. Fortunately, we do not have to look far afield for a more challenging problem. Even a closely related language like German presents us with a far richer system of inflectional morphology. So rich, indeed, that Mark Twain (1935) once complained that:

> a person who has not studied German can form no idea of what a perplexing language it is . . . . Every noun has a gender, and there is no sense or system in the distribution; so the gender of each must be learned separately and by heart. There is no other way. To do this, one has to have memory like a memorandum book. In German, a young lady has no sex, while a turnip has. Think what overwrought reverence that shows for the turnip, and what callous disrespect for the girl. (p. 21)

Anyone who has studied German, be it in the context of the classroom or in the country itself, has probably reached a very similar conclusion.

The vagaries of German gender are compounded by the fact that German still clings to a system of case-marking only slightly simpler than that found in Classical Latin. For example, the definite article is declined through all four cases and all three genders in the singular and across all four cases with gender neutralized in the plural. The result of these various obligatory markings is the following paradigm for the definite article:

	Masc	*Fem*	*Neut*	*Plural*
Nom	der	die	das	die
Gen	des	der	des	der
Dat	dem	der	dem	der
Acc	den	die	das	die

This paradigm is rife with homonymy. The six forms of the definite article *(der, die, das, dem, des, den)* must cover the 16 cells in the paradigm. This is done by having a single form cover several meanings. For example, the article *der* can mean either masculine singular nominative, feminine singular genitive, feminine singular dative, or plural genitive.

In order to select the correct form of the definite article, the language learner has to know three things about the noun—its case, its number, and its gender. Number is the easiest category, since it bears an straightforward relation to real-world properties. Case is somewhat more abstract, but it can generally be figured out through a combination of cues from the verb, related prepositions, and some word order patterns. However, there is little in the external situation that can help the child figure out the gender of a noun (Maratsos & Chalkley, 1980). It is possible that the noun's gender could be simply memorized or even inferred on the basis of its use within the paradigm. However, recent work by Köpcke and Zubin (Köpcke, 1982, 1988; Köpcke & Zubin, 1983, 1984, in press; Zubin & Köpcke, 1981, 1986) has shown that Mark Twain's view of gender as arbitrary and unpredictable is incomplete and partially incorrect.

In fact, Köpcke and Zubin have shown that there are dozens of phonological cues that can be used to predict the gender of a German noun. For example, almost all nouns ending in -e are feminine, as in *die Sonne, die Ente,* and *die Tante*. Almost all nouns beginning with *dr-, tr-,* and *kn-* are masculine, as in *der Knecht, der Trieb,* and *der Drang*. There are dozens of other cues like these. In addition to these purely phonological cues, there are derivational endings such as *-chen, -lein, -ett, -tum, -ei,* and so on, each of which reliably specify a particular gender.

MacWhinney, Leinbach, Taraban, and McDonald (1989) constructed a series of models of the acquisition of German gender. The first model dedicated a series of nodes to the cues enumerated by Köpcke and Zubin, along with a series of nodes for case and number cues. The second model made no explicit coding of the Köpcke–Zubin cues, instead simply encoding the phonological form of the base in the manner of the MacWhinney–Leinbach model for English. Much to our surprise, the network with no hand coding of features outperformed the hand-crafted network in terms of both learning and generalization. These results provide nice support for the view of connectionist networks as providing emergent self-organizing characterizations of linguistic systems. Similar results for hand-wired vs. emergent solutions are reported by Daelemans, Gillis, and Durieux (in press) for the learning of Dutch stress by a connectionist network. The architecture of the successful nonhandcrafted German simulation is given in Fig. 2.2. The input to the network was a pattern across the 143 phonological units to represent the noun stem and the 11 phonological units to represent suffixes attached to the noun. In addition, there were 5 semantic units representing inherent gender and 17 cues that provided a distributed pattern of surface structure information helpful in determining the case for the noun. However, the actual identity of the case was not given. This network was trained with 2,000 German nouns from all cells in the paradigm. It learned the training set completely. When tested with 200 new nouns, the system was able to guess the gender of the new words with 70% accuracy. This compares with a level of 80% accuracy that could be expected from a native German speaker.

The model also succeeded in capturing a variety of important developmental phenomena. Like the children studied by MacWhinney (1978a) and Mills (1986), the model showed early acquisiiton of the nominative and delayed acqui-

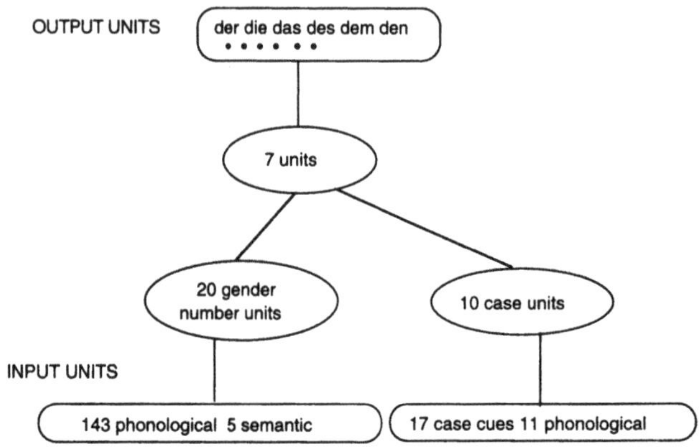

FIG. 2.2. Architecture of the model for German.

sition of the genitive. These acquisitional order effects are undoubtedly due to the fact that the frequencies of the four cases in the training corpus were based on their actual distribution in German corpora. Also, like German children, the model made good use of reliable cues to gender such as final -e or some of the derivational markers. Like children, the model was able to use the paradigm to infer word class. For example, given the accusative form *den Bauer,* the model could produce the genitive singular form *des Bauers*. Native speakers can do this on the basis of only one exposure to the word and the model displays similar behavior. Like children, the model frequently omitted the article. This occurred when the output units did not reach threshold. Finally, the model demonstrated the same tendency toward overgeneralization of the feminine gender often found in children. This is apparently due to the fact that the similarity of the feminine to the plural lends it enough frequency and paradigmatic support to tend to overcome the effects of the other two genders.

When evaluating the success of these connectionist models of language acquisition, it is important to consider the extent to which symbolic models are able to address similar problems. For the learning of English verb morphology, Ling (1994) presents a model that performs about as well as the MacWhinney–Leinbach model for English. Although Ling's model is based on a conventional symbol-passing architecture, it uses an automatic learning algorithm, thereby avoiding problems with hand-wiring. However, this also means that Ling's model has no clear representation of rules and would probably not be accepted as a full symbolic model by many linguists and psycholinguists. Nonetheless, the head-on comparison of models conducted by Ling is quite interesting and further connectionist work by Bullinaria (in press) shows that the competitive testing of symbolic and connectionist models can be quite instructive.

LEXICAL ITEMS: AN ACHILLES HEEL?

Despite its basic successes, there are several properties of the MacWhinney models that should give us serious cause for worry. In this sense, these weaknesses of the model are actually more instructive than its successes. These weaknesses play a parallel role in both the model for English and the model for German.

Problem #1—Homophony. Because both of the models are based on a system that converts from phonology to phonology without using discrete representations for lexical items, both models run into serious problems with homophonous forms. Consider the three ways in which we can form the past tense of "ring" in English. We can say "the maid wrung out the clothes," "the soldiers ringed the city," or "the choirboy rang the bell." These three different past tense forms all have the same sound /rIN/ in the present, but each takes a different form in the past.

A similar problem arises in German. The stem *Bund* can be either *der Bund* or *das Bund,* depending on whether it is an "alliance" or a "bundle or sheaf of wheat." And the stem *Band* can be either *der Band* or *das Band* depending on whether it means a "volume of a book" or a "rubber band." The problem here is that, in order to control this variation, one needs to distinguish the meanings of the two homophonous lexical items involved. If the network has no concept of "lexical item" this is difficult to do. These problems also affect the formation of the plural. For example, the singular form *das Wort* has two plural forms: *die Wörter* (several words) and *die Worte* (connected words or speech).

Problem #2—Compounds. A parallel problem crops up in the formation of the past tense of compound words. The English training set included several compounds based on irregular verbs such as "undcrgo," "rcthink," and "undo." The fact that the past tense of "undergo" is "underwent" depends on the fact that "undergo" is a variant of the stem "go." If the compound itself is high enough in frequency, the network can learn to treat it as an irregular. However, the network had a hard time learning the past tense of low frequency irregular compounds. At the end of training, the model was still not producing "underwent" correctly, even though it had learned "went" early in training. It is clear that the model was not able to use its learning about "go–went" to facilitate learning of the far less frequent form "undergo-underwent."

A similar problem emerged in the learning of the gender of compounds in German. The model quickly learned that *Mutter* (mother) was feminine, because the noun was so frequent. However, there is a competing tendency to treat words with final -er as masculine. And this tendency led the model to treat the less frequent form *Grossmutter* (grandmother) as masculine, although it is clearly a variant of *Mutter* and should be feminine.

Problem #3—Derivational status. The model was also not capable of utilizing information regarding the derivational status of lexical items. As Kim, Pinker, Prince, and Prasada (1990) have noted, the past tense forms of denominal verbs are uniformly regular. For example, the word "ring" can be used as a verb in a sentence such as "the groom ringed her finger" and we would never say "the groom rung her finger." However, as we noted earlier, the network of the MacWhinney–Leinbach simulation cannot use the derivational status of the verb "ring" to make this distinction.

German provides even clearer examples of the importance of derivational status. All German nouns that derive from verbs are masculine. For example, the noun *der Schlag* (blow, cream) derives from the verb *schlagen* (to hit). However, there is no motivated way of indicating this in the model. In general, the model includes no independent way of representing derivational suffixes and prefixes. Thus, no distinction is made between true phonological cues such as final -e or initial kn- and derivational markers such as *-chen* or *-ett*. This leads to some very clear confusions. For example, masculines such as *der Nacken* (neck) and *der Hafen* (harbor) end in phonological /en/, whereas neuters such as *das Wissen* (knowledge) and *das Lernen* (learning) end in the derivational suffix *-en*. Confusion of these two suffixes leads to inability to correctly predict gender for new nouns ending in *-en*.

Problem #4—Early irregulars. A well-known child language phenomenon is the u-shaped learning curve for irregular verbs in English. For a verb such as "go," children may begin with "went," then show some occasional usage of "goed," and finally settle in on correct usage with "went." During the period of oscillation between "goed" and "went," it is usually "went" that predominates. However, not all irregular verbs show this pattern and not all overregularizations enter at the same time. The MacWhinney–Leinbach model showed the oscillation between "goed" and "went" terminating in correct usage, but it did not show early use of "went." The reason for the failure of the model to produce early "went" is that the network is configured to construct the past tense as a variation on the phonological form of the present tense. A more accurate model would allow direct learning of "went" as a rote form. But the capacity to learn rote associations between sound and meaning involves the capacity to learn lexical items and this means that we will need a connectionist architecture specifically designed for this type of learning.

The Core Problem. These four weaknesses we have discussed can be linked to a single core problem: the absence of any way of representing lexical items. Because these models have no lexical items, they are forced to rely on sound features as the only way to determine inflectional morphology. It would be a mistake to imagine that the sound form of words has no impact on inflection and derivation. In fact, it seems that what really happens during both production and comprehension is that both the sound and meaning of stems and affixes are available in parallel, although the time course of their activation may vary (Kawamoto, 1993).

One way of addressing this problem is to mix both sound features and meaning features into the model without providing any explicit representation of lexical items. Attempts to achieve lexical access without lexical representations may be partially effective in models of reading (Kawamoto, 1993; Plaut & McClelland, 1993) and spelling (Seidenberg & McClelland, 1989), but they run into more serious problems (Cottrell & Plunkett, 1991; Hoeffner, 1992), when dealing with language learning and word production. The Hoeffner model displays this problem most clearly. It learns to associate sound to meaning and stores these associations in a distributed pattern in the hidden units. This approach works well enough until the model is given more than about 700 forms. At this point, the large pool of hidden units is so fully invested in distinguishing phonological and semantic subtypes and their associations that there is simply no room for new words. Adding more hidden units doesn't solve this problem, since all the interconnections must be computed and eventually the learning algorithm will bog down. Perhaps what we have here is the soft underbelly of connectionism—its inability to represent Islands of Stability in the middle of a Sea of Chaos. Perhaps the problem of learning to represent lexical items is the Achilles' heel of connectionism.

A SOLUTION TO THE LEXICAL LEARNING PROBLEM

Given the seriousness of these problems and the extent to which they have limited the full effectiveness of network models for English and German, we decided to confront the problem directly. The core assumption in our new approach is that the lexical item serves a central controlling and stabilizing role in language learning and processing. We can refer to this revised approach as *lexicalist connectionism*. Predecessors to lexicalist connectionist models can be found in localist connectionist models of the type developed by Dell (1986) and Stemberger (1985) where a central role is given to the lexical item. However, because of their localist node-based architecture, these models were forced to rely on hand-wiring. The Competition Model (MacWhinney, 1987, 1988; MacWhinney & Anderson, 1986; MacWhinney & Bates, 1989) also relies on localist, hand-wired connections. These models provide good descriptions of particular experimental results, but at the price of violating the basic constraint on self-organization that is one of the important attractions of connectionism to the developmental psychologist.

A First Attempt. For the last two years, I have been researching ways of integrating lexical items into self-organizing connectionist networks. The first approach to this problem was a model developed by Gupta and MacWhinney (1992) to coordinate German article marking with the learning of the case and number markings on the noun. The basic idea behind this work was to explore whether inclusion of lexical items in a simulation would make a signficant difference in learning and generalization. In order to do this, Gupta and I took the MacWhinney, Leinbach, Taraban, and McDonald model for German and "grafted" on a system of lexical items. In addition, we provided the network with a way of learning case-gender-number configurations. The crucial comparison was between a form of the model that used lexical category units and one that did not. With these units present, the model was able to learn all the articles for a 2,094 word corpus in 65 epochs and all the noun markings in 70 epochs. Without lexical categories, there were still 34 article errors at 65 epochs and there were still 53 noun inflection errors at 70 epochs. With a larger input corpus, errors would further increase and the network without lexical categories would then be unable to even learn the training set. This comparison made it clear that the availability of lexical items and lexical categories is crucial for the successful learning of the full German inflectional system.

Self-Organizing Feature Maps. This model demonstrated the importance of lexical items, but it provided us with no clues on how to implement this learning in connectionist hardware. For further ideas on this topic we turned to the self-organizing feature map framework of Kohonen (1982) and Miikulainen (1990; Miikulainen & Dyer, 1991). In this framework, word learning is viewed as the association of a large number of phonological features to a large number of semantic features. These many features constitute a high-dimensional space. However, the association of these many dimensions can be conveniently represented on a 2-D feature map in which nearby vectors in the input space are mapped onto nearby units in the 2-D map. The two dimensions of the visible representation do not have any direct relation to features in the input data set, rather they preserve the topological relations inherent in the high-dimensional space.

Schematically, one can think of the map as a 2-D compression that associates sound and meaning as in Fig. 2.3. Learning involves the strengthening of weights between particular inputs and units on the map. This can be done in strict accord with established biological principles of lateral inhibition and the redistribution of syntactic resources (Kohonen, 1982) and a computationally efficient algorithm can be implemented that is faithful to these biological principles (Miikkulainen, 1990).

Using the self-organizing feature map algorithm of Kohonen and Miikulainen, Franklin Chang and I have found that a network with 10,000 nodes can learn up to 6,000 lexical associations with an error rate of less than 1%. In this particular

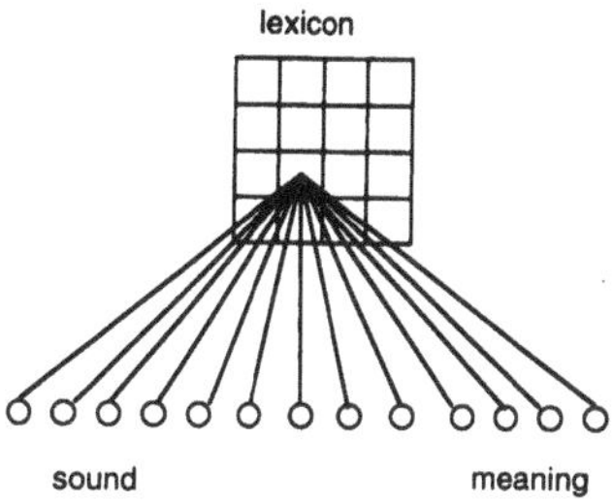

FIG. 2.3. A two-dimensional compression of a multidimensional association space.

implementation, we used four floating-point numbers to represent sound and four additional floating-point numbers to represent meaning. The shape of these eight numbers for each item was generated randomly. At the beginning of learning, the first input vector of eight numbers would lead by chance to somewhat stronger activation on one of the 10,000 cells. This one slightly more active cell would then inhibit the activation of its competitors. Once it has won this particular competition, its activation would be negatively damped to prevent it from winning for all of the items. Then, on the next trial, another cell would win in the competition for the next lexical item. This process would repeat until all 6,000 items had developed some "specialist" cell in the feature map. During this process, the dynamics of self-organization would make it so that items that shared features would end up in similar regions of the feature map.

One way of following the development of the feature map is to track the average radius of the individual items. After learning the first 700 words, the average radius of each word was 70 cells; after 3,000 words, the radius was 8; after 5,000 words the radius was 3; and after 6,000 words the radius was only 1.5 cells. Clearly, there is not much room for new lexical items in a feature map with 10,000 cells that has already learned 6,000 items. However, there is good reason to think that the enormous number of cells in the human brain makes it so that the size of the initial feature map is not an important limiting constraint on the learning of the lexicon by real children.

Using Maps for Retrieval. The self-organizing feature map solves only one part of the problem of lexical learning. It shows us how uncommitted cortex can be organized to have localist representations for individual lexical items. But this algorithm fails to provide us with a feasible way of retrieving lexical information without violating the prohibition against symbol passing. Given a sound and a meaning, we can activate a lexical item, but we cannot take a sound and retrieve a meaning. Nor can we take a meaning and retrieve the corresponding sound.

In order to permit full use of the lexicon, we need to supplement the basic feature map architecture with additional connections. We do this by simultaneously building up three identical parallel feature maps. We call these the sound map, the meaning map, and the association map. During training, all three maps are given full input patterns. They then come to take on very parallel forms of internal organization. Then we use Hebbian learning between the maps to form inter-item associations between sound, meaning, and the central association map. Up to this point, we are assuming that all lexical learning is occurring with both sound and meaning being copresent. Once this type of learning is complete, we begin auto-associative learning. The four meaning numbers are blanked out and the sound net is trained to produce the correct activation in the association net just on the basis of the sound input. The association net then activates the corresponding item in the meaning net and this item then activates its meaning. In this way, we can retrieve meaning from sound. Retrieval of sound from meaning involves the opposite form of processing.

IMPLICATIONS OF THE MODEL

This implementation of Miikulainen's model allows us to put aside our earlier worries regarding lexical learning as an Achilles' Heel for connectionist models of language learning. We now have self-organizing structures that look very much like lexical items. We cannot manipulate these items with standard symbol-passing techniques, but we can develop their use through connections to other processes. In this section, I will discuss some of these additional processes.

Input Phonology Scaffolds Output Phonology. When a child learns a new word, the initial association is between an auditory form and some referential content. At first, the child knows how to "hear" the word, but does not know how to "say" it. It is safe to assume that the featural representation of auditory forms derives from basic properties of the auditory system and auditory cortical processing (Kuhl & Miller, 1975; Werker, Gilbert, Humphrey, & Tees, 1981). On the other hand, there is no evidence for a rich innate mapping of auditory form to articulatory gestures. Instead, learning of some of these associations of individual auditory–articulatory correspondences occur in the period before the onset of the first words (Oller, 1991; Oller & Eilers, 1988). These mappings provide the basis for a transduction of auditory form to articulatory form, but they are only partially adequate for the full task of lexical phonology. They must be supplemented by a process of auditory scaffolding.

When the child tries to use her tongue and mouth to produce the required sound, her articulatory activities can be closely guided by the sequential structure of the auditory form. When the child listens to the word, the auditory units become activated in their correct order in a chained fashion (Houghton, 1990; McClelland & Elman, 1986; Rumelhart & Norman, 1982). When the child tries to produce the word, this auditory chain can be used as a scaffold for the articulatory process. During articulation, each auditory unit stimulates some closely matching articulatory unit. In this way, activation of the articulation for a new word being learned is more or less on track initially. Eventually, connections from output phonology can become directly associated to the core lexical feature map, thereby obviating reliance on the auditory scaffold.

Buffering and Segmentation. Another basic process that must be incorporated in a connectionist model of language processing is lexical "masking." If our models assume a single central lexicon, we will need to have some process that deactivates each lexical item immediately after it is activated. The trace of this masked item must then be stored provisionally in some separate form apart from the main lexicon. The simplest way to do this is to activate a second copy of the original item (Burgess & Hitch, 1992). As Grossberg (Cohen & Grossberg, 1986, 1987; Grossberg, 1978, 1987; Grossberg & Stone, 1986a, 1986b) has noted, masking can be used as a way of accounting for segmentation. For example, when the system hears the form "cats," the item "cat" can be masked out. This leaves the suffix "-s" as the residue which is then a candidate for lexical learning. In effect, masking has led to the segmentation of "cats" into "cat" and "-s." Subsequent lexical learning involves association of the residual semantics with the residual phonology, as outlined in MacWhinney (1978a). In general, segmentation involves building up a contrast between lexical items that are already known and material that is new and unfamiliar. For example, if the child already knows the words "Mommy" and "Daddy," but does not know the word "like" the sentence "Daddy likes Mommy" would be represented in this way:

d a d i	l aɪ k s	m a m i
Daddy	unknown	Mommy

For the known stretches, there are two lexical items that successfully compete. These strings and the semantics they represent are masked. The unknown stretch stimulates lexical learning of the new word "likes." In this way, the use of the lexicon leads to the correct segmentation of the input and further lexical learning.

Recovery From Overgeneralization. A well-discussed phenomenon in both cognitive and linguistic development is the u-shaped curve (Strauss, 1981). U-shaped curves involve performance that, for a period, gets worse as the child gets older. For example, the young child may begin with "went" as the past tense of "go." Months later, we begin to hear the form "goed" intermingled with "went." Finally, the child stops using "goed" and produces only "went." In the language learning literature, "goed" is called a overgeneralization error. Followers of the Chomskyan nativist approach to language learning (Baker & McCarthy, 1981; Gleitman, 1990; Gleitman, Newport, & Gleitman, 1984; Morgan & Travis, 1989; Pinker, 1984, 1989; Wexler & Culicover, 1980) have called the problem of recovering from overgeneralization "the logical problem of language acquisition." In their view, the linguistic input is so impoverished that many types of errors could never be corrected on the basis of positive evidence alone. These writers also cite observational evidence that children do not immediately benefit from "negative evidence" attempting to correct their errors.

The account of language learning being developed here is in a position to present a full alternative solution to the so-called "logical problem." This solution assumes that lexical items are represented as complete auditory traces. For example, the word "went" has a full episodic representation as an auditory input form. At the same time, the extraction of the suffix "-ed" by masking and segmentation allows the system to produce the form "go-ed" by combination of lexical items. This form is further supported by the overall system of analogic processing of inflectional morphology in the MacWhinney–Leinbach model that we reviewed earlier. When this occurs, there is a competition between the output form and residual auditory form, as schematized in Fig. 2.4. Children's language is full of competitions of this type. The child must learn to stop saying things like "*I poured the tub with water," "*I unsqueezed the ball," or "*I recommended him a soup" (Bowerman, 1988). Our connectionist account holds that recovery occurs when the episodic support for exceptions is strengthened against the analogic pattern. Many children are conservative in the first place and tend to limit the total number of overgeneralizations they produce. Other children must work on a case-by-case basis to strengthen auditory forms against analogic pressures.

Although there is no true "logical problem" underlying language acquisition and although one cannot use recovery from overgeneralization as an argument for nativist constraints, it is helpful to look at areas of persistent overgeneraliza-

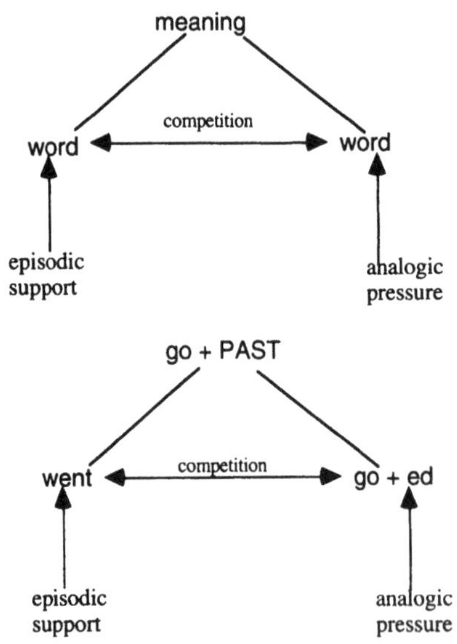

FIG. 2.4. The competition between rote and analogy.

tions as indicators of underlying connectionist analogic pressures. For this reason, it makes sense for language researchers to continue to focus on overgeneralizations as an important source of data about crucial processes in language learning.

LINKING UP WITH THE COMPETITION MODEL

During the 1980s, Elizabeth Bates and I collaborated with colleagues in over a dozen countries to examine crosslinguistic differences in sentence processing. This work is summarized in an edited volume by MacWhinney and Bates (1989). The core idea underlying this work is the notion of cue validity. Cue validity is simply the conditional probability of a category, given a cue. In dozens of published studies, we showed that languages differ markedly in the relative reliance they place on basic cues to sentence interpretation. For example, a sentence like "The eraser chases the dog" is interpreted as a strange case of Subject-Verb-Object order in English, whereas it is readily seen as involving Object-Verb-Subject order in the corresponding Italian sentence. This is because Italian tends to ignore the word order cue and places relatively more reliance on Animacy.

Although we provided formal mathematical models of cue integration at the end of sentence processing (McDonald & MacWhinney, 1989), we did not provide an explicit computational mechanism that showed how these cues would be used during the on-line processing of sentence interpretation. There is a good reason why we avoided this additional step. We were convinced that parsing models based on a standard symbol-passing architecture (Marcus, 1980) were cognitively implausible. Moreover, many of these models (Frazier, 1987) made heavy use of constructs from universal grammar that went directly against the strong evidence we had for language differences in sentence processing. We believed that the best implementation of our model would be one based on connectionist principles. However, we were not satisfied by the performance and scalability of the various attempts to build connectionist models of sentence processing (Hanson & Burr, 1990; Houghton, 1993; McClelland & Kawamoto, 1986).

A Competition Model Net. Recently, Janice Johnson and I have made some progress in developing a connectionist implementation of the Competition Model. The network not only models the learning of syntax by the first language learner, but also the acquisition of a second language. The model uses a recurrent network of the type examined by Elman (1991). The basic idea behind the system is given in Fig. 2.5.

Processing in this type of recurrent net works in terms of cycles, with each word in the sentence triggering one cycle through the net. When the first word

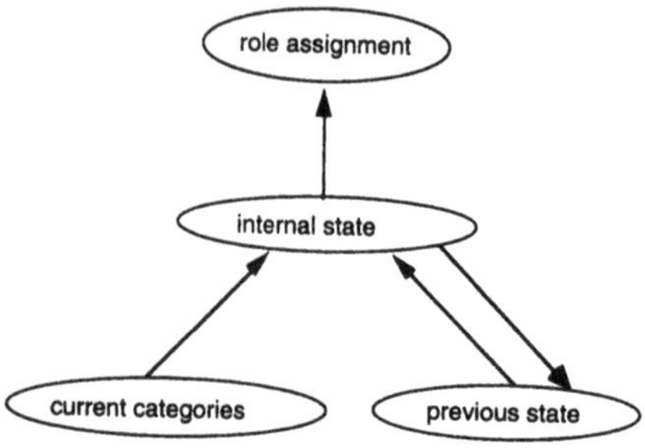

FIG. 2.5. A recursive network for role assignment.

comes in, its grammatical categories become activated and these turn on the "current categories" as input. These categories activate some "internal state" units and these in turn activate some provisional "role assignment" decisions. At the same time, the "internal state" units are copied to the "previous state" units in order to provide a short-term memory. On the next pass through the network with the next word, the input categories are activated in a new way. This time, they work together with the "previous state" units to determine the activation of the "internal state" units and then the provisional role assignments.

The input to the net was a set of lexically based grammatical categories. Our use of grammatical categories as input is based on our assumption that this category of information can become associated with the lexical feature map network using the FGREP technique developed by Miikulainen and Dyer (1991). The 14 input units were:

0 flag for first item in a sequence
1 noun
2 verb
3 animate
4 inanimate
5 singular morphology
6 plural morphology
7 subject case morphology
8 object case morphology
9 passive voice morphology
10 active voice morphology
11 relative pronoun
12 English
13 Dutch

Units 2, 9, 10, and 11 were always set off for nouns. Units 1, 3, 4, 7, 8, and 11 were always set off for verbs.

The system included a pool of 100 internal state units and a parallel set of 100 units for preserving the previous state. The output units were used to designed to provide the type of sentence interpretation recorded in Competition Model studies of sentence processing. In particular, we wanted to model the patterns of sentence choice observed in English adults and children by Bates, McNew, MacWhinney, Devescovi, and Smith (1982) and in English and Dutch second language learners by McDonald (1987). The output units we included in our net were:

Unit	Value
0–2	N1 role in main clause—Agent, Patient, and/or Perspective
3–5	N1 role in relative clause—Agent, Patient, and/or Perspective
6–8	N2 role in main clause—Agent, Patient, and/or Perspective
9–11	N2 role in relative clause—Agent, Patient, and/or Perspective
12–14	N3 role in main clause—Agent, Patient, and/or Perspective
15–17	N3 role in relative clause—Agent, Patient, and/or Perspective
18–22	V1 status: main/relative agrees N1, N2, or N3
23–27	V2 status: main/relative agrees N1, N2, or N3
28	English language input
29	Dutch language input

We trained the network on a richly patterned corpus including actives, passives, animacy variations (AA, AI, IA), agreement variations (first, second, both), imperatives, intransitives, and four relative clause structures (SS, SO, OS, and OO). All sentences were grammatical and all used NVN word order. The Dutch corpus differed from the English corpus primarily in its greater use of OVS word order and its restriction of relative clause orders to SOV patterns.

Results for L1 Learning of English and Dutch. Using the back-propagation algorithm, we were able to train the network to make the correct role assignments for all of the patterns in the training set. In addition to looking at correctness of decisions, we could examine the relative strength of assignments across time, since the output units changed in their activation after each word. We found that the network trained on the English corpus quickly moved toward a very strong activation of N1 as agent, whereas the network trained on the Dutch corpus was much slower to reach this decision. Again, this result is based directly on the fact that the Dutch corpus contains many grammatical OVS sentences as input.

Our testing of the model paralleled the testing of subjects in our experiments by using ungrammatical VNN and NNV orders as ways of testing cue competition. In English, VNN order weakly activates a VOS interpretation, just as it does in our experimental data. In NNV sentences, however, the network initially begins with a SOV interpretation and then shifts in midstream to a strong OSV interpretation. This not only provides evidence that the recurrent net can recover quickly from "garden pathing," but also matches well with our experimental data from English-speaking subjects. Of course, the reasons for these patterns can be traced directly to the shape of the input corpus where NNV orders occur only in relative clauses without relativizers where they always have OSV interpretations. If the relativizer is included in the corpus, we find that generalization is blocked. In general, this type of network displays very little generalization for patterns that do not have similar linear orders.

We also found that the English agreement and case cues were numerically weaker at each step during processing that the corresponding cues in Dutch. Again, these are facts about the structure of the input corpus. The one mismatch we encountered between the model and our empirical data on the learning of English and Dutch was with the NNV order in Dutch. The problem here was that we were deriving NNV order in both languages primarily from relative clauses. However, for Dutch, the strength of the SOV interpretation of NNV patterns is based on interpretation of nouns in subordinate clauses, which are almost always in SOV order. Future attempts to construct a fuller input corpus will obviously need to include examples of subordinate clauses, along with relative clauses. This type of problem underscores the extent to which we can only hope to have a fully accurate model if we have a truly representative input corpus. Deriving such a corpus empirically and coding it computationally is a massive undertaking, but one that must be done if we are to understand the limits of data-driven models.

Results for Second Language Learning. Connectionist networks face a major obstacle when attempting to model the acquisition of a second language. This is the tendency for networks to display "catastrophic interference" when the training corpus undergoes a sudden radical change of state. This radical change of state can occur in the real world when an Dutch-speaking child goes to live with friends in the United States and suddenly is immersed in an English-speaking world where virtually no one speaks Dutch. Of course, the sharpness of this shift can vary a great deal in reality. Even in the sharpest cases of transition, the learner continues to use the first language internally and it is probably unrealistic to think that input from the first language ever ceases altogether. Because of this, we decided to model the shift between languages in a somewhat gradual fashion. After 20 cycles, when the L1 corpus was fully learned, we began to expose the network to a mixed training corpus for another 10 cycles before shifting to only Dutch. When we trained in this way and when we included language units in both the input and output, we found that we were able to minimize catastrophic interference of L1 and closely model the L2 learning patterns described by McDonald (1987).

LIMITATIONS AND PROSPECTS

This modeling work with connectionist nets has advanced to the point where it can compete on an equal footing with the more powerful rule-based symbolic models. These networks minimize hand-wiring and maximize self-organization. Because of this, they are attractive to developmental psychologists. They also avoid reliance on hardware address and symbol-passing. And it is this that makes them attractive to cognitive neuroscientists. But they are still incomplete in many ways. In our modeling of language learning, we have made good progress in the areas of lexical learning, inflectional morphology, and role assignment. Our models of transfer and learning for a second language show a remarkably good fit to the experimental data. But there is still much work to be done. We need to link up the high-level modeling of role assignment to detailed aspects of lexical processing and local role assignment and attachment. We need to model the learning of more different types of inflectional structures. And we need to deal in great detail with lexical effects on syntax. There may still be an Achilles' Heel that will doom this whole process to failure. But, for now, we can look at the progress we have made as grounds for cautious optimism.

REFERENCES

Anderson, J. (1978). Arguments concerning representations for mental imagery. *Psychological Review, 85*, 249–277.

Baker, C. L., & McCarthy, J. J. (Eds.). (1981). *The logical problem of language acquisition*. Cambridge: MIT Press.

Bates, E., McNew, S., MacWhinney, B., Devescovi, A., & Smith, S. (1982). Functional constraints on sentence processing: A cross-linguistic study. *Cognition, 11*, 245–299.

Bowerman, M. (1988). The "no negative evidence" problem. In J. Hawkins (Ed.), *Explaining language universals*. London: Blackwell.

Bullinaria, J. (in press). Learning the past tense of English verbs: Connectionism fights back. *Journal of Artificial Intelligence Research*.

Burgess, N., & Hitch, G. (1992). Toward a network model of the articulatory loop. *Journal of Memory and Language, 31*, 429–460.

Cohen, M., & Grossberg, S. (1986). Neural dynamics of speech and language coding: Developmental programs, perceptual grouping, and competition for short-term memory. *Human Neurobiology, 5*, 1–22.

Cohen, M., & Grossberg, S. (1987). Masking fields: A massively parallel neural architecture for learning, recognizing, and predicting multiple groupings of patterned data. *Applied Optics, 26*, 1866–1891.

Cottrell, G. (1985). *A connectionist approach to word sense disambiguation*. Unpublished doctoral dissertation, University of Rochester.

Cottrell, G., & Plunkett, K. (1991). Learning the past tense in a recurrent network: Acquiring the mapping from meaning to sounds. In *Proceedings of the Thirteenth Annual Conference of the Cognitive Science Society*. Hillsdale, NJ: Lawrence Erlbaum Associates.

Daelemanns, W., Gillis, S., & Durieux, G. (in press). The acquisition of stress: A data-oriented approach. *Computational Linguistics*.

Dell, G. (1986). A spreading-activation theory of retrieval in sentence production. *Psychological Review, 93*, 283–321.

Elman, J. (1991). *Incremental learning, or the importance of starting small* (CRL Tech. Rep. 9101). Unpublished manuscript, University of California, San Diego.

Fodor, J. A., Bever, T. G., & Garrett, M. F. (1974). *The psychology of language: An introduction to psycholinguistics and generative grammar*. New York: McGraw-Hill.

Francis, W., & Kučera, H. (1982). *Frequency analysis of English usage: Lexicon and grammar*. Boston: Houghton Mifflin.

Frazier, L. (1987). *Sentence processing: A tutorial review*. Hove, UK: Lawrence Erlbaum Associates.

Gleitman, L. (1990). The structural sources of verb meanings. *Language Acquisition, 1*, 3–55.

Gleitman, L. R., Newport, E. L., & Gleitman, H. (1984). The current status of the motherese hypothesis. *Journal of Child Language, 11*, 43–79.

Goldsmith, J. (1976). An overview of autosegmental phonology. *Linguistic analysis, 2*, 23–68.

Grossberg, S. (1978). A theory of human memory: Self-organization and performance of sensory-motor codes, maps, and plans. *Progress in Theoretical Biology, 5*, 233–374.

Grossberg, S. (1987). Competitive learning: From interactive activation to adaptive resonance. *Cognitive Science, 11*, 23–63.

Grossberg, S., & Stone, G. (1986a). Neural dynamics of attention switching and temporal-order information in short-term memory. *Memory and Cognition, 14*, 451–468.

Grossberg, S., & Stone, G. (1986b). Neural dynamics of word recognition and recall: Attentional priming, learning, and resonance. *Psychological Review, 93*.

Gupta, P., & MacWhinney, B. (1992). Integrating category acquisition with inflectional marking: A model of the German nominal system. In *Proceedings of the Fourteenth Annual Conference of the Cognitive Science Society*. Hillsdale, NJ: Lawrence Erlbaum Associates.

Gupta, P., & Mozer, M. C. (1993). Exploring the nature and development of phonological representations. In *Proceedings of the Fifteenth Annual Conference of the Cognitive Science Society*. Hillsdale, NJ: Lawrence Erlbaum Associates.

Hanson, S. J., & Burr, D. J. (1990). What connectionist models learn: Learning and representation in connectionist networks. *Behavioral and Brain Sciences, 13*, 471–518.

Harley, T., & MacAndrew, S. (1992). Modelling paraphasias in normal and aphasic speech. In *Proceedings of the Fourteenth Annual Conference of the Cognitive Science Society*. Hillsdale, NJ: Lawrence Erlbaum Associates.

Hertz, J., Krogh, A., & Palmer, R. (1991). *Introduction to the theory of neural computation*. New York: Addison-Wesley.

Hinton, G., & Shallice, T. (1991). Lesioning an attractor network: Investigations of acquired dyslexia. *Psychological Review, 98*, 74–95.

Hoeffner, J. (1992). Are rules a thing of the past? The acquisition of verbal morphology by an attractor network. In *Proceedings of the Fourteenth Annual Conference of the Cognitive Science Society*. Hillsdale, NJ: Lawrence Erlbaum Associates.

Hopfield, J. J. (1982). Neural networks and physical systems with emergent collective computational abilities. *Proceedings of the National Academy of Sciences, 79*, 2554–2558.

Houghton, G. (1990). The problem of serial order: A neural network model of sequence learning and recall. In R. Dale, C. Mellish, & M. Zock (Eds.), *Current research in natural language generation*. London: Academic Press.

Houghton, G. (1993). A constraint-satisfaction model of grammatical role assignment in language production. Manuscript submitted for publication.

Jaeger, J. J. (1984). Assessing the psychological status of the vowel shift rule. *Journal of Psycholinguistic Research, 13, No.1*, 13–36.

Kawamoto, A. (1993). Non-linear dynamics in the resolution of lexical ambiguity: A parallel distributed processing account. *Journal of Memory and Language*, *32*, 474–516.

Kim, J., Pinker, S., Prince, A., & Prasada, S. (1990). Why no mere mortal has ever flown out to center field. *Cognitive Science*, *15*, 173–218.

Klahr, D., & Kotovsky, K. (1991). *Complex information processing: The impact of Herbert A. Simon*. Hillsdale, NJ: Lawrence Erlbaum Associates.

Kohonen, T. (1982). Self-organized formation of topologically correct feature maps. *Biological Cybernetics*, *43*, 59–69.

Köpcke, K.-M. (1982). *Untersuchungen zum Genussystem der deutschen Gegenwartssprache*. Tübingen: Niemeyer.

Köpcke, K.-M. (1988). Schemas in German plural formation. *Lingua*, *74*, 303–335.

Köpcke, K.-M., & Zubin, D. (1983). Die kognitive Organisation der Genuszuweisung zu den einsilbigen Nomen der deutschen Gegenwartssprache. *Zeitschrift fur germanistische Linguistik*, *11*, 166–182.

Köpcke, K.-M.,& Zubin, D. (1984). Sechs Prinzipien für die Genuszuweisung im Deutschen: ein Beitrag zur natürlichen Klassifikation. *Linguistische Berichte*, *93*, 26–50.

Köpcke, K.-M., & Zubin, D. (in press). Zur Frage der psychologischen Realität von Genuszuweisenden Regeln zu den einsilbigen Nomen der deutschen Gegenwartssprache. *Linguistische Berichte*.

Kuhl, P., & Miller, J. (1975). Speech perception by the chinchilla: Voiced-voiceless distinction in alveolar plosive consonsants. *Science*, *190*, 69–72.

Lamb, S. (1966). *Outline of stratificational grammar*. Washington: Georgetown University Press.

Linell, P. (1979). *Psychological reality in phonology: A theoretical study*. Cambridge: Cambridge University Press.

Ling, C. (1994). Learning the past tense of English verbs: The symbolic pattern associator vs. connectionist models. *Journal of Artificial Intelligence Research*, *1*, 209–229.

Ling, C., & Marinov, M. (1993). Answering the connectionist challenge. *Cognition*, *49*, 267–290.

MacWhinney, B. (1978a). The acquisition of morphophonology. *Monographs of the Society for Research in Child Development*, *43*, Whole no. 1.

MacWhinney, B. (1978b). Conditions on acquisitional models. In *Proceedings of the 1978 annual conference*. New York: Association for Computing Machinery.

MacWhinney, B. (1987). The competition model. In B. MacWhinney (Ed.) *Mechanisms of language acquisition*. Hillsdale, NJ: Lawrence Erlbaum Associates.

MacWhinney, B. (1988). Competition and teachability. In R. Schiefelbusch & M. Rice (Eds.), *The teachability of language*. New York: Cambridge University Press.

MacWhinney, B. (1993). Connections and symbols: Closing the gap. *Cognition*, *49*, 291–296.

MacWhinney, B. (1994). The dinosaurs and the ring. In R. Corrigan, S. Lima, & M. Noonan (Eds.), *The reality of linguistic rules*. Amsterdam: John Benjamins.

MacWhinney, B., & Anderson, J. (1986). The acquisition of grammar. In I. Gopnik & M. Gopnik (Eds.), *From models to modules*. Norwood, NJ: Ablex.

MacWhinney, B., & Bates, E. (Eds.). (1989). *The crosslinguistic study of sentence processing*. New York: Cambridge University Press.

MacWhinney, B., & Leinbach, J. (1991). Implementations are not conceptualizations: Revising the verb learning model. *Cognition*, *29*, 121–157.

MacWhinney, B., Leinbach, J., Taraban, R., & McDonald, J. (1989). Language learning: Cues or rules? *Journal of Memory and Language*, *28*, 255–277.

Maratsos, M., & Chalkley, M. (1980). The internal language of children's syntax: The ontogenesis and representation of syntactic categories. In K. Nelson (Ed.), *Children's language: Volume 2*. New York: Gardner.

Marchman, V. (1992). Constraint on plasticity in a connectionist model of the English past tense. *Journal of Cognitive Neuroscience*, *5*, 215–234.

Marcus, M. (1980). *A theory of syntactic recognition for natural language*. Cambridge, MA: MIT Press.

Marslen-Wilson, W. D. (1987). Functional parallelism in spoken word-recognition. *Cognition, 25*, 71–102.

McClelland, J., & Elman, J. (1986). Interactive processes in speech perception. In J. McClelland, & D. Rumelhart (Eds.), *Parallel distributed processing*. Cambridge, MA: MIT Press.

McClelland, J., & Kawamoto, A. (1986). Mechanisms of sentence processing: Assigning roles to constituents. In J. McClelland & D. Rumelhart (Eds.), *Parallel distributed processing*. Cambridge, MA: MIT Press.

McDonald, J. (1987). Sentence interpretation in bilingual speakers of English and Dutch. *Applied Psycholinguistics, 8*, 379–414.

McDonald, J., & MacWhinney, B. (1989). Maximum likelihood models for sentence processing research. In B. MacWhinney & E. Bates (Eds.), *The crosslinguistic study of sentence processing*. New York: Cambridge University Press.

Miikkulainen, R. (1990). A distributed feature map model of the lexicon. In *Proceedings of the 12th Annual Conference of the Cognitive Science Society*. Hillsdale, NJ: Lawrence Erlbaum Associates.

Miikkulainen, R., & Dyer, M. (1991). Natural language processing with modular neural networks and distributed lexicon. *Cognitive Science, 15*, 343–399.

Mills, A. E. (1986). *The acquisition of gender: A study of English and German*. Berlin: Springer-Verlag.

Morgan, J., & Travis, L. (1989). Limits on negative information in language input. *Journal of Child Language, 16*, 531–552.

Nespor, M., & Vogel, I. (1986). *Prosodic phonology*. Dordrecht: Foris.

Newell, A., & Simon, H. (1972). *Human problem solving*. Englewood Cliffs, NJ: Prentice-Hall.

Ohala, J. (1974a). Phonetic explanation in phonology. In A. B. et al. (Eds.) *Papers from the parassession on natural phonology*. Chicago: Chicago Linguistic Society.

Ohala, J. J. (1974b). Experimental historical phonology. In J. M. Anderson & C. Jones (Eds.)., *Historical linguistics II*. New York: American Elsevier.

Ohala, M. (1974c). The abstractness controversy: Experimental input from Hindi. *Language, 50*, 225–235.

Oller, K. (1991). Similarities and differences in vocalizations of deaf and hearing infants: Future directions for research. In J. Miller (Ed.), *Research on child language disorders: a decade of progress* (pp. 277–285). Austin, TX: Pro-Ed.

Oller, D. K., & Eilers, R. E. (1988). The role of audition in infant babbling. *Child Development, 59*, 441–449.

Pinker, S. (1984). *Language learnability and language development*. Cambridge, MA: Harvard University Press.

Pinker, S. (1989). *Learnability and cognition: The acquisition of argument structure*. Cambridge, MA: MIT Press.

Plaut, D., & McClelland, J. (1993). Generalization with componential attractors: Word and non-word reading in an attractor network. In *Proceedings of the Fifteenth Annual Conference of the Cognitive Science Society*. Hillsdale, NJ: Lawrence Erlbaum Associates.

Rumelhart, D., Hinton, G., & Williams, R. (1986). Learning internal representations by back propagation. In D. Rumelhart & J. McClelland (Eds.), *Parallel distributed processing: Explorations in the microstructure of cognition*. Cambridge, MA: MIT Press.

Rumelhart, D., & McClelland, J. (1986a). *Parallel distributed processing*. Cambridge, MA: MIT Press.

Rumelhart, D. E., & McClelland, J. L. (1986b). On learning the past tense of English verbs. In J. L. McClelland & D. E. Rumelhart (Eds.), *Parallel distributed processing: Explorations in the microstructure of cognition*. Cambridge, MA: MIT Press.

Rumelhart, D., & McClelland, J. (1987). Learning the past tenses of English verbs: Implicit rules or parallel distributed processes? In B. MacWhinney (Ed.), *Mechanisms of Language Acquisition*. Hillsdale, NJ: Lawrence Erlbaum Associates.

Rumelhart, D., & Norman, D. (1982). Simulating a skilled typist: A study of skilled cognitive-motor performance. *Cognitive Science, 6*, 1–36.

Seidenberg, M., & McClelland, J. (1989). A distributed, developmental model of word recognition and naming. *Psychological Review, 96*, 523–568.

Squire, L. (1987). *Memory and brain*. New York: Oxford University Press.

St. John, M. (1992). The story gestalt: A model of knowledge-intensive processes in text comprehension. *Cognitive Science, 16*, 271–306.

Stemberger, J. (1985). *The lexicon in a model of language production*. New York: Garland.

Strauss, S. (Ed.). (1981). *U-shaped learning curves*. Hillsdale, NJ: Lawrence Erlbaum Associates.

Touretzky, D. (1990). BoltzCONS: Dynamic symbol structures in a connectionist network. *Artificial Intelligence, 46*, 5–46.

Trammell, R. (1978). The psychological reality of underlying forms and rules for stress. *Journal of Psycholinguistic Research, 7*, 79–94.

Twain, M. (1935). The awful German language. In *The family Mark Twain*. New York: Harper & Brothers.

von Neumann, J. (1956). Probabilistic logics and the synthesis of reliable organisms from unreliable components. In C. Shannon & J. McCarthy (Eds.), *Automata studies*. Princeton, NJ: Princeton University Press.

Werker, J. F., Gilbert, J. H. V., Humphrey, K., & Tees, R. C. (1981). Developmental aspects of cross-language speech perception. *Child Development, 52*, 349–355.

Wexler, K., & Culicover, P. (1980). *Formal principles of language acquisition*. Cambridge, MA: MIT Press.

Zubin, D., & Köpcke, K. (1981). Gender: A less than arbitrary grammatical category. In C. M. R. Hendrick & M. Miller (Eds.), *Papers from the Seventeenth Regional Meeting*. Chicago: Chicago Linguistic Society.

Zubin, D. A., & Köpcke, K. M. (1986). Gender and folk taxonomy: The indexical relation between grammatical and lexical categorization. In C. Craig (Ed.), *Noun classes and categorization*. Amsterdam: John Benjamins.

3 Systems Learning Symbol Systems: Commentary on MacWhinney and Smith

Karen Freeman
Gedeon Deák[1]
Institute of Child Development
University of Minnesota

We are in the difficult position of commenting on two excellent papers, both of which center on intriguing and convincing empirical evidence. We restrict our comments to questions about the data and approaches presented, ideas for future developments, and a few concerns about interpretations and conceptual issues.

This pair of papers, which explore two distinct problems in language acquisition—word learning (Smith) and inflectional morphology (MacWhinney and Chang)—exemplify a paradigm very different from that which dominated the language acquisition literature 15 to 20 years ago. In the new paradigm, rules, constraints, and homuncular control processes have been replaced by bottom-up, subsymbolic computation and associations. MacWhinney and Chang use a connectionist system with an articulated architecture to model the use of phonological and semantic input in determining articles. Smith examines the role of physical features in the extension of novel words, and argues that knowledge, associations, and context, rather than innate biases, jointly constrain these extensions. We examine each of these contributions in turn, and finally consider their implications for language learning and education.

HAND-WIRING AND RULES: A PREMATURE DEATH?

MacWhinney and Chang's application of a connectionist model to the problem of language acquisition assumes and asserts the implicit nature of language acquisition: connectionist networks are pattern-matching systems built up by progres-

[1]Order of authorship was random.

sive, gradual modification based on repeated, patterned input. They do not require conscious processing of or reflection about discrete symbols. Instead they register input and incrementally construct associations. The authors point out that connectionist systems are more promising in their explanatory powers than are traditional systems in which thoughts follow discrete rule-based flowcharts (see also, e.g., Churchland, 1986; Rumelhart & McClelland, 1986; Smolensky, 1988). What *is* unique about their approach is that they have maintained an associationist pattern-matching system while conceding the connectionist ideal of a general system (that is, a single, homogeneous network that can handle all verbs). Theirs is a less parsimonious system, with more articulated architecture, in which patterns of important verb features—bindings, morphophonology, and even semantic attributes—are learned on a verb-by-verb basis.

In the past connectionist models have relied on hand-wiring (e.g., Dell, 1986; MacWhinney, 1987, 1988; MacWhinney & Anderson, 1986; MacWhinney & Bates, 1989; Stemberger, 1985). Hand-wiring is a process of setting specific parameters in order to achieve the desired input-output patterns. MacWhinney and Chang are opposed to the use of hand-wiring for several reasons. They argue that hand-wiring does not reflect the way humans learn, which they describe as "self-organizing" (i.e., parameters are not set by a programmer). If organisms are self-organizing, only minimum hand-wiring is allowable (note that hand-wiring seems analogous to imposing constraints; we return to this point below). Further, MacWhinney and Chang do not think that rules direct language learning. In a connectionist system rules can be incorporated through hand-wiring. If rules are to be completely exorcised from language learning, hand-wiring must be avoided. On the basis of a comparison between a hand-wired and nonhand-wired model of German gender acquisition (MacWhinney, Leinbach, Taraban, & McDonald, 1989), the authors assert that hand-wiring is not necessary or even beneficial for learning.

Or is it? In some sense, hand-wiring might not be completely disposable. To illustrate this, we cite a behavior that is very difficult to program into a connectionist system: repeat-signs in written music.[2] In written music there are discrete symbols that occur in pairs that inform the musician to repeat the section of music bounded by the symbols. These pairs can occur anywhere in a piece of music. Importantly, they are relatively easy for even novice musicians to learn.

How might a connectionist network learn to read correctly repeat symbols? There are at least two possibilities. First, when the system encounters the initial repeat sign of a pair, it might begin binding a variable to every subsequent note until it encounters the closing repeat sign. Over multiple encounters with repeat signs, the system might eventually learn that when it reaches the last variable-bound note, it should begin moving backward until it reaches the first

---

[2]We thank Michael Maratsos for this example.

variable-bound note. Then it should begin to move forward again, simultaneously erasing the variable. It seems unlikely that this is how humans deal with repeat signs. For example, this process would predict a correlation between the length of the repeated section and the time taken to begin the repeat. Although we know of no empirical data on this possibility, it seems unlikely that such a relation exists.

A second possibility is that a network might learn, upon encountering the first of a pair of repeat signs, to enter all subsequent notes into a memory buffer of the sort described by Elman (1991). In a buffer of this kind, the output would be stored for some interval of time before being used as input. The network would continue entering notes into the buffer until it reaches the closing repeat sign. Then it would output the entire contents of the memory buffer and continue forward. It is also unlikely that this is how humans deal with repeat signs. Such a system would require memorizing the repeated section the first time through, a difficult feat for most musicians playing passages of even moderate length.

Let us raise another example, one that might involve a process analogous to hand-wiring in human language learning. One of us (G.D.) recalls more-easily learning the genders of many German nouns after being told by an instructor that nouns ending in *-chen* are neuter, those ending in *-e* are feminine, and so on. Was Deák "hand-wired" to associate *-chen* with neuter? Can we consider this an example of "installation" of a discrete rule (one that, unlike MacWhinney et al.'s, 1989, rule-based network, was relatively successful)? Perhaps, but this is an oversimplification. Deák presumably could have ignored the input provided by his teacher. Some predisposition (intense dislike of memorizing German nouns?) presumably led him to attend to and internalize the instructor-provided rules. A computer, on the other hand, cannot choose to ignore or not ignore hand-wiring. Thus, there may be an important difference between hand-wiring Deák and hand-wiring artificial connectionist networks: the ability of the system to choose whether or not, and how, to integrate rules. It might be argued that toddlers, like artificial networks, lack deliberate self-control over the integration and application of rules. Nevertheless, it appears to us that a major challenge for connectionist modelers is to reconcile the reality of discrete and easily learned rules with the protracted process of association-building that is required to learn complex symbol systems.

The critical point of these examples is that repeat signs and (a few) phonological noun features are discrete signals to apply a simple, categorical *rule*, and it is quite easy for humans to learn to apply these rules in response to the appropriate signals. Humans do not need extended learning or many exposures to learn to read repeat signs or to learn that words ending in *-chen* are neuter. The same can be said for stop signs, social gestures such as an outstretched, open hand, and any number of other signals to apply simple rules. Humans are good at quickly learning and using such symbols, whereas nonhand-wired connectionist networks are not.[3] Connectionist systems might eventually be able to model seemingly-rule-based behavior, but to date they are not compelling in this regard. In contrast, rule-learning and -use are very easy for symbol-based systems (notwithstanding the shortcomings of such systems noted by MacWhinney and Chang). Our argument for the utility of categorical symbols for discrete actions is not meant to suggest a return to the age of the "big bad rules." Rather, we wish to point out that there is a need to reevaluate the role of hand-wiring in learning, which may entail careful analysis of what counts as hand-wiring, and what function hand-wiring plays in a system.

We should note the possibility that both associationist and rule-like processes (of an unknown nature) operate in the learning of symbol systems. Perhaps rules and associationist networks underlie language learning under different circumstances. Connectionist processes might direct primarily implicit, subsymbolic learning, whereas rule-based processes may direct explicit, "top-down" learning. In general, first language learning seems to be better described by connectionist models: It is a gradual and largely implicit process. In contrast, formal learning of second languages or other symbol systems (such as written music) typically relies on learning explicit rules (although it no doubt also relies on associative processes). It is possible that subsymbolic connectionist networks will someday be able account for fast rule learning, and it is also possible that a hypothetical grounded, neurologically plausible symbol-passing system will be created. Currently, though, we lack a single model that is able to account for these two kinds of language learning behaviors.

We began by discussing the extent to which hand-wiring can (or should) be eliminated. Accepting that in general hand-wiring is not desirable, we now ask a slightly different question: to what extent have MacWhinney and Chang truly eliminated hand-wiring? It seems that they have, in a sense, traded one form of hand-wiring for another. It is true that their model does not incorporate input-based rules. Yet hand-wiring can be defined more generally as the *a priori* imposition of arbitrary constraints that have not been shown to have psychological reality. This definition would include the practice of imposing an architecture that lacks psychological reality. There is at least one example of this in their lexical connectionist model.

The authors create an architecture in which three initial identical parallel feature maps correspond to sound, meaning and association, respectively. Initially these nets are given both sound and meaning input. As a result of training on the initial input patterns, the maps develop parallel forms of organization. In order to allow associative mapping between the parallel feature maps, the mean-

[3]We realize that MacWhinney, Leinbach, Taraban, and McDonald (1989) found a feature-based network superior to a cue-based network for learning German gender. This was, however, a "toy model," to use MacWhinney's term. It is unclear whether this finding would hold up in a more contextualized and grounded system.

ing units are "blanked out." Subsequently the sound net is trained to create the correct activation in the association net in the absence of meaning. Eventually this process allows the retrieval of meaning from sound. We question whether this suppression of a discrete set of units mirrors any known psychological process. Such a process seems like an arbitrary structural imposition. Without empirical verification of the existence of such a process in human learning, the psychological validity of their model is in question. To some extent, then, their model relies on a form of hand-wiring. We are left wondering whether any ungrounded system (e.g., any artificial system) can completely avoid hand-wiring.

MacWhinney and Chang's lexical connectionist model is nevertheless an exciting step towards a more realistic model of inflectional morphology and related aspects of language (e.g., morphophonology, syntactic binding). The specification of stable locations for individual words may be necessary for any plausible model, and their model therefore offers improvement over completely distributed models (e.g., Rumelhart & McClelland, 1986). We believe that the major challenge for this approach will be to build a lexical connectionist system with a physiologically and psychologically plausible architecture. Ultimately, any such model also will have to be integrated into a larger system that can account for other psychological phenomena involving lexical items, such as lexical priming effects. Furthermore, it remains to be seen how more complex and nebulous aspects of lexical items, such as meaning and connotation, can be incorporated in an extension of this model.

W(H)ITHER CONSTRAINTS? LEARNING IS NOT INDUCTION

Smith's paper adds to a lively debate in the early word learning literature about the existence and role of constraints on word learning (e.g., Behrend, 1990; Keil, 1979; Kuczaj, 1990; MacWhinney, 1991; Maratsos, 1992; Markman, 1989, 1992; Markman & Wachtel, 1988; Merriman, 1991; Merriman & Bowman, 1989; Nelson, 1988, 1990; Woodward & Markman, 1991). Constraints have been conceptualized by developmentalists as biases or tendencies internal to an organism, which place limits on or guide the ways in which the organism construes an ambiguous or indeterminate situation (e.g., Markman, 1989; Bloom, 1993). Within the domain of word learning, constraints have been proposed as a means of solving a problem of induction (i.e., how to limit the possible meanings of an unknown word). Constraints are thought to "solve" this problem by reducing the possible meanings that children will consider for a new word. Smith rejects the problem of induction as irrelevant, thereby denying the premise that supports constraints: "Learning is not hypothesis testing. Development is not induction." (p. 00). She rests her argument on evidence against the existence of a stable shape bias that constrains early word learning.

Smith's general contention is that the shape bias does not exist in any static manner. Instead she argues that the appearance of constrained patterns of behavior rests on the nonlinear, interactive effects of many forces on children's shifting attention. She bases this partly on evidence of changes in patterns of novel-word generalization that result from contextual changes such as syntactic frame (noun or adjective), task (similarity or word generalization), and stimulus attributes (plain, eyes, sneakers, or glitter). In sum, Smith rejects both the problem of induction and the shape bias; the latter rejection rests on three arguments (which, by extension, inveigh against constraints in general): (a) the shape bias first appears after first words are learned, (b) the shape bias can be learned and therefore is not innate, and (c) the shape bias varies as a function of context and therefore is not robust or parsimonious. After considering her rejection of the induction problem, we will assess the effectiveness and support for each of these arguments, and raise other relevant findings.

Is There an Induction Problem?

To begin with, young children rapidly learn words beginning halfway through the second year, and in spite of some errors (e.g., overextensions and underextensions), their meanings are usually close enough to the adult meaning to allow communication. The question therefore remains: Why do (presumably) so few children interpret "rabbit" to mean, for instance, "the rabbit's left hind leg and the ground directly underneath it," or something similarly implausible to our adult sensibilities? Children's errors are relatively systematic, and by the time they are three, gross errors are relatively rare. Because adults spend relatively little time carefully teaching children the exact meanings (i.e., intensions and extensions) of words, it is important to determine why children seldom hold implausible but nevertheless conceivable meanings for words.

By limiting the possible meanings of a word, constraints have been offered as a solution to the induction problem. Smith rejects the very existence of the induction problem, arguing that children do not explicitly hypothesize word meanings at all. We agree that it is unlikely that explicit hypothesis testing plays a substantial role in determining word meanings, particularly for young children. However, we suggest that the problem of "induction" does not necessarily rest on induction (or hypothesis testing). Regardless of the process by which words are linked to meanings, we may ask: How does an organism that lacks symbols, has little shared communication, and limited knowledge of the world or other people, learn the meaning of its first few words, given the indeterminacy of the input? This is a serious question regardless of whether word meanings are induced or arise by some other process (such as that proposed by Smith).

Of course, although we maintain that there is a problem of indeterminacy, the solution to this problem need not be innate language-specific constraints. Rather, it could be the convergence of certain general abilities that emerge by 12 to 18 months in normally developing children, abilities that are not specifically linguistic in nature. For example, although children may not possess a language-specific whole-object bias (Markman, 1989), their general expectation that countable objects persist and are not transitory (Baillargeon, 1991; Baillargeon, Spelke, & Wasserman, 1985) and that objects are stable, bounded, and unitary (Spelke, 1988) could result in performance that would resemble such a bias. Furthermore, children's ability to focus attention on the object to which an adult is attending (e.g., Butterworth & Jarrett, 1991; Murphy & Messer, 1977; Scaife & Bruner, 1975) might limit the indeterminacy of a novel word taught by ostention. In sum, although language-specific shape biases would clearly speed the process of first-word learning, they probably are not necessary. Children's first words might rest on a convergence of other (more general) abilities, so that each word would require more effort and perhaps more trials and errors (see Dromi, 1987). Thus, the shape bias is not needed to solve the indeterminacy problem, but this does not mean that the indeterminacy problem (at least the version of it posed earlier) evaporates—rather, it is circumvented, at least in part, by infants' growing knowledge of objects and by their social-cognitive skills.

First Words Precede the Shape Bias

Smith argues that if the shape bias were an essential constraint on word learning, it should exist prior to learning first words. She cites evidence from a human longitudinal study and a connectionist network that the shape bias emerges after first words have been produced. On the basis of these findings, she argues that the shape bias is not innate, and first word learning does not depend on constraints. Instead, the shape bias is learned.

The first finding to support the learnability of the shape bias is a developmental finding that the shape bias emerges out of word learning instead of preceding it: In a longitudinal study, the shape bias was found to covary with the course of vocabulary growth. The second is a connectionist model that successfully learns a shape bias (Gasser & Smith, 1991). Smith's conclusion, that the shape bias is learned in the course of word learning, is also consistent with data from the categorization literature. We turn briefly to this literature in search of converging lines of evidence for Smith's hypothesis.

We propose that the shape bias should support categorization at the "basic level" but impede categorization at the "superordinate level." The basic level has been defined as the level at which within-category similarity and between-category difference are maximized. At this level, shape is relatively uniform between category members (Rosch, Mervis, Gray, Johnson, & Boyes-Braem, 1976), whereas it is less so at the superordinate level. A shape bias therefore would be expected to help young children categorize at the basic level. There are data to indicate that the onset of basic-level categorization is correlated with the 18-month vocabulary spurt (Gopnik & Meltzoff, 1987). Prior to the vocabulary spurt, infants typically do not succeed at basic-level categorization tasks. This conclusion is supported by Freeman and Bauer (1994), who found that all 24-month-olds sort at the superordinate level, but only those with above average productive vocabulary sort at the basic level. In addition, because members of superordinate categories have less similar shapes than do members of basic-level categories, a shape bias would predict that infants perceive basic-level categories better than superordinate categories. Mandler and her colleagues (Mandler & Bauer, 1988; Mandler, Bauer, & McDonough, 1991) have demonstrated that 1- to 2-year-olds categorize at the superordinate or global level earlier than the basic level. In sum, the results of categorization research are consistent with Smith's assertion that a shape bias is not present during the early period of word learning. Further, like Smith's results, these findings suggest that the development of a shape bias might arise from word learning.

It is important to note, however, that arguments about age-of-onset of the shape bias do not conclusively inform debates about whether a hypothetical shape bias is innate or learned (note that most constraint theorists seem to agree that constraints are innate; for example, Behrend, 1990; Keil, 1992; Markman, 1992). Woodward and Markman (1991) point out that some innately driven developments, such as the onset of puberty, occur relatively late in life. Thus, not all late developments are attributable to learning. By the same token, of course, early development need not indicate innateness (see, e.g., Gottlieb, 1991; Lickliter, 1991). Thus, timing does not conclusively address innateness versus learnedness. More importantly, the "innate versus learned" debate is itself problematic, because the idea that behaviors are "innate" is flawed (Johnston, 1987; Oyama, 1988). This is not to say that genes are unimportant, or that environment is all-important to behavior. In many ways, however, the expression of genes depends upon the environment—from the intercellular environment to the external environment (Gottlieb, 1991; Greenough, 1991). A particular combination of genes, the history of an organism, and environmental factors all determine the expression of any species-wide behavior. Thus, no behavior is strictly (or even mostly) innate; every behavior emerges from a complex interaction among genetic, historical, and environmental factors.

Furthermore, it is unclear, as Smith points out, how a constraint on the possible interpretations of a new word would be embodied in genetic code. It is also completely unclear how such a genetic sequence might eventually contribute to a child's attention to shape. Consequently, it does not add anything to our understanding of word learning to claim innateness, although certainly any species-specific cognitive tendency will be contributed to by genetic factors. In this sense, we agree with Smith that the concept of innate constraints is inherently problematic. Yet by the same token, invoking age-of-onset data as an argument against constraints implies an acceptance of the same concept of innateness. We therefore take the strong stance that arguments about age-of-onset, and of learnability, will not add to our understanding of biases in word learning, because they imply a dichotomous, nature versus nurture picture of phenotypic development. Consequently, Smith's strongest argument against constraints lies in her empirical demonstrations of the context-dependence of the shape bias.

Context-Dependence of the Shape Bias

Smith and her colleagues have generated elegant evidence that attention to shape is partly dependent upon the context in which novel word generalization occurs (see especially Jones, Smith & Landau, 1991; Landau, 1993). We believe that these data are quite problematic for the constraints position. Markman and her colleagues have argued, first, that constraints are applied probabilistically, and second, that some as-yet-incomplete and indeterminately large set of circumstances can override any given constraint (see, e.g., Liittschwager & Markman, 1994; Markman, 1992; Markman & Wachtel, 1988). This places the position dangerously close to the line of falsifiability. Smith's arguments against a shape bias exemplify this weakness of constraints theories, but it is a general problem, as an example will make clear.

To underscore the general weakness of constraints theories (as conceived with the qualifications stated above) we turn our attention to a different constraint: mutual exclusivity. This constraint is thought to prevent children from applying a novel word to an object for which they already know a word. According to Markman, the mutual exclusivity constraint rests on a belief that one object can only have one name. The evidence for mutual exclusivity originally presented by Markman and Wachtel (1988) is far from absolute: In some experiments their subjects acted in a manner consistent with the proposed constraint on less than 70% of all trials. Thus, the constraint is applied probabilistically. Furthermore, Markman argues that the constraint can be overridden, so that children learn, for example, hierarchically nested terms for the same object (Au & Glusman, 1990; Banigan & Mervis, 1988; Waxman & Hatch, 1992). There is also evidence that children will learn (Mervis, Golinkoff, & Bertrand, 1994) and spontaneously apply (Deák & Maratsos, 1994) multiple basic-level words to the same objects. Furthermore, in a recent study, Liittschwager and Markman (1994) found that the mutual exclusivity constraint is applied by 16- and 24-month-olds only when the processing load is high (i.e., when they must remember several novel words).

These data can be framed in a manner consistent with Markman's account (the constraint is applied probabilistically and can be overridden in certain situations), although they certainly make the mutual exclusivity hypothesis unparsimonious. However, what is most damaging to the hypothesis is the fact that some of the overriding factors (e.g., processing load) were never predicted by Markman, and are not deductively obvious. These qualifications have been tacked onto the mutual exclusivity hypothesis *post hoc*, placing the falsifiability of mutual exclusivity in question. As more extenuating circumstances are discovered, apparently they can be added to the hypothesis without *a priori* theoretical justification. In its current state, there is no limit to the number and kind of extenuating circumstances that can be incorporated into the mutual exclusivity hypothesis. Unless such limitations are specified, the hypothesis is unfalsifiable.

For every proposed constraint on word meaning that has been examined in some detail (e.g., mutual exclusivity, taxonomic constraint, whole object constraint, shape bias), context effects (such as those demonstrated by Smith) and probabilistic use (rather than universal application) have been found. The shape bias is an excellent example because Smith and her colleagues have generated compelling evidence about the age-, task-, and context-specificity of the bias. As we have just argued, though, Smith's point can be generalized: Constraints on word meaning typically are not the best or most parsimonious explanation for the total set of data about children's word learning. In spite of this strong statement, there are a few points about Smith's data and argument that deserve mention.

Are 24-Month-Olds Constrained?

This shape bias is not present in all of the contexts, tasks, or age groups tested by Smith and her colleagues. In fact, 12- and 18-month-olds show an almost total disregard to shape. However, 24-month-olds do seem to rely predominantly on shape across contexts and tasks (see Smith's Fig. 1.13, p. 19), a finding not discussed by Smith. Although Smith interprets her evidence as inconsistent with a shape bias, the performance of 24-month-olds seems to be fairly consistent with some such constraint. The pattern of findings could suggest the possibility of a transient shape preference that evolves around 24 months in English-speaking children. Following the first fifty words, during a period of rapid word learning, children might make default assumptions about the meanings of new count nouns. As they pass through these few months and learn more about syntax and stimulus associations (e.g., the salience of texture in animate beings), the shape bias becomes weaker and much more situation-specific, or more finely tuned.

How Many Contexts?

It is unclear, based on the evidence presented, how extensive or far-reaching is context sensitivity. One of the contextual factors explored—adding eyes to an object—seems straitforward, assuming children have learned that these features are usually found on animate things and that texture is an important property of animate things (e.g., texture allows you to differentiate bugs, fish, birds, and mammals). Another contextual factor explored by Smith and her colleagues is more curious; specifically, covering an item with glitter, placing it in a dark chamber and shining a spotlight on it while using an adjectival context to present a new word. This seems an extreme and unnatural manipulation to compel children to attend to color. We might reiterate the possibility that at some age(s) children have a default tendency to attend to shape, which is typically overruled only under relatively extreme circumstances. We suggest this not because we believe it is highly likely, but because it is a logical possibility. It is also, unfortunately, a possibility that is difficult to falsify: The best one could do is to try to demonstrate a large enough number of intervening contexts that such a possibility becomes less and less likely.

Stability and Flexibility: Unlikely Bedfellows

Another potential issue regarding Smith's account of word learning is how to reconcile a context-sensitive, dynamic system for word learning with the apparent stability that results. That is, the knowledge that results from the dynamic, multivariate process of word learning is a relatively stable lexicon consisting of words and meanings shared by members of a linguistic community. Such a process, if unconstrained by universal, fast-and-hard principles, *could* result in much more confusion than it does. Although this might appear, at first glance, to be a problem, actually it is not: The system proposed by Smith (see Fig. 1.14, p. 20) takes into account four kinds of input. Three of these—knowledge of specific words, syntactic knowledge, and knowledge of relations between properties—are not necessarily context sensitive (although they certainly are not static), and these therefore ground the system and prevent contextual factors from leading the system to wildly different and potentially erroneous decisions in unusual situations.

Ultimately, Smith's research program exemplifies the principle that with regard to complex, probabilistic behaviors such as generalizing word meanings, simple one-factor models probably will not accurately account for the data. Children's interpretations of word meanings are sensitive to changes in task, context, set of available information, and individual characteristics. The challenge in the study of this and other complex dynamically shifting behaviors will be discovering powerful, theoretically interesting principles that go beyond the generality, "Word meaning is a dynamic process that depends on interactions among many factors." One danger is that word meaning researchers will continue to investigate any number of contextual factors and interactions among factors, each of which may be interesting in and of itself but fails to elucidate general principles about word learning that lead to powerful theories.

WHAT IS MISSING FROM SYSTEMS AND NETWORKS?

A potential shortcoming of the models presented by Smith and MacWhinney and Chang is their seeming difficulty with integrating certain overarching factors into the word learning system. These factors include reasons for wanting to learn and/or apply a particular word or words (with particular inflections), practical and communicational intentions and goals in word-learning and word-using situations, and motivational states. This loose, interrelated conglomeration of factors, which, for example, might be expected to guide attention, does not have a clear role in Smith's system. In fact, dynamic systems in general (of which Smith's model is an example) and connectionist systems in general (of which MacWhinney and Chang's model is an example) have difficulty integrating goals, motivations and intentions (see Aslin, 1993). One strategy, then, is to eliminate these as epiphenomena, but this only begs the question (i.e., why does the system produce output that is apprehended as *intentional*?). Most people phenomenologically experience some degree of intentional control over some kinds of learning (if only in the motivation to learn), and it is not clear how these phenomena can be integrated into connectionist and dynamic systems.

IMPLICIT LANGUAGE LEARNING AND FORMAL LEARNING OF SYMBOL SYSTEMS

Smith's and MacWhinney and Chang's chapters represent a relatively new approach to language acquisition because both discard rules, constraints, and symbol-passing in favor of dynamic, associationist, subsymbolic processes. Language acquisition is an appropriate domain for this approach: It is inevitable and occurs prior to the development of sophisticated metalinguistic and symbolic abilities. These features make it likely that language acquisition rests more on implicit (i.e., subsymbolic and associationist) than explicit (i.e., rule-using) processes. It is thought provoking that young children, relying largely on implicit processes, learn a complex system that involves syntax, morphophonology, semantics, and pragmatics in less time than it takes older children to learn the far simpler rules of arithmetic. There are many possible reasons for this discrepancy (e.g., children spend less time using the mathematical representation system, they are less motivated to learn math, etc.). However, it is also possible that the difficulty with these later achievements lies in making explicit what children already know implicitly. This possibility has broad implications for second language and math instruction.

The focus placed on explicit tuition and rule induction in traditional education might not foster the acquisition of second languages and mathematics. In American math education formal rules are traditionally taught in a didactic manner: Children are instructed about certain rules and then given problems upon which to use these rules. This reliance on "top-down," rule-based induction bears little resemblance to the conditions under which children learn first languages. If learning the formal principles of arithmetic requires the conversion of everyday knowledge about changes in numerosity into an abstract symbol system, we should seek methods of instruction that facilitate this implicit-to-explicit mapping (see Resnick's chapter 4, this volume, and Gelman & Gallistel, 1986, for evidence that preschoolers know a great deal about number and arithmetic).

We posit that bottom-up or emergent learning conditions might facilitate second language and arithmetic learning more than do didactic conditions. By emergent instruction (our term) we mean methods that encourage extensive experience with the fundamental units and procedures of the symbol system in practical problem-solving situations, situations which eventually allow principles to emerge via multiple concrete examples. This approach, which is essentially that favored by Resnick (this volume), allows more room for implicit processing: rather than being taught rules, students "discover" regularities and functional solutions (the Japanese system also utilizes aspects of this approach by beginning lessons with concrete examples rather than rules, see Stigler & Fernandez, this volume).

Although the idea of allowing children to infer principles through problem solving is far removed from the dynamic and connectionist models of Smith and MacWhinney and Chang, the emergent approach is certainly more amenable to such models than is the didactic approach. For example, emergent approaches emphasize extensive experience with basic units (e.g., numbers) and procedures (e.g., counting). This repeated input of fundamental units in order to build up higher-order patterns is essentially a connectionist approach. However, our purpose is not to try to apply the findings or approaches of these authors directly to second language and mathematics learning—they are very different problems. Our point is simply that the approaches taken by Smith and MacWhinney and Chang emphasize the subsymbolic, associationist nature of first language learning. First language acquisition proceeds without the benefit of explicit tuition of rules. Second languages and mathematics, like first languages, are complex, formal symbol systems. Therefore, the instruction of second languages and mathematics might benefit from attempts to duplicate implicit learning conditions in instruction. We suspect that there is a great deal of research to be done by educational psychologists in order to determine whether, and how, principles of implicit symbol-system learning should be imported into educational programs in order to make learning more efficient and effective.

CONCLUSIONS

In sum, these chapters exemplify promising approaches to the study of language acquisition. MacWhinney and Chang's model overcomes what has been a serious drawback to connectionist models (see Pinker & Prince, 1988); their difficulty in learning exceptions to patterns. Their approach relies on carefully crafted architecture that allows a high level of precision in the growth of the system. However, this feature also raises questions about the psychological plausibility of such architectural specifications. Smith offers a serious empirical challenge to constraints theorists and, more importantly, provides a reasonable alternative. Although her account raises questions (e.g., what about 24-month-olds, what role do intentions and motivations play, how pervasive are context effects), it has the substantial advantages of, first, taking into account additional factors that are involved in word meaning acquisition, and, second, not relying on problematic assumptions (e.g., innatism). Perhaps the most noteworthy aspect of these chapters is their rejection of symbol passing and rule representations. Although this rejection raises the unsettling question of why people are often very good at learning rules, we optimistically hope that this is a solvable problem. On the whole, it is more important to avoid a return to implausible representational theories and "big bad rules."

ACKNOWLEDGMENTS

The authors thank Maria Sera for helpful feedback.

REFERENCES

Aslin, R. (1993). Commentary: The strange attractiveness of Dynamic Systems to development. In L. Smith & E. Thelen (Eds.), *A dynamic systems approach to development: Applications*. Cambridge MA: MIT Press.

Au, T. K., & Glusman, M. (1990). The principle of mutual exclusivity in word learning: To honor or not to honor? *Child Development*, 61, 1474–1490.

Baillargeon, R. (1991). Reasoning about the height and location of a hidden object in 4.5- and 6.5-month-old infants. *Cognition, 38*, 13–42.

Baillargeon, R., Spelke, E. S., & Wasserman, S. (1985). Object permanence in five-month-old infants. *Cognition, 20*, 191–208.

Banigan, R. L., & Mervis, C. B. (1988). Role of adult input in young children's category evolution: II. An experimental study. *Journal of Child Language, 15*, 493–504.

Behrend, D. A. (1990). Constraints and development: A reply to Nelson. *Cognitive Development, 5*, 313–330.

Bloom, P. (1993). Where do constraints on word meaning come from? In E. V. Clark (Ed.), *Child language research forum, Vol. 24*. Stanford, CA: CSLI.

Butterworth, G., & Jarrett, N. (1991). What minds have in common is space: Spatial mechanisms serving joint visual attention in infancy. *British Journal of Developmental Psychology, 9*, 55–72.

Churchland, P. S. (1986). *Neurophilosophy*. Cambridge, MA: MIT Press.

Deák, G., & Maratsos, M. (1994, April). *Plurality of reference: Preschoolers apply multiple labels to the same object*. Poster presented at the Thirteenth Biennial Conference on Human Development, Pittsburgh, PA.

Dell, G. (1986). A spreading-activation theory of retrieval in sentence production. *Psychological Review, 93*, 283–321.

Dromi, E. (1987). *Early lexical development*. New York: Cambridge University Press.

Elman, J. L. (1991). Incremental learning, or the importance of starting small (Tech. Rep. 9101). Center for Research in Language, University of California, San Diego.

Freeman, K. E., & Bauer, P. J. (1994). Sorting out language and level: Examining the relation between productive vocabulary and category differentiation. Manuscript.

Gasser, M., & Smith, L. B. (1991). The development of a notion of sameness: A connectionist model. In *Proceedings of the 13th Annual Conference of the Cognitive Science Society* (pp. 719–723). Hillsdale, NJ: Lawrence Erlbaum Associates.

Gelman, R., & Gallistel, C. R. (1986). *The child's understanding of number* (2nd ed.) Cambridge, MA: Harvard University Press.

Gopnik, A., & Meltzoff, A. (1987). The development of categorization in the second year and its relation to other cognitive and linguistic developments. *Child Development, 58,* 1523–1531.

Gottlieb, G. (1991). The experimental canalization of behavioral development. *Developmental Psychology, 27,* 4–13.

Greenough, W. T. (1991). Experience as a component of normal development: Evolutionary considerations. *Developmental Psychology, 27,* 14–17.

Johnston, T. D. (1987). The persistence of dichotomies in the study of behavioral development. *Developmental Review, 7,* 149–182.

Jones, S., Smith, L. B., & Landau, B. (1991). Object properties and knowledge in early lexical learning. *Child Development, 62,* 499–516.

Keil, F. C. (1979). *Semantic and conceptual development: An ontological perspective.* Cambridge, MA: Harvard University Press.

Keil, F. C. (1992). The origins of an autonomous biology. In M. R. Gunnar & M. Maratsos (Eds.), *Modularity and constraints in language and cognition: The Minnesota Symposium on Child Psychology* (Vol. 25). Hillsdale, NJ: Lawrence Erlbaum Associates.

Kuczaj, S. A. (1990). Constraining constraint theories. *Cognitive Development, 5,* 341–344.

Landau, B. (1993). Learning the language of space. In E. V. Clark (Ed.), *Child language research forum* (Vol. 24). Stanford, CA: CSLI.

Lewkowicz, D. J., & Lickliter, R. (Eds.). (1994). *The development of intersensory perception.* Hillsdale, NJ: Lawrence Erlbaum Associetes.

Lickliter, R. (1991). Context and animal behavior II: The role of conspecifics in species-typical perceptual development. *Ecological Psychology, 3*(1), 11–23.

Liittschwager, J. C., & Markman, E. M. (1994). Sixteen- and 24-month-olds' use of mutual exclusivity as a default assumption in second-label learning. *Developmental Psychology, 30*(6), 955–968.

MacWhinney, B. (1987). The competition model. In B. MacWhinney (Ed.), *Mechanisms of language acquisition.* Hillsdale, NJ: Lawrence Erlbaum Associates.

MacWhinney, B. (1988). Competition and teachability. In R. Shiefelbusch & M. Rice (Eds.), *The teachability of language.* New York: Cambridge University Press.

MacWhinney, B. (1991). A reply to Woodward and Markman. *Developmental Review, 11,* 192–194.

MacWhinney, B., & Anderson, J. (1986). The acquisition of grammar. In I. Gopnik & M. Gopnik, (Eds.), *From models to modules.* Norwood, NJ: Ablex.

MacWhinney, B., & Bates, E. (Eds.). (1989). *The crosslinguistic study of sentence processing.* New York: Cambridge University Press.

MacWhinney, B., Leinbach, J., Taraban, R., & McDonald, J. (1989). Implementations and not conceptualizations: Revising the verb learning model. *Cognition, 29,* 121–157.

Mandler, J. M., & Bauer, P. J. (1988). The cradle of categorization: Is the basic level basic? *Cognitive Development, 3,* 247–264.

Mandler, J. M., Bauer, P. J., & McDonough, L. (1991). Separating the sheep from the goats: Differentiating global categories. *Cognitive Psychology, 23,* 263–298.

Maratsos, M. (1992). Constraints, modules, and domain specificity: An introduction. In M. R. Gunnar & M. Maratsos (Eds.), *Modularity and constraints in language and cognition: The Minnesota Symposium on Child Psychology* (Vol. 25). Hillsdale, NJ: Lawrence Erlbaum Associates.

Markman, E. M. (1989). *Categorization and naming in children.* Cambridge, MA: MIT Press.

Markman, E. M. (1992). Constraints of word learning: Speculations about their nature, origins, and domain specificity. In M. Gunnar & M. Maratsos (Eds.), *Modularity and constraints in language and cognition: The Minnesota Symposium of Child Psychology* (Vol. 25). Hillsdale, NJ: Lawrence Erlbaum Associates.

Markman E. M., & Hutchinson, J. E. (1984). Children's sensitivity to constraints on word meaning: Taxonomic versus thematic relations. *Cognitive Psychology, 16,* 1–27.

Markman E. M., & Wachtel, G. F. (1988). Children's use of mutual exclusivity to constrain the meaning of words. *Cognitive Psychology, 20,* 121–157.

Merriman, W. E. (1991). The mutual exclusivity bias in children's word learning: A reply to Woodward and Markman. *Developmental Review, 11,* 164–191.

Merriman, W.E., & Bowman, L. L. (1989). The mutual exclusivity bias in children's word learning. *Monographs of the Society for Research in Child Development, 54*(3–4. Serial No. 220).

Mervis, C. B., Golinkoff, R. M., & Bertrand, J. (1994). Two-year-olds readily learn multiple labels for the same basic-level category. *Child Development, 65,* 1163–1177.

Murphy, C. M., & Messer, D. J. (1977). Mothers, infants, and pointing: A study of gesture. In H. R. Schaffer, (Ed.), *Studies in mother-infant interaction.* London: Academic Press.

Nelson, K. (1988). Constraints on word learning? *Cognitive Development, 3,* 221–246.

Nelson, K. (1990). Comment on Behrend's "constraints and development." *Cognitive Development, 5,* 331–339.

Oyama, S. (1988). Ontogeny and the central dogma: Do we need the concept of genetic programming in order to have an evolutionary perspective? In M. R. Gunnar & E. Thelen (Eds.), *Systems and development: The Minnesota Symposium on Child Psychology* (Vol. 22). Hillsdale, NJ: Lawrence Erlbaum Associates.

Pinker, S., & Prince, A. (1988). On language and connectionism: Analysis of a parallel distributed processing model of language acquisition. *Cognition, 28,* 73–193.

Rosch, E., Mervis, C.B., Gray, W.D., Johnson, D.M., & Boyes-Braem, P. (1976). Basic objects in natural categories. *Cognitive Psychology, 8,* 382–439.

Rumelhart, D. E., & McClelland, J. L. (1986). On learning the past tenses of English verbs. In J. L. McClelland & D. E. Rumelhart (Eds.), *Parallel distributed processing* (Vol. 2). Cambridge, MA: MIT Press.

Scaife, M., & Bruner, J. S. (1975). The capacity for joint visual attention in the infant. *Nature, 253,* 265–266,

Smolensky, P. (1988). On the proper treatment of connectionism. *Behavioral and Brain Sciences, 11,* 1–74.

Spelke, E. S. (1988). The origins of physical knowledge. In L. Weiskrantz (Ed.), *Thought without language.* Oxford: Clarendon Press.

Stemberger, J. (1985). *The lexicon in a model of language production.* New York: Garland.

Waxman, S. R., & Hatch, T. (1992). Beyond the basics: Preschool children label objects flexibly at multiple hierarchical levels. *Journal of Child Language, 19,* 153–166.

Woodward, A. L., & Markman, E. M. (1991). Constraints on learning as default assumptions: Comments on Merriman and Bowman's "The mutual exclusivity bias in children's word learning." *Developmental Review, 14,* 57–77.

4 Inventing Arithmetic: Making Children's Intuition Work in School

Lauren B. Resnick
University of Pittsburgh

I begin this chapter with an apparent contradiction: School mathematics—especially beyond the primary grades—seems difficult and inaccessible to many people. Yet most young children entering school have a great deal of knowledge about quantities and their relations. What is more, children's knowledge of quantity relations seems to be organized in ways that are coherent with the formal structures of mathematics, including some fundamental laws of algebra. How can it be that children know so much about mathematics and yet have such a hard time learning it in school? My efforts to answer this question raise a series of fundamental questions about the nature of knowledge and cognitive competence, the relations between cognition and social processes, and the role of schooling in adaptive sociocognitive development.

KNOWING MATHEMATICS: A SOCIOCOGNITIVE INTERPRETATION

In the mid-1980s, an important article by a group of Brazilian developmental psychologists made a distinction between mathematical performances "in the streets" and "in the school" (Carraher, Carraher, & Schliemann, 1985). They documented stunning, flexible computational skill by child street vendors who could not manage school arithmetic. This group and other investigators subsequently documented extensive practical arithmetic among children (e.g., Saxe, 1988) and adults (Lave, 1988; Nunes, Schliemann, & Carraher, 1993; Scribner, 1984) and showed how such performances were embedded in the demands of everyday life. They also documented nearly error-free computation, often on large numbers and in complex situations, among *street math* performers. But the status of street math as "real mathematics" was not clear at first. Perhaps these arithmetic strategies were just tricks of the trade, convenient procedures passed on within a working culture but not requiring much mathematical understanding on the part of those who used them.

About the same time that the street math studies were becoming known, mathematics educators and students of mathematical cognition were combining forces to challenge common school math practices as also not being real mathematics (e.g., Charles & Silver, 1988; National Council of Teachers of Mathematics, 1989; Schoenfeld, 1985). These reformers and scholars wanted to recraft mathematics education to focus on underlying principles, rather than on computation, and on strategies for mathematical problem solving and communication, rather than on routine procedures. The gist of their agenda might be described as wanting to replace school math with *math math*, that is, child-accessible versions of the kind of thinking that mathematicians do.

The distinctions among *street math, school math,* and *math math* serve as a starting point for my consideration of what it means to know mathematics. I try to show that street math—a version of which can be observed in school children if we capture their everyday intuitions about number and quantity—is based on substantial conceptual knowledge of mathematical principles. Street math is, however, a different kind of *social* practice than math math. American school children sometimes engage in math math practices, but such practices are very rare among unschooled street math performers.

Street Math: Practical Performances Based on Intuitive Principles

The top of Fig. 4.1 gives an example of numerical reasoning by a 9- or 10-year-old selling coconuts on the streets of a northeastern Brazilian city. This child was not "playing store." He was engaged in real work, part of the informal economy that is vital in the life of very poor communities in much of the world, work that is essential to the welfare of his family. Errors in pricing cannot be tolerated, for the child would lose money for his family either by receiving too little for the coconuts sold (profit margins are very small in the informal economy) or by driving customers away to a competitor likely to be waiting just a few steps away.

In Recife, coconuts are customarily sold in bunches of three, so the children learn the price of a single coconut and of a bunch of three. Because of rampant inflation, these prices may change every few days. There is little opportunity to memorize the prices of bundles of coconuts other than the standard group of three. This means that the question asked by the interviewer, posing as a customer, is a true problem for the child.

The bottom of Fig. 4.1 shows an analysis of this apparently simple exchange,

How much is one coconut? *35.* **I'd like ten. How much is that? [Pause]** *Three will be 105; with three more, that will be 210.* **[Pause]** *I need four more. That is . .* **[Pause]** *315. . . . I think it is 350.*

Coconuts	Cruzeiros
3 coconuts	*105 cruzeiros*
3 more coconuts	(105 more cruzeiros) *210 cruzeiros so far*
(6 coconuts so far)	
6 needs 4 more to reach 10	
(3 more coconuts)	(105 more cruzeiros) *315 cruzeiros so far*
(9 coconuts so far)	
(9 needs 1 more to reach ten)	
(1 more coconut)	(35 cruzeiros)
(10 coconuts in all)	*350 cruzeiros in all*

FIG. 4.1. Numerical reasoning by a child coconut vendor. From Carraher, Carraher, and Schliemann (1985, p. 23).

which reveals a surprisingly complex level of mathematical thinking. Underlying everything the child does is a mathematical principle of *additive composition*. Stated in ordinary language, this principle specifies that quantities and numbers are compositions of other quantities and numbers (e.g., 9 is composed of 4 and 5; 5 is composed of 2 and 3; 9 can also be combined with another 9 to yield 18 and so on for larger and larger numbers). This principle permits both decomposition of a target amount (10 coconuts are made up of 3 coconuts, plus 3 more, plus 3 more, plus 1 more) and composition of a new amount by adding known amounts (350 cruzeiros, plus 350 more, plus 350 more, plus 35 more).

The problem, however, was not presented to the child vendor as an exercise in rules of numerical composition, as it might be in school (e.g., "What combinations add up to 10?" or "What is 3 times 350 cruzeiros plus 35?"). This means that the child needed additional knowledge: about how two series of composed numbers relate to one another. The bottom part of Fig. 4.1 schematizes the relational knowledge that this child vendor possessed. The analysis reveals a form of *protoratio* reasoning (see Singer, Kohn, & Resnick, in press). The child vendor cannot (or at least does not) construct a relational equation such as 35::1 = 350::10 (cf. Vergnaud, 1983). But he solves a ratio-like problem by treating it as a problem in coordinating two additive compositions.

In this scale, you see, each two centimeters will be worth one meter. Four meters will be eight centimenters. But it is nine centimeters here, that means half a meter more. Nine centimeters is a wall four and a half meters.

blueprint size	wall size
2 cm	*1m*
8 cm	*4m*
(1 cm more) *9 cm*	
	1/2m more
9 cm	*4-1/2m*

FIG. 4.2. Protoratio reasoning by an uneducated construction worker. From Carraher (1986, p. 22).

The same basic strategy is used by minimally educated adults in Brazil working as construction foremen and thus needing to use scale information on architectural plans to decide on the length of sections of walls they are building. Fig. 4.2 gives an example. This man is working from a mental table of the kind shown in the bottom part of the figure. It is basically the same kind of *protoratio* table as the coconut example—two decomposed series of numbers are coordinated to yield a correct answer—although in this particular case, the foreman also expresses the ratio directly at one point.[1]

Protoratio reasoning is also the most common way that school children solve ratio problems, at least until a certain point in their education. A particularly clear example comes from a study by Ricco (1982), who presented to French school children in grades 2 to 5 (roughly 7- to 11-years-of-age) problems in which, given the price of a certain number of pens, they had to calculate the price of other multiple-pen purchases. The problems were presented in tabular form with some lines filled in and others left for the child to complete. For example, one problem was presented as shown in Table 4.1.

From third grade on, the most common method used by Ricco's subjects was to compute a constant difference that was added to successive rows in the Price Paid column, taking into account the "jumps" in the Number of Pens Bought rows: for example, "Five pens cost 20 francs . . . because there is 4 francs difference between 12 and 16. Six pens . . . 24; I add 4. Eight will cost 28 francs. Oh, no! Seven is missing. Seven . . . 28 francs, 8 pens . . . 32 francs. . . ."

---

[1]There is no developmental connection claimed between child performance of street math and adult performance. These studies have not followed individuals through different life-stages.

TABLE 4.1
Type of Table Used by Ricco to Assess Ratio Reasoning

Number of Pens Bought	*Price Paid*
1	?
2	?
3	12
4	16
5	?
6	?
8	?
10	?
15	?
16	?
18	?
71	?
72	?
75	?

School Math: Errors and Alienation

In the Brazilian research, children and adults whose everyday work required mathematical performances of the kind just described carried them out without errors. Yet many of the same individuals, when given written arithmetic probems in school form, with identical numbers in them, could not do the arithmetic at all (Nunes et al., 1993). The contrast between nearly perfect performance on street math and highly errorful performance on school math highlights an almost total disjunction of everyday and school competence that, at first glance, calls into question the entire venture of school mathematics.

Such total disjunctions are more rare in more fully schooled societies, probably because there is less compelling economic reason to practice street math and because the school forms of mathematical knowledge dominate our lives so much. Most Americans, for example, eventually learn to do written school arithmetic without undue error. But they attain nothing like the sense of nearly perfect command that the Brazilian street mathematicians—child and adult—display. What is more, the learning process for school arithmetic is not a smooth one. Most children make many errors along the way, errors that have come to be called *buggy algorithms* (Brown & VanLehn, 1982; VanLehn, 1990) because they are systematic transformations of correct algorithms, made, apparently, because children are *not* applying schemas of additive composition (Resnick & Omanson, 1987).

Math Math: Beyond Utility

Yet there is plenty of evidence that American and European school children know the principles of additive composition and can use them to think about numbers and arithmetic (Resnick & Greeno, 1990). To learn this, we have had to get

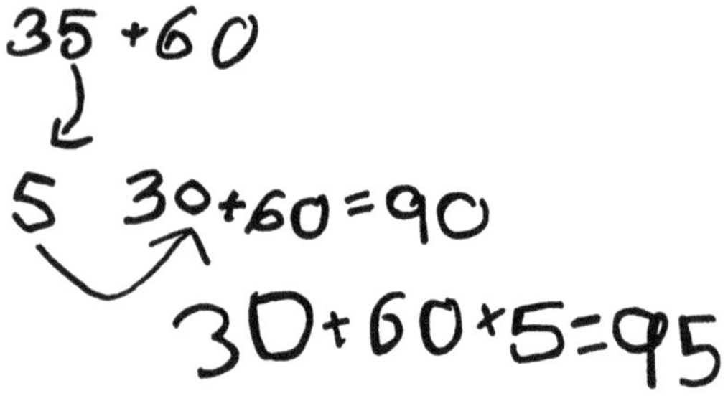

FIG. 4.3. Additive composition reasoning by a first grader.

ahead of school math, interviewing children about procedures and concepts they have not yet encountered in school. Fig. 4.3 gives an example of a first grader, Pitt, who has not yet been taught two-digit addition, explaining in words and numerical symbols how he mentally solved the problem 30 plus 65. Pitt's writing appears in Figure 4.3. His accompanying verbal description was, "I would take away the 5 from the 35. Then I'd add the 60 and the 30, which equals 90. Then I'd bring back the 5 and put it on the 90, and it equals 95."

What Pitt did was to temporarily remove a component from one of the numbers, allowing him to use a known "number fact" (60 + 30 = 90). He then added back the removed component at the end. Thus, he knew that it is permissible to change a number in the course of calculation, as long as a compensating change is made at another point to preserve the total quantity. The constraints and permissions that guided Pitt's invented procedure derive from the mathematical principles of additive composition of number.

A feature of Pitt's performance that is rarely encountered among unschooled street math performers is that he was clearly reasoning about *numbers* as such and not about quantities of material, such as coconuts or pens. This is one of the features of math math. Pitt demonstrated a command of and a taste for math math in many other interviews. For example, his explanation of why 2 × 3 and 3 × 2 yield the same answer (Fig. 4.4) does not reach the status of a proof, but he was

What's two times three? ***Six.*** **How did you get that?** ***Well, two threes . . . one three is three; one more equals six.*** **Okay, what's three times two?** ***Six.*** **Anything interesting about that?** ***They each equal six, and they're different numbers. . . . I'll tell you why that happens. . . . Two has more ways; well, it has more adds . . . like two has more twos, but it's a lower number. Three has less threes, but it's a higher number. . . .*** **Alright, when you multiply three times two, how many adds are there?** ***Three . . . and in the other one there's two. But the two--that's two threes--but the other one is three twos, 'cause twos are littler than threes, but two has more . . . more adds, and then the three has less adds but it's a higher number.***

FIG. 4.4. A child's informal reasoning about commutativity of multiplication.

searching for justifications for why certain procedures work, explaining the relations among numbers. In short, he was exploring the properties of numbers as a domain of interest in and of itself, beyond any immediate practical utility.

THE SCHOOL MATH PROBLEM: COGNITIVE OR MOTIVATIONAL?

Let us return now to my opening contradiction: Why is school math so difficult when street math, apparently based on intuitive appreciation of fundamental mathematical principles, is available to children? The by-now traditional answers to this question come in separate categories that we can roughly label *cognitive* and *motivational.* Although I begin with these categories, I do not mean to accept the traditional separation between them but rather want to show that cognitive and motivational factors interact in ways that produce an unproductive *situation* for mathematical performance in school.

The Cognitive Disconnect. On the cognitive side, there is evidence that the forms of school math teaching do not connect well with the street math that children have acquired at home. Arithmetic (nearly the only math that is in the American elementary school curriculum) is taught as if children come to school knowing nothing at all about it—none of the counting principles that Gelman and Gallistel (1978), for example, have documented for preschool children; none of the language of quantity that Sera, Troyer, and Smith (1988) and others have established; none of the intuitive schemas that even the most "deprived" children have for understanding additive composition of material in the physical world (Resnick, 1992).

Instead, arithmetic (and later algebra) is taught as a series of rules for manipulating the written numerical symbols. Learning the particular procedural rules that have been handed down over the years, mainly as ways to insure reliability in written calculation, and applying them correctly have become the major goals of instruction. There is nothing wrong with the rules per se. In fact, every one of the algorithms taught in elementary school reflects a systematic and elegant application of some subset of the basic principles of additive composition (see Resnick & Omanson, 1987, for an analysis of some of these). But only minimal efforts to help children understand the algorithms as principled derivations are usually made. Furthermore, because math is viewed by educators as an exact subject, there is little invitation to children to talk—in their necessarily imprecise and nonmathematical language—about what they are practicing, except to recite the rules they are expected to learn (Resnick, 1988). All in all, little is done either to use children's street math knowledge or to cultivate math math practice in the classroom.

The Motivational Disconnect. The failure of much of our present teaching to make a cognitive connection between children's own math-related knowledge and the school's version of math feeds a view held by many children that what they know does not count as mathematics. This devaluing of their own knowledge is especially exaggerated among children from families that are traditionally alienated from schools, ones in which parents did not fare well in school and do not expect—however much they may desire—their children to do well, either. In the eyes of these children, math is what is taught in school. Because they do not encounter much at home that resembles school math, they are inclined to discount the street math that surrounds them and that they are learning as not real math. What they do know, often rich and robust, does not count as school knowledge, and so they do not try to use it to make sense of what they encounter in school.

This point is illustrated by the responses we encountered in a set of informal interviews with African-American children about their perceptions of mathematics. Interested in the ways in which home activities might relate to school math learning, we asked several fifth graders to tell us whether they did math at home and what that math was like. All said they did math at home, but when asked for examples, all but one described only their own school homework or the homework of family members enrolled in adult education programs. One girl broke out of the mold, describing how she used math to "prove" that her mother could afford the new dress she wanted, by calculating the cost of clothing items the whole family needed from the Sears catalog and then comparing the total cost of those items with the amount budgeted for family clothing. The specifics of the arithmetic are not particularly interesting in this case. What is important is that this child understood the very practical and desire-motivated activity of pricing clothing to be math, whereas the others did not. For them, only the school-like activity counted as math.

RECONNECTING: FROM STREET MATH TO MATH MATH

The cognitive and motivational disjunctions between what children bring from home and what the school offers can be overcome. Victoria Bill is an elementary school teacher who studied the body of research I have just summarized and then worked to invent a new way of teaching math that would actively use children's street math intuition. The children with whom Bill worked were from an inner-city school. Almost all were African-American, and about 70% were eligible for free or subsidized lunch. In Bill's first year of work, the median first-grade class percentile rankings on the school district's standardized tests moved from around the 30th percentile to above the 80th, with the lowest child scoring at the 66th percentile (Resnick, Bill, & Lesgold, 1992). Similar gains in test performance were made with children in several different grades that Bill taught in succeeding years using her new approach.

These test-based successes—we might call them school math successes—were obtained despite a program that spent little time on the activities typical in school math programs. Bill's method can be characterized as setting up sequences of situations in which street math can be done by children and then, via a carefully structured form of classroom discourse, pushing them toward math math. There is almost no school math intervening.

Principles for Teaching Math Math

Everyday Problems. Figure 4.5 shows some typical work of second graders. The page is copied from a child's notebook dated in January of the school year. The work results from a typical day's lesson, lasting perhaps 40 minutes. The lesson was built around a single problem that the children analyzed under the teacher's direction and then developed solutions to in small groups. The theme of the problem for January 24, 1990, like most problems used in Bill's teaching, came from the children, who are encouraged to bring problems to school that they have encountered or made up. Bill does not necessarily use the problems as given. She reworks them somewhat (keeping them recognizable in such content as children's names, barrettes and other materials being dealt with, and the like) in order to represent a particular mathematical structure. This way of developing problems illustrates one of the principles on which the program is based:

> Encourage everyday problem finding.

The goal is to undo the disconnection between home or street learning and school learning: to bring street math to school. By using problems that the children bring to school as the basis for a formal lesson, Bill teaches the children implicitly that what they do and think about at home *is* math. The same message is carried in other program practices, such as miniprojects that children are expected to do with parents or other family members. For the youngest children, miniprojects might include finding matching sets of four objects in the household or recording the numbers and types of items removed from a grocery bag after a shopping trip.

Accelerated Introduction of Concepts. The problem shown in Fig. 4.5 is a compound problem involving both multiplication and subtraction. This problem is substantially more complex (because it involves multiplication and because it involves two separate arithmetic steps) than children would normally encounter in a typical second-grade textbook. This means that most children will require substantial *scaffolding* in order to solve the problem. Scaffolding is provided through guided class discussion, which is also the teacher's opportunity to evoke and shape mathematical thinking and mathematical explanation by the children.

Monique told her friend TaRae that she would give her 95 barrettes. Monique had 4 bags of barrettes and each bag had 9 barrettes. Does Monique have enough barrettes?

The class first developed an estimated answer. Then they were asked, "How many more does she need?" The solutions below were generated by different class groups.

Group 1 first solved for the number of barrettes by repeated addition. Then they decomposed *4 x 9* into *2 x 9* plus *2 x 9*. Then they set up a missing addend problem, *36 + __ = 95*, which they solved by a combination of estimation and correction.

Group 2 set up a subtraction equation and then developed a solution that used a negative partial result.

Group 4 began with the total number of barrettes needed and subtracted out the successive bags of 9.

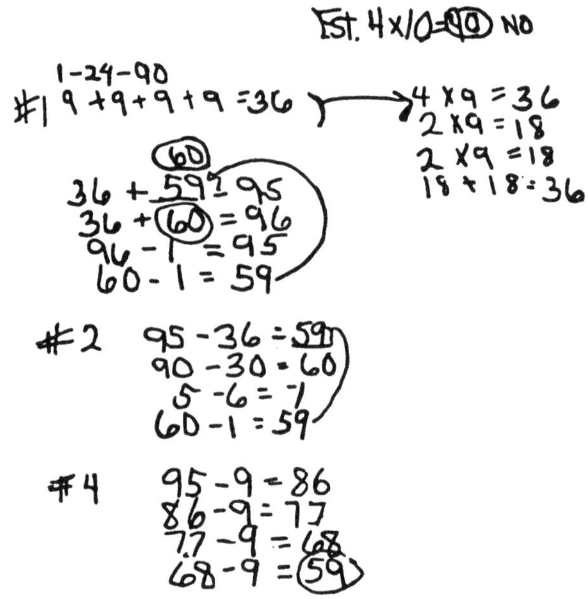

FIG. 4.5. A second-grade problem and several solutions.

Children also scaffold each other's thinking as they work in independent small groups to develop numerical solutions. The choice of a problem as complex as this one for children at this age is guided by another principle:

> Introduce key mathematical structures as quickly as possible.

According to the research alluded to here, young children come to school already knowing a lot about the additive composition of physical material in the world (Resnick & Greeno, 1990). But this knowledge about physical material is not about numbers. In her first grade teaching, Bill tries to help children see how what they know about physical material also applies to numbers, which, at this age, they appreciate mainly via counting. For children, additive composition is not broken down into separate arithmetic rules such as addition, subtraction, and multiplication. To help them develop the connection between their additive composition knowledge and what can be done with numbers, it is important to help them glimpse, even before they can master, the additive composition structure at work across several arithmetic operations and in large as well as small numbers. For this reason, Bill introduces concepts, always embedded in a familiar problem, at a very fast pace. Commutativity, distributivity, and additive inverse form part of the conceptual curriculum beginning in first grade. The concepts are revisited over time to allow full mastery to develop.

Use Street Math Knowledge. In solving the problem shown in Fig. 4.5, after some discussion designed to insure that most of the children understand the *story* structure (not necessarily the numbers yet), children work in table groups to figure out solution approaches. The class first began with an estimation: *9 is close to 10, and 4 tens are 40, 40 is far from the 95 barrettes Monique needs to give to TaRae, so, "No, there are not enough barrettes."* Bill encourages estimation as one of several forms of *number sense* that she treats as integral goals of her teaching. Most days' lessons include at least one occasion in which children develop an estimated solution to a problem or part of a problem.

Group 1 wanted to "prove" that their estimation was correct, and they did so in two ways. First, they added 9 four times to get 36. Then, they proved that 36 was correct in another, more sophisticated way. They added 9 and 9 to make 18, building on their very accessible knowledge of doubles. They repeated the 9 plus 9 to yield another 18. And then they added the two 18s! This solution builds directly and obviously on the children's knowledge of additive composition. They are combining numbers to form partial sums and then combining those to form yet larger sums. This reliance on informally acquired, intuitive knowledge about doubling and accumulation illustrates another principle:

> Draw children's informal knowledge, developed outside school, into the classroom.

In some ways, this is the central precept of Bill's program. It is the foundation principle, drawn from the research discussed earlier, showing that children have good intuitional foundations for mathematical thinking and reasoning about numbers. The usual approach to teaching, in which children must master the "standard" or "correct" procedures for arithmetic, not only fails to use the cognitive resources children bring to school but also creates a motivational problem, because children come to believe that their home-acquired knowledge does not count in school.

Equations at an Early Age. The algebraic notation used to record children's thinking illustrates yet another principle:

> Use formal notations (identity sentences and equations) as a public record of discussions and conclusions.

Early use of algebraic notation is the aspect of Bill's teaching practice that people usually find most surprising. It seems to run counter to the emphasis many developmentalists and mathematics educators place on manipulatives and avoidance of meaningless symbolic manipulation. In Bill's classroom, however, equations are introduced as a shared public record, in mathematically exact language, of ideas that have already been discussed and that therefore have meaning for the children. Public records that can be referred to by everyone are essential in discussion-based learning. Without them, talk is ephemeral, and there is no intellectual accountability for ideas. The use of standard mathematical notation as a shorthand record introduces mathematical precision but permits children to speak in their ordinary language during classroom discussions. The use of formal mathematical notation comes easily to children under these circumstances and is a source of pride to them. It is also, of course, a painless way to introduce a powerful tool for later mathematical use. Equation notations support reasoning about purely mathematical relationships that cannot be observed directly in physical material (Resnick, Cauzinille-Marmeche, & Mathieu, 1987).

The next step in Bill's lessons is to develop specific numerical solutions. In this case, the class was seeking an answer to a question that was not made explicit in the problem statement but was implied in the story structure of the problem: *How many more barrettes does Monique need?* The nonspecification of the *how many* question mimics the way in which problems come up in the real world. The situation typically makes clear what questions should be asked and answered; it provides a mutually understood *common ground* (Clark & Brennan, 1991) for activity. If Monique has to provide 95 barrettes for TaRae and she knows she has only 36, she obviously needs to get enough more to reach 95.

To work on this solution, children return to their table groups to develop their ideas. They know that, although they are expected to reach a mathematically correct answer, there are several ways to reach it. Group 1 interpreted the problem as a "missing addend" addition problem: In effect, how many are needed to get from 36 to 95? (The underlined number was initially a blank space, the class's conventional way of showing the "unknown" in an equation.) They then estimated 60 (a circled number is, by classroom convention, an estimate). But this, added to 36, produced one more than the necessary number of barrettes. Knowing that subtracting 1 from 96 would produce 95, the children also subtracted 1 from the estimated 60, to produce an exact answer of 95. This solution uses intuitive knowledge of *equivalence classes of differences,* one of the algebraic concepts that is rooted in the general principle of additive composition of number.

Group 2 set up the problem as a subtraction problem, 95 minus 36 equals *unknown*, a conversion based on a conceptual understanding of the inverse relationship between addition and subtraction. Next, they worked on the *tens place*, subtracting 30 from 90 to yield 60. Beginning there runs contrary to the computational practice normally taught in school, which begins at the right: thus, with the *ones place*. But it is perfectly sensible mathematically and is actually a more convenient way to proceed when doing arithmetic mentally. These children's next step is an even more startling departure from standard school arithmetic practice. Moving to the ones place, Group 2 proposed subtracting 6 from 5 to yield a *negative* 1. The standard school algorithm teaches children that "You can't take a large number from a small one," so you have to "borrow" (or "regroup"), moving *10* from the tens place over to the ones place. Some of the Group 2 children had been exposed to the concept of negative numbers while working with a computer program and, as far as we know, tried out the idea in the context of subtraction for the first time in the course of this lesson.

Build Confidence in Street Math as Knowledge that Counts. As is clear from these examples, correct answers are sought in Bill's classroom but not just a single correct solution path. Indeed, variety and invention are encouraged. Bill always asks for another way to solve the problem, and the groups are likely to favor new solutions over ones they have encountered before. No standard algorithms are taught. The strongest reason for this practice is another of the program's principles:

> Develop children's trust in their own knowledge.

Children need to believe that what they know is real math and that it counts in school. The only effective way to foster such a belief is to let them use what they know in school and to celebrate what they can do with it. That approach bridges the motivation gap that I discussed earlier. We have often been asked if it would not be just as effective to teach children one or another of the standard computational procedures—which are, after all, both efficient and mathematically correct—and then work with them to analyze how mathematical principles are exemplified in the procedure learned. We believe that such a practice would be perfectly reasonable for adults and perhaps for children who are extremely confident about their ability to cope well with school. But for children who have any doubt about themselves as competent school learners—and this includes most children who come from less privileged homes—the implicit message is that the procedure taught is the one that counts as real, school-sanctioned knowledge, which means that other procedures based on their home-acquired knowledge do not.

Talk is Central. The written material reproduced in Fig. 4.5 is the record, as made by one child in the class, of an extended discussion lasting about 40 minutes and orchestrated by the teacher. The discussion is a reflection of a final principle of Bill's program:

> Talk about mathematics; don't just do arithmetic.

In traditional elementary school practice, math class is devoid of the normal chatter of children, the talk by which they learn most naturally. The focus in school math on performing procedures drives out talk. So does a false but widely held belief that mathematical talk must always be precise. It is true that the end result of mathematical thinking and talking is a set of precise statements. But conversation among mathematicians about their subject is full of the hesitations, restarts, and partially formulated ideas that characterize any conversation in which people are grappling with new ideas and trying to build explanations.

The Structure of Classroom Discourse

Communal Concept Building. To bring talk about mathematical ideas into the classroom, Bill has developed a special form of classroom discourse. She leads discussions designed to engage children in a form of shared problem solving in which the class as a whole, building on contributions from individuals and small working groups, constructs solutions and justifications to a problem. Like many other classroom discussions (see, e.g., Griffin & Humphrey, 1978; Mehan, 1979; Poole, 1990; Sinclair & Coulthard, 1975), Bill's classroom discourse is substantially controlled by the teacher. The teacher generally alternates turns with the children, whose contributions are much shorter than hers; thus, she controls the topic and direction of classroom talk. Unlike the standard school recitation form of discourse that consists of a series of unrelated questions and answers, however, Bill incorporates the children's contributions into relatively extended lines of reasoning that may last across several teacher–student exchanges.

Figure 4.6 schematizes the flow of conversation in a typical lesson. This diagram distinguishes teacher talk, student talk, and full class talk (almost always choral counting). Topically related turns are connected by lines. One can see in this diagram that very few turns are unconnected. Almost every statement is part of a chain that runs over several exchanges.

Revoicing. A look inside this general pattern uncovers another outstanding feature of the discourse: the teacher's frequent repeating or *revoicing* (Bill, Leer, Reams, & Resnick, 1992) of children's contributions. Each teacher contribution in a discussion can be coded as a repetition (P), revoicing (V), question (Q), challenge (CH), or explanation (E). Repetitions are counted when the teacher restates exactly what a child said; adds some term that functions deictically, such

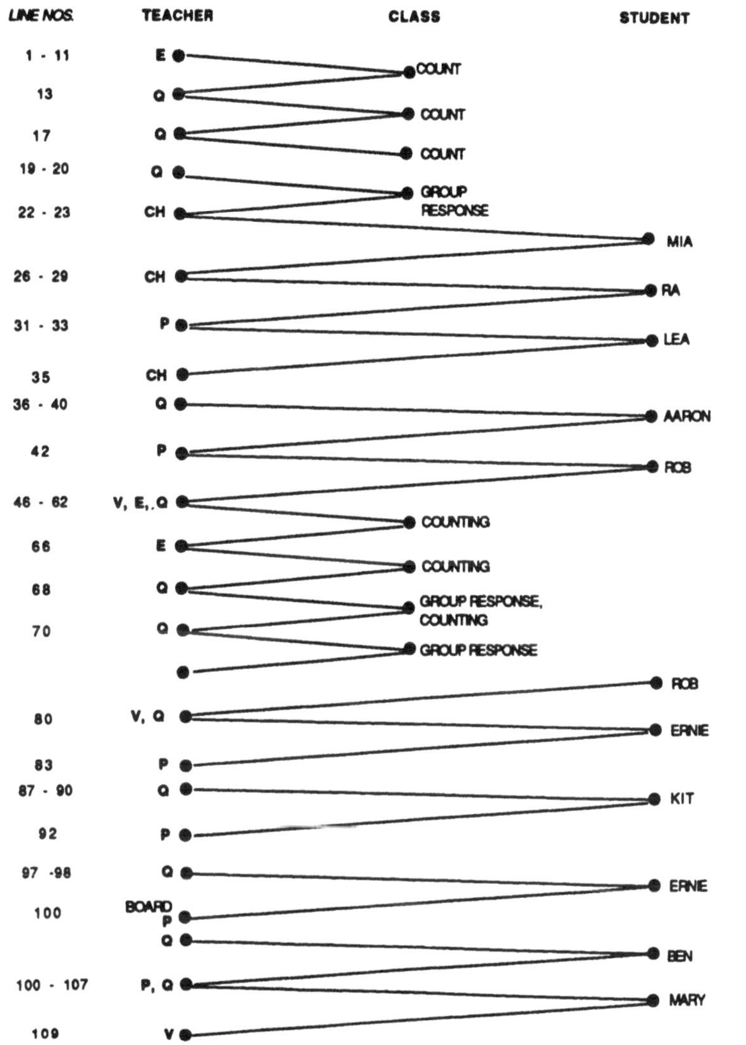

Note. E = Explanation; Q = Question; CH = Challenge; P = Repetition; V = Revoicing

FIG. 4.6. Pattern of conversation in Victoria Bill's math classroom.

as *here*, *now*, or *again*; or writes what a child has said on the blackboard. These repetitions seem to serve several functions. In the general flow of conversation, they function as acceptances of a child's response to a teacher request. In addition, because children often speak in soft or indistinct voices in classroom settings, repeating their words is often necessary if their contributions are to become public: available to all members of the class and not just to the teacher.

Revoicing carries the process of incorporating children's responses even further. Revoicing refers to occasions when the teacher rephrases or otherwise modifies the children's contributions. We regard the following kinds of rephrasings as revoicing:

- providing a label for a quantity after a child utters only a number
- rephrasing from dialect to standard English
- repeating only a part of what the child said
- making a mathematical restatement (e.g., changing a child's statement of repeated addition into a mathematically equivalent multiplication statement)

In a representative 10 min of classroom talk that we coded for one of Bill's lessons, 84% of all children's contributions were incorporated into the discussion. Of these, more than half were repeated by the teacher, and almost a third were revoiced. In three of the revoicing incidents, the teacher provided a label for a quantity stated by the child as only a number. These are potentially crucial discourse moves, because they serve to keep the class's attention focused on the semantics of the story problem, not just on the numerical arithmetic. One revoicing was a restatement in standard English ("Ones that don't have the icing") of a statement given by a child in vernacular dialect ("Ones that don't have *no* icing"). This kind of revoicing also serves to maintain the focus on meaningful communication while the teacher standardizes the language used.

Revoicings can be considered a form of conversational scaffolding (cf. Wood, Bruner, & Ross, 1976). Such scaffolding permits children to participate in a conversation that is beyond their current individual cognitive capacities. Other forms of conversational scaffolding are common in ordinary conversation, for example, the occasions on which a person provides the word or phrase for which a conversational partner seems to be searching. Repetition and revoicing are particularly prominent forms in teacher-controlled classroom discourse.

Revoicings sometimes serve as tools in the teacher's effort to maintain continuity in the conceptual content of the conversation. In these cases, Bill reformulates a child's contribution so that she can use it to forward her own pedagogical goal. For example, in a lesson focused on multiplication, the children are asked to figure out how many children are in the class, and one child proposes, "You could count them *by groups*." (He is referring to the table seating groups in the room.) Accepting his idea, Bill also transforms it, saying, "Oh. Oh, he says *by fours* . . . . So this is a group of four . . . ." This transformation allows her to pursue her pedagogical goal of showing the relationship between repeated addition and multiplication.

Linking Representations. Another special feature of Bill's teaching is her particular strategy for linking different representations—verbal, concrete, graphic, and formal—of quantities and their relations. Figure 4.7 schematizes 3 min of a discussion in which Bill led the class through several different ways of determining how many cupcakes there were on a tray. In these few minutes, five different representations were linked: a written equation; the children's oral language; the teacher's oral language; the actual tray of cupcakes; and a transparency graphic showing the cupcake tray schematically as a 3×7 array of squares.

In the course of the conversation, the equation $5 + 5 + 5 = 15$ was produced. But this happened slowly, with each element in the equation written down only after child language and teacher language were carefully linked to the cupcakes and to the transparency graphic. In the opening line, Rob suggested that one could start the process of finding the total number of cupcakes by "do[ing] five plus five plus five." At this point, Rob had stated all of the left side of the equation. But Bill did not proceed directly to writing what Rob had said. Instead, she linked his words to their physical referent, the uniced cupcakes, saying "So when he's thinking of five plus five plus five, he's thinking of . . . ." As she said this, Bill pointed to the 3 rows of uniced cupcakes. She thus revoiced Rob's contribution and simultaneously attributed a particular referent (the 3 rows of cupcakes) to it. She also insisted on a label, "not iced," for the particular cupcakes, thus linguistically specifying the referent of Rob's statement.

Next, Bill analyzed the uniced cupcakes to show more precisely to what the 5s refer. First, she specified a row of 5, pointing carefully to one row. The class counted. The choral counting used frequently in this lesson served to reiterate the quantitative meaning of the 5s that Rob had spoken; they are the cardinals arrived at by counting each of the rows. After the children counted one row of cupcakes, the exercise was repeated, but this time the squares in the transparency schematic were counted. This shift highlights the fact that the schematic stands for the cupcake tray and can be used as if it were the tray itself. In other words, the second count refers to the same row of five cupcakes.

In just about one minute of talk, one row of 5 was selected for attention. Teacher and child language was linked to both displays. And only after all of this was done was a single 5 written into the developing equation.

THE DEVELOPMENTAL ROOTS OF MATH MATH

Bill's teaching approach is based on a developmental theory of how mathematical knowledge develops through a sequence of levels characterized by changes in representational content (see Resnick & Greeno, 1990). This theory is distinguished from Piaget's theory of mathematical development in two important ways. First, what develops over time is mainly the *kinds* of conceptual entities that are recognized and reasoned about rather than logical structures. In fact, fundamental logical or relational structures are maintained across the levels of mathematical development. Second, the different representational forms develop

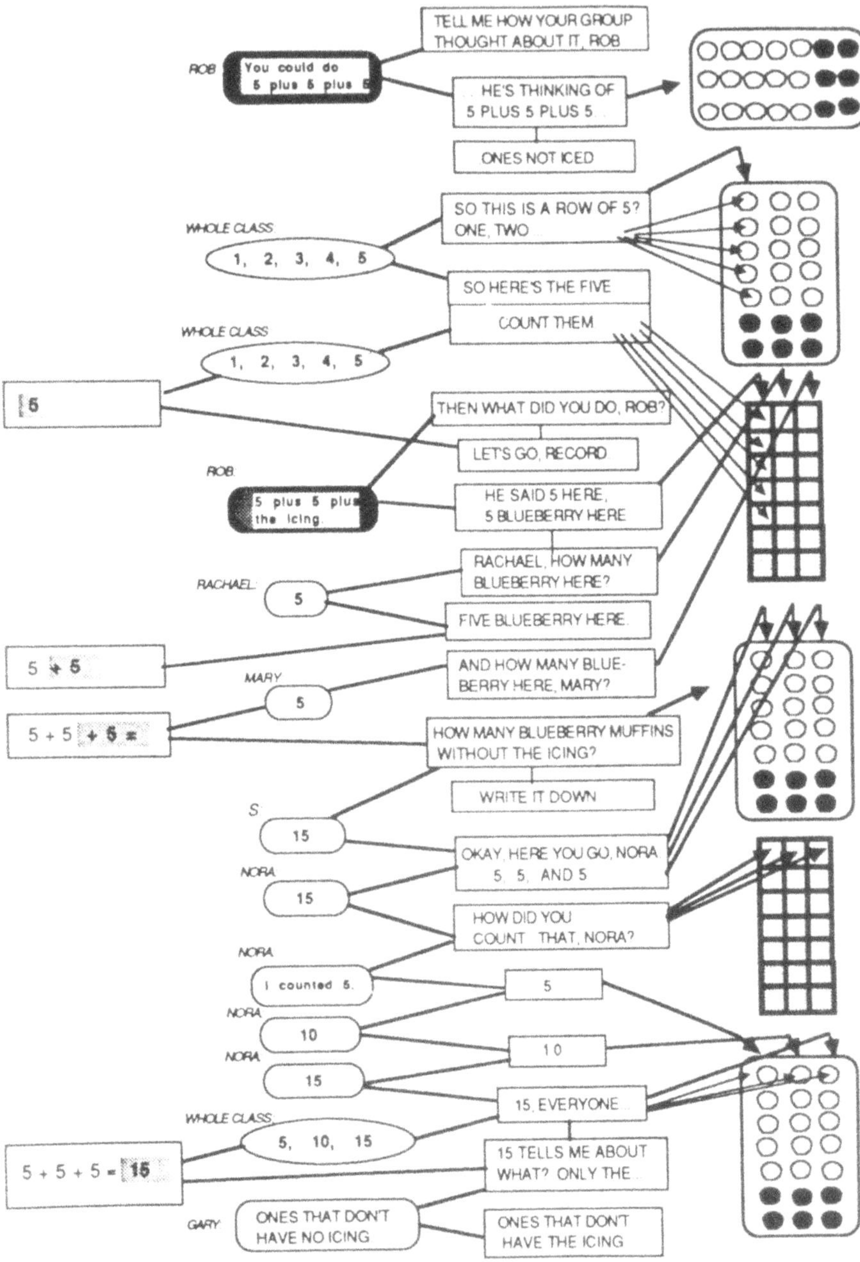

FIG. 4.7. Linking representations in three minutes of classroom talk.

unevenly for different numbers and operations, and the levels, therefore, can coexist in the same child.

Four Levels of Mathematical Thinking. Our ideas about the importance of representational structures in mathematical development are shared by a number of theorists (e.g., Fuson, 1988; Steffe, Cobb, & von Glasersfeld, 1988; Steffe, von Glasersfeld, Richards, & Cobb, 1983). Most of those accounts, however, have focused heavily on the representations underlying counting and the transitions from counting objects to reasoning about cardinalities of sets. Our analysis is compatible with other representational development theories but extends them to include both a form of reasoning about quantity that precedes the ability to count individual objects or sets and an advanced form of reasoning in which operators and relations are represented as conceptual entities. The four kinds of mathematical thinking that Resnick and Greeno identified are summarized in Table 4.2.

In the *mathematics of protoquantities*, reasoning is about amounts of physical material. Comparisons of amounts are made and inferences can be drawn about the effects of various changes and transformations on the amounts; but no numerical quantification is involved. The language of protoquantitative mathematical thinking is a language of descriptive and comparative terms applied directly to the physical objects or amounts: a big doll, many eggs, more milk. In the mathematics of protoquantities, operations are actions that can be performed directly on physical objects or material: increasing and decreasing, combining and separating, comparing, ordering, pairing. The simplest form of protoquantitative reasoning is direct perceptual comparison of objects or sets of different sizes. More advanced protoquantitative reasoning works on a mental representation of amounts of material and allows one to reason about the results of imagined increases and decreases in amounts of material. Thus, protoquantitative reasoners can say that there *will be* more apples after mother gives each child some additional ones, or that some mice *must have been* removed if there are now less than before, without being able to look simultaneously at the objects in their before and after states. Similarly, mental combining and separating operations permit children to reason protoquantitatively about the relations between parts and whole: for example, more fruits in the bowl than either apples or oranges (Fuson, Lyons, Pergament, Hall, & Kwon, 1988; Markman & Siebert, 1976; McGarrigle, described in Donaldson, 1978).

In the *mathematics of quantities*, reasoning is about numerically quantified amounts of material. Numbers are used as measures: 4 dolls, 3 feet of board, 7 pounds of potatoes. In the mathematics of quantities, numbers function as adjectives; they describe a property (the measured amount) of a physical quantity. The numbers take their meaning from the physical material they refer to and describe. Terms from formal mathematics, such as *add* or *divide*, may be used, but their reference is to action on physical material. Operations in the mathematics of quantities are actions on measured amounts of material.

TABLE 4.2
Four Types of Mathematical Thinking

Mathematics of:	*Objects of Reasoning*	*Linguistic Terms*	*Operations*
protoquantities	physical material	much, many, more, less, big, small, etc.	increase, decrease, combine, separate, compare, order
quantities	measured physical material	*n* objects, *n* inches, *n* pounds, etc. Add, take away, divide	increase and decrease quantified sets by specific numbers of objects; increase and decrease measured amounts of material by measured amounts combine and partition quantified sets or measured amounts divide a set or measured amount into equal shares
numbers	specific numbers	*n* more than, *n* times, plus *n*, minus *n*, times *n*, *n* plus *m*, *n* divided by *m*	actions of adding, subtracting, multiplying, dividing, applied to specific numbers
operators	numbers in general, operations, variables	addition, subtraction, multiplication, division, difference, equivalence, times greater than, times less than, 1/nth of	commute, associate, distribute, compose, decompose

By contrast, in the *mathematics of numbers*, numbers function not as adjectives, describing something else, but as nouns. That is, numbers are conceptual entities that can be manipulated and acted on. One can add 3 and 4 (not 3 apples and 4 apples) or multiply 3 (not 3 books) by another number. In the mathematics of numbers, numbers themselves have properties rather than being properties of physical material. The properties of numbers are defined in terms of other numbers. Numbers have magnitudes in relation to one another: For example, 12 is *8 more than* 4; it is *3 times* 4; it is 1/3 of 36. Numbers are also compositions of other numbers: thus, 12 is 8 + 4, 7 + 5, 6 + 6, and so forth. Operations in the mathematics of number are actions taken on numbers, resulting in changes in those numbers. Thus, 12 can be changed to 4 by subtracting 8 or, alternatively, by dividing by 3; it can be changed to 36 by multiplying by 3 or by adding 24. The numbers being compared, composed, and changed in these examples are purely conceptual entities. Their meaning derives entirely from their relations to one another and their place within a system of numbers. Physical material need not be imagined.

The final type of mathematical thinking that we identify is the *mathematics of operators*, in which not only numbers but also operations on numbers are conceptual entities that can be reasoned about. In the mathematics of numbers, operations are like transitive verbs. They describe actions that can be performed on numbers. But they are not themselves objects with properties, objects on which actions can be taken. Similarly, in the mathematics of numbers, one can describe relations between numbers, but the relations are essentially adjectives describing properties of the numbers. They are not themselves noun-like objects with properties that can be reasoned about. In the mathematics of operators, operations do behave like nouns. They can be reasoned about and not just applied. For example, it can be argued that the operation of addition by combining is always commutative, no matter what pair of numbers is composed. In the mathematics of operators, relations between numbers also are objects to reason about. A *difference of* 3, for example, can be understood as a property of the pair 11 and 8. Differences can be compared, so that one can recognize that [11 − 8] is less than [24 − 20], or even operated on so that [11 − 8] can be subtracted from [24 − 20]. This kind of reasoning about relations as mental objects is what it takes to understand functions.

Coexistence of the Levels. There is no reason to suppose that people pass all at once from a protoquantitative way of thinking to the mathematics of quantities or from the mathematics of quantities to the mathematics of numbers. There might be some developmental limits—of the kind developed by Case (1985) and Fischer (1980), for example—on how many chunks of information can be thought about at once, and this would be a brake of sorts on the pace at which new objects and properties could be incorporated into the mental system. But most evidence suggests that mathematical mental objects are built up specific bit by specific bit rather than emerging in discrete stages. So, for example, children may be doing the mathematics of quantity on dimensions such as manyness and length while still reasoning only protoquantitatively about weight or speed. Furthermore, they may convert small integers (e.g., 1, 2, 3, and 4) into mental entities and perform the mathematics of number on them while still using higher numbers only as descriptors of amounts of physical material. Similarly, operators may be transformed from verbs to nouns, one at a time. Children can, for example, reason generally about the commutativity of addition well before they can reason about multiplicative functions. Furthermore, as each new kind of number—for example, positive integers, negative integers, fractions—is encountered, it is likely that learning will entail passage through the successive layers of the mathematics of protoquantities, quantities, numbers, and operators. Thus, at any given moment, a child can be functioning at several different layers of mathematical thought.

Even more important, as more advanced forms of mathematical reasoning are developed, the earlier ones are not discarded but remain part of the individual's total knowledge system. People able to think abstractly about numbers and operators as conceptual entities can also use numbers to refer to specific measured quantities. This capacity to move back and forth among the mathematics of quantities, numbers, and operators is crucial in enabling people to relate their abstract mathematical knowledge to practical situations. When scientists use numbers, for example (cf. Schwartz,1988), they are almost always referring to specific, measured quantities (the mathematics of quantities); their reasoning about functional relations (the mathematics of operators) refers back to these physical quantities. Engineers often reason protoquantitatively about physical systems (e.g., deKleer & Brown, 1985; Forbus, 1985), using the conclusions reached about how quantities should change or relate to one another to constrain and check the results of more formal calculations.

Coherence Across Levels. One reason that people can move back and forth easily across the four levels of mathematical thinking is that the basic logical relations are the same at all levels. This can be seen most clearly if we express the four levels as sets of equations, as in Fig. 4.8, which shows the evolution of the mathematical concepts of commutativity and associativity.

At the level of protoquantitative reasoning, before they can reliably quantify physical material, children know that a whole quantity (W) can be cut into two or more parts and that the parts can be recombined to make the whole (Equation 1). They also know that the order in which the parts are combined does not matter in reconstituting the original amount (Equations 2 and 3). Equation 2 is a protoquantitative version of the commutativity of addition property; Equation 3 is a protoquantitative version of the associativity of addition property.

In the mathematics of quantities, relations are between measured or counted amounts of material. However, all of the relationships among protoquantitative parts and wholes are maintained. As a result, children can now reason using quantified equations, such as Equations 4 through 6. Equations 5 and 6 constitute versions of the commutativity and associativity properties within the mathematics of quantities. Note that they maintain the identical form to Equations 2 and 3.

In the mathematics of numbers, the same schemas organize knowledge about relations among numbers. This is evident in Equations 7 through 9, which exactly parallel the structure of Equations 1 through 3 and 4 through 6. Equations 8 and 9 constitute versions of commutativity and associativity in the mathematics of numbers.

Finally, in the mathematics of operators, attention switches from actions on particular numbers to more general relations between numbers. Commutativity

Mathematics of Protoquantities

(1) $P1 + P2 + P3 = W$
(2) $P1 + P2 = P2 + P1$
(3) $(P1 + P2) + P3 = P1 + (P2 + P3)$

Mathematics of Quantities

(4) 3 apples + 5 apples + 4 apples = 12 apples
(5) 3 apples + 5 apples = 5 apples + 3 apples
(6) (3 apples + 5 apples) + 4 apples = 3 apples + (5 apples + 4 apples)

Mathematics of Numbers

(7) $3 + 5 + 4 = 12$
(8) $4 + 7 = 7 + 4$
(9) $(3 + 5) + 4 = 3 + (5 + 4)$

Mathematics of Operators

(10) $n + m = m + n$
(11) $(n + m) + p = n + (m + p)$

FIG. 4.8. Four levels of reasoning about commutativity and associativity.

and associativity are *always* true for addition, no matter what the numbers. Thus, Equations 10 and 11 express in formal mathematical terms the same relationships that were expressed in protoquantitative Equations 2 and 3.

Emergent Math Math. So where, exactly, is math math? At first blush, it might seem to emerge with the mathematics of operators, where reasoning is about general patterns of relations among quantities and not about any specific quantities or even specific numbers. But Victoria Bill's young students were engaging in an emergent form of math math: noticing relations and justifying procedures. Their talk was about quantities and numbers, sometimes even protoquantities, but it concerned the same fundamental relations as would advanced students' or mathematicians' talk about operators. With this observation, we are in a position to reconsider the role of schooling in children's sociocognitive development.

IN CONCLUSION: BACK TO SCHOOL?

My analysis has been intended to make it clear that even young children have the cognitive wherewithal to engage in forms of thinking that contain many of the features of true mathematical reasoning. They can, under the right evoking and supporting conditions, practice intellectually honest forms of math math even in elementary school. They can also perform analogs of street math that depend on and help to develop fundamental mathematical concepts.

Yet, in today's schools, neither street math nor math math is usually the order of the day. Instead, children spend their time practicing forms of school math that many have trouble learning—for reasons of both cognitive and motivational disconnect—and that are increasingly hard to defend as useful tools for the lives they will lead outside school. This is clear from studies of modern work places, which suggest that the mathematics most people actually use looks more like Brazilian street math—highly accurate, tuned to specific situations rather than abstractions, dependent on tools and instruments—than like the ritualized, repetitive arithmetic drills of the schools.

Suppose we were to do away with all or most of this school math drill. What, if anything, would we substitute and to what ends? To answer this question sensibly, we need to return to my opening questions about the nature of knowledge and cognitive competence. In mathematics, as in other fields, *knowledge*, or even *conceptual understanding*, does not adequately define cognitive competence. Cognitive competence is also a matter of knowing how to *use* concepts and knowledge in ways that are socially and culturally adaptive. I have shown that, in some fundamental respects, the street math practiced by Brazilian children and adults is based on conceptual structures—such as additive composition—that are mathematically sound. Yet these individuals fail at school math and would almost certainly have difficulty participating in the kind of discourse that would qualify as math math. The only way, then, to make sense of the very different forms of mathematical competence discussed in this chapter is to think of them as different forms of mathematical *practice*, each valued in different communities, each with its own preferred ways of using knowledge.

In mathematical practice, as in other domains, cognitive competence and social competence are ineluctably intertwined. To be good at street math is to be good at participating in a particular set of activities that involve both certain kinds of knowledge and specific ways of interacting with other people. A good practitioner of street math knows not only how to calculate the price of coconuts or the length of building walls but also how to convince others (e.g., customers) that the calculation is an appropriate one. Similarly, a good practitioner of math math is someone who knows how to engage in particular kinds of discussions about the nature of numbers, or about operators and relations, that are sanctioned as "mathematical" in nature. These discussions are likely to focus on justifications, demonstrations, and, eventually, proofs that follow certain accepted rules for both logical relations and forms of presentation. School math, too, is a form of social practice. It has its particular rules of participation, ones that, by and large, tend to discourage both the practical and familiar activity of street math and the more intellectual, valued-for-its-own-sake, activity of math math discussions.

There is no way to acquire social practices except to participate in them. Children learn street math by participating in street math activities. They can learn math math competencies in the same way: by participating in the social practices that define math math. In any given social practice, beginners are not, of course, very expert. To participate, they need scaffolding of various kinds. Older siblings may help beginning street math participants in their price calculations, for example. Or, a teacher's revoicing may allow a young child to participate in an early form of math math discussion. The important point about participation is that it is just that: actual participation, not *preparation* for participation. This means that learning and cognitive development may be productively viewed as particular forms of *socialization*—specifically, socialization into practices that involve the use of concepts and forms of reasoning that we habitually study as cognitive achievements.

This, finally, brings us back to school. Where in the world might children be socialized into math math practice? We might send older children out into apprenticeships or internships to learn modern forms of street math or use simulations of workplaces in school. But math math cannot be learned in those environments. Math math is a social practice of its own, one that values discussion, rational justification, and reflection, all in pursuit of understanding for its own sake. To socialize children into math math requires deliberately creating places where math math is practiced in a form in which children can participate. That is what Victoria Bill has done in her classroom. Bill's young students were engaging in an emergent form of math math: noticing relations, constructing formal representations of these relations, justifying procedures.

In this era in which information is freely available from so many other sources, providing deliberately planned environments for cognitive socialization is arguably the central purpose of the school. And among the kinds of environments that schools can uniquely provide are those designed to socialize children into a culture of rational inquiry and reasoned debate. Using school in this way will require exchanging the social practices of school math for those of math math. There are several models, in addition to the one described here, of what such reorganized school practice might look like for mathematics. Leading mathematics educators such as Alan Schoenfeld (1992) and Magdalene Lampert (1986) have described how math math discourse can be organized in the classroom and how mathematical concepts can emerge within that discourse. Similar cases can be made for changed practice in other subject matters. These are fundamental changes, not just fine-tuning of the curriculum. The challenge of bringing about such change, in socially and politically responsible ways, is great. It is a challenge worthy of our best efforts.

REFERENCES

Bill, V. L., Leer, M. N., Reams, L. E., & Resnick, L. B. (1992). From cupcakes to equations: The structure of discourse in a primary mathematics classroom. *Verbum, 15*(1), 63–85.

Brown, J. S., & VanLehn, K. (1982). Towards a generative theory of "bugs." In T. P. Carpenter, J. M. Moser, & T. A. Romberg (Eds.), *Addition and subtraction: A cognitive perspective* (pp. 117–135). Hillsdale, NJ: Lawrence Erlbaum Associates.

Carraher, T. N. (1986). From drawings to buildings: Working with mathematical scales. *Instructional Journal of Behavioral Development, 9*, 527–544.
Carraher, T. N., Carraher, D. W., & Schliemann, A. D. (1985). Mathematics in the streets and in schools. *British Journal of Developmental Psychology, 3*, 21–29.
Case, R. (1985). *Intellectual development: Birth to adulthood*. New York: Academic Press.
Charles, R. I., & Silver, E. A. (Eds.). (1988). *The teaching and assessing of mathematical problem solving*. Hillsdale, NJ/Reston, VA: Erlbaum/National Council of Teachers of Mathematics.
Clark, H. H., & Brennan, S. E. (1991). In L. B. Resnick, J. M. Levine, & S. D. Teasley (Eds.), *Perspectives on socially shared cognition* (pp. 127–149). Washington, DC: American Psychological Association.
deKleer, J., & Brown, J. S. (1985). A qualitative physics based on confluences. In D. Bobrow (Ed.), *Qualitative reasoning about physical systems* (pp. 7–84). Amsterdam: Elsevier Science Publishers.
Donaldson, M. (1978). *Children's minds*. New York: Norton.
Fischer, K. W. (1980). A theory of cognitive development: The control and construction of hierarchies of skills. *Psychological Review, 87*, 477–531.
Forbus, K. D. (1985). Qualitative process theory. In D. Bobrow (Ed.), *Qualitative reasoning about physical systems* (pp. 85–168). Amsterdam: Elsevier Science Publishers.
Fuson, K. C. (1988). *Children's counting and concepts of number*. New York: Springer-Verlag.
Fuson, K. C., Lyons, B., Pergament, G., Hall, J., & Kwon, Y. (1988). Effects of collection terms on class-inclusion and on number tasks. *Cognitive Psychology, 20*, 96–120.
Gelman, R., & Gallistel, C. R. (1978). *The child's understanding of numbers*. Cambridge, MA: Harvard University Press.
Griffin, P., & Humphrey, F. (1978). Task and talk. In R. Shuy & P. Griffin (Eds.), *The study of children's functional language and education in the early years*. Final Report to the Carnegie Corporation of New York. Arlington, VA: Center for Applied Linguistics.
Lave, J. (1988). *Cognition in practice: Mind, mathematics, and culture in everyday life*. Cambridge, England: Cambridge University Press.
Lampert, M. (1986). Knowing, doing, and teaching mathematics. *Cognition and Instruction, 3*, 305–342.
Markman, E. M., & Siebert, J. (1976). Classes and collections: Internal organization and resulting holistic properties. *Cognitive Psychology, 8*, 516–577.
Mehan, H. (1979). *Learning lessons: Social organization in the classroom*. Cambridge, MA: Harvard University Press.
National Council of Teachers of Mathematics. (1989). *Curriculum and evaluation standards for school mathematics, K-12*. Reston, VA: Author.
Nunes, T., Schliemann, A. D., & Carraher, D. W. (1993). *Street mathematics and school mathematics*. New York: Cambridge University Press.
Poole, D. (1990). Contextualizing IRE in an eighth-grade quiz review. *Linguistics and Education, 2*, 185–211.
Resnick, L. B. (1988). Treating mathematics as an ill-structured discipline. In R. I. Charles & E. A. Silver (Eds.), *The teaching and assessing of mathematical problem solving* (pp. 32–60). Hillsdale, NJ/Reston, VA: Erlbaum/National Council of Teachers of Mathematics.
Resnick, L. B. (1992). From protoquantities to operators: Building mathematical competence on a foundation of everyday knowledge. In G. Leinhardt, R. Putnam, & R. A. Hattrup (Eds.), *Analysis of arithmetic for mathematics teaching* (pp. 373–429). Hillsdale, NJ: Lawrence Erlbaum Associates.
Resnick, L. B., Bill, V., & Lesgold, S. (1992). Developing thinking skills in arithmetic class. In A. Demetriou, M. Shayer, & A. Efklides (Eds.), *Neo-Piagetian theories of cognitive development: Implications and applications for education* (pp. 210–230). London: Routledge.
Resnick, L. B., Cauzinille-Marmeche, E., & Mathieu, J. (1987). Understanding algebra. In J. A.

Sloboda & D. Rogers (Eds.), *Cognitive processes in mathematics* (pp. 169–203). Oxford, England: Clarendon Press.

Resnick, L. B., & Greeno, J. G. (1990). *Conceptual growth of number and quantity*. Unpublished manuscript.

Resnick, L. B., & Omanson, S. F. (1987). Learning to understand arithmetic. In R. Glaser (Ed.), *Advances in instructional psychology* (Vol. 3, pp. 41–95). Hillsdale, NJ: Lawrence Erlbaum Associates.

Ricco, G. (1982). Les premiere acquisitions de la notion de fonction lineaire chez l'enfant de la 7 a 11 ans [Initial acquisitions of the linear function concept by children 7 to 11 years old]. *Educational Studies in Mathematics, 13*, 289–327.

Saxe, G. B. (1988). The mathematics of child street vendors. *Child Development, 59*, 1415–1425.

Schoenfeld, A. H. (1985). *Mathematical problem solving*. New York: Academic Press.

Schoenfeld, A. H. (1992). Learning to think mathematically: Problem solving, metacognition, and sense-making in mathematics. In D. Grouws (Ed.), *Handbook for research on mathematics teaching and learning* (pp. 334–370). New York: Macmillan.

Schwartz, J. L. (1988). Intensive quantity and referent transforming arithmetic operations. In M. Behr & J. Hiebert (Eds.), *Number concepts and operations in the middle grades* (pp. 41–52). Reston, VA: National Council of Teachers of Mathematics.

Scribner, S. (1984). Studying working intelligence. In B. Rogoff & J. Lave (Eds.), *Everyday cognition: Its development in social context* (pp. 9–40). Cambridge, MA: Harvard University Press.

Sera, M., Troyer, D., & Smith, L. (1988). What do two-year-olds know about the sizes of things? *Child Development, 59*, 1489–1496.

Sinclair, J. M., & Coulthard, R. M. (1975). *Toward an analysis of discourse*. New York: Oxford University Press.

Singer, J. A., Kohn, A. S., & Resnick, L. B. (in press). Knowing about proportions in different contexts. In P. Bryant & T. Nunes (Eds.), *How do children learn mathematics?* Hillsdale, NJ: Lawrence Erlbaum Associates.

Steffe, L. P., Cobb, P., & von Glasersfeld, E. (1988). *Construction of arithmetical meanings and strategies*. New York: Springer-Verlag.

Steffe, L. P., von Glasersfeld, E., Richards, J., & Cobb, P. (1983). *Children's counting types: Philosophy, theory, and applications*. New York: Praeger.

VanLehn, K. (1990). *Mind bugs*. Cambridge, MA: MIT Press.

Vergnaud, G. (1983). Multiplicative structures. In R. Lesh & M. Landau (Eds.), Acquisition of mathematics concepts and processes (pp. 127–174). London: Academic Press.

Wood, D., Bruner, J. S., & Ross, G. (1976). The role of tutoring in problem solving. *Journal of Child Psychology and Psychiatry, 17*, 89–100.

5 Learning Mathematics From Classroom Instruction: Cross-Cultural and Experimental Perspectives

James W. Stigler
Clea Fernandez
University of California, Los Angeles

In this chapter we explore the question of how children learn mathematics from classroom instruction. Although we know a great deal from a cognitive-psychological perspective about how children's mathematical knowledge develops over the elementary school years (Carpenter, Moser, & Romberg, 1982; Ginsburg, 1983); and although we know a fair amount from the field of educational research about how mathematics is taught in elementary school classrooms (Brophy & Good, 1986; Dunkin & Biddle, 1974), we know very little about the mechanisms by which teaching and learning are related. Indeed, despite the now predominant view that children construct knowledge—as opposed to merely receiving it—from their environment; and despite the fact that much of this process, at least in the industrialized world, must surely go on inside classrooms, we know almost nothing about *how* children construct knowledge during classroom instruction, that is, about the processes by which a child builds meaning from classroom activities.

We believe there are at least two reasons for this dearth of knowledge. One reason is that we have lacked tools for describing classroom instruction in terms that allow us to relate the instruction to students' learning and construction of meaning. Many descriptions of instruction lack a theoretical rationale, or, if they contain such a rationale, refer to it only implicitly. There are many ways one might describe classroom instruction, only some of which might be relevant for student learning. It seems to us that the quest to describe instruction would most profitably be carried out in the context of attempts to develop theories of how children learn from instruction, and thus far this has not been the rule.

A second problem that has hindered attempts to understand the processes by which students construct knowledge in classrooms concerns the difficulty of studying such processes in naturalistic contexts. Classrooms are complex environments that contain a diversity of students who no doubt process the same instruction in a slightly different way. Many of the techniques used by cognitive scientists to study cognitive processing—for example, on-line questioning of the learner, or think-aloud protocols produced by the learner during instruction—appear difficult to use during instruction in a typical classroom. Most such techniques would be disruptive at best, and highly impractical.

In this chapter we do not answer the question of how knowledge is constructed in classrooms, nor do we provide a well-developed theory. Instead, we present a progress report on our efforts to overcome these two obstacles that have slowed the development of theory and empirical research on how children learn mathematics from classroom instruction.

The chapter is divided into two major parts. In the first part we discuss our efforts to describe mathematics classrooms in meaningful ways, by which we mean ways that capture dimensions that are relevant for student learning. We have grappled with the problem of how to describe classrooms meaningfully in the context of cross-cultural comparisons of mathematics instruction in Asian and American classrooms. In this work we have studied classrooms in Japan, China, Taiwan, and the United States. We present illustrative examples from these studies, emphasizing the comparison of Japanese and American classrooms.

In the second part of the chapter we discuss some of our most recent work in which we attempt to explore the processes by which students learn from classroom instruction. This work begins where our cross-cultural work leaves off: The differences we have found between Japanese and American classrooms are great, and they are, of course, associated with well-known mathematics achievement differences between students in the two countries (Stevenson, Lee, & Stigler, 1986). But do the differences in teaching methods cause the differences in achievement, or are they merely associated spuriously? By trying to answer this question we can gain a better understanding of the link between teaching and learning, which ultimately is our goal.

Why Cross-Cultural Comparison?

Before continuing, however, let us pose one additional question that may be on the reader's mind: Why cross-cultural comparisons, and why Japan, if our goal is to understand mathematics teaching and learning in the United States?

Teaching in the United States is surprisingly homogeneous, with most U. S. mathematics teachers appearing to follow some variant of a "direct instruction" approach to teaching. Of course there are critiques of the direct instruction approach, most notably from so-called "constructivist" mathematics educators.

But while these critics are able to define a form of instruction they consider ideal—in such documents as the National Council of Teachers of Mathematics *Standards*, or the California *Framework*—there is a void when it comes to finding actual examples of what the new instruction should look like. We believe that American research on classroom instruction is hindered by this lack of examples.

The study of Japanese instruction helps to mitigate this problem. Although instruction in Japan is not rare or exotic—in fact, it fits very well into the constructivist frameworks described in current American reform documents—it does differ greatly from that found in U.S. classrooms. Simply increasing the variability of examples has an important positive effect on research. It increases our awareness of what consistencies there are among American classrooms. It helps us to identify new variables that might affect learning. And it keeps us from focusing on false dichotomies—for example, rote vs. understanding—that do not necessarily describe actual variations in classroom teaching.

But this is not the only reason to study education in Japan: Studies of mathematics achievement that compare Japanese and American children show that Japan is remarkably successful in achieving the same goals that we set for our educational system. Historians of education (e.g., Graham, 1992) tell us that our goals for education in the United States have changed over the past several decades: At the turn of the last century our focus was on attainment—how many of our youth graduated from each level of school—instead of achievement—how much students actually learn in school. At that time education was also considered to be for the elite, not as a force that could close the gap between advantaged and disadvantaged students. Today these goals have changed. Today we care about achievement, not just about attainment, and we see schooling as having an equalizing function in our society.

These changes in our own goals may make Japanese education more relevant today than it ever was for efforts to improve American education. Recent studies have demonstrated beyond doubt that Japanese students far outperform their American counterparts on tests of academic achievement, especially in the areas of mathematics and science. In one study of fifth-grade elementary school students, for example, the highest performing school in the U.S. sample did less well on a test of mathematics achievement than the lowest peforming school in Japan (Stevenson & Stigler, 1992). These differences were not limited to computational skills; they were equally large or larger when tests assessed novel problem-solving skills or conceptual understanding of mathematical principles. Further, the variabilty in performance was far greater among American schools and students than it was in Japan. Thus, the Japanese schools not only produce high achievement, but produce it across broad segments of the population. For both of these reasons, processes of teaching and learning in Asian schools merit our serious attention.

CULTURAL DIFFERENCES IN CLASSROOM INSTRUCTION

Most of what Japanese and American children know about mathematics they learn in classrooms. Thus, in seeking to explain the Japanese advantage in mathematics achievement we have focused on comparing mathematics instruction as it occurs in Japanese and American classrooms. In this section we present an overview of this comparison, which has sought to identify dimensions that differentiate teaching between these two countries and that might be important for student learning.

Our description is based on several large observational studies in classrooms, studies that have involved more than 5000 hours of observation in more than 300 mathematics classrooms. We have employed several different methods, each of which yields a slightly different view of classroom instruction. In our first study (Stigler, Lee, & Stevenson, 1987) we used a time-sampling approach, coding randomly selected 10-sec intervals according to a predefined set of categories. Although this gave us reliable estimates of the percentage of time teachers and students spent in different kinds of activities, it did not give us a very good sense of what happens in the typical mathematics lesson of each country.

Our next two studies filled out this picture. In the second study we collected narrative observations of 800 mathematics lessons in Japan, Taiwan, China, and the United States (Stigler & Perry, 1988). In our third, and most recent, study we collected videotapes of Japanese and American teachers teaching the same topics. For example, we have tapes of 20 Japanese teachers and 20 American teachers introducing the topic of how to find the area of a triangle (Stigler, Fernandez, & Yoshida, in press). We do not say more here about the methods used in these studies; more details can be found in the referenced publications. Together, these studies provide a rich view of instruction in these different cultures.

We begin by describing some fundamental differences in the educational contexts within which instruction unfolds in these two countries. We then move to a more detailed comparative analysis of teaching practices.

The Organization of Schooling

In order to understand educational differences between Asia and the United States one must first understand fundamental differences in our assumptions about the nature of human abilities. If we had to choose the single most important characteristic that distinguishes Asian and American educational systems it would be this: In the United States we place a strong emphasis on the importance of individual differences in ability among students, whereas Asian cultures tend to stress the similarities among students. As we will see, this single difference has great implications for the ways that schools are organized in these cultures.

The American emphasis on innate differences in abilities is omnipresent though not immediately obvious; it becomes much clearer in the context of cross-cultural comparisons. Take, for example, a question we have asked in numerous studies of students, parents, and teachers: How would you rate the importance of ability, and effort in explaining students' achievement in school? Regardless of how we ask the question or of who the respondents are, we always get the same pattern of cross-cultural differences, as illustrated in Fig. 5.1 (from Stevenson & Stigler, 1992). Asians consistently rate the importance of innate ability lower than do Americans, and rate the importance of effort higher. Americans do believe effort is important; indeed, the American mothers (whose data are presented in Fig. 5.1) rate effort as slightly more important than ability. But the relative emphasis on effort over ability differs greatly across cultures, with the largest gap being in Japan.

This emphasis in American culture on the significance of innate individual differences has had a profound impact on the design of our educational system, a fact that had not loomed so large in our minds before we began our study of Asian schools. Indeed, we would now argue that American schools are to a large extent structured around the idea that children differ in important ways from each other, and that the goal of education is, first, to diagnose the nature of these individual differences, and second, to provide differentiated educational experiences according to the needs of individuals.

There are a number of practices common in American schools that almost never occur in Asian schools and that follow from this individualized model of education. These practices include:

Tracking. American children commonly are tracked according to ability into different classrooms, even as early as kindergarten. We don't usually label the classes high and low ability, preferring instead to invoke constructs such as "readiness," but the assumption is the same: Children are best served when they are placed in homogeneous groups and given instruction that is tailored to their needs. Tracking does not occur in Asian schools until much later, usually high school.

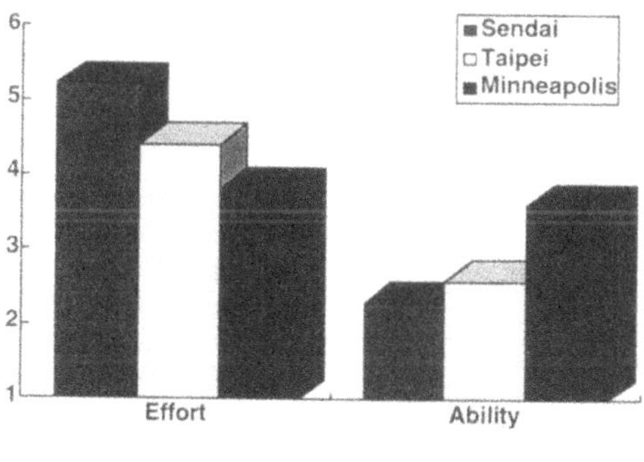

FIG. 5.1. Mothers' importance ratings of factors influencing children's performance in school.

Special Education. Again, special education is based on the assumption that there are different kinds of children who need different educational experiences. American children are routinely diagnosed and pulled out of regular classrooms because they are gifted, retarded, poor, learning disabled, etc. Asian educators assume that high quality education is high quality education, and that all children need just that. Pulling children out of their regular classrooms for specialized instruction is extremely rare.

Ability Grouping. Within classrooms American teachers often group children for instruction according to their abilities or levels of preparation. Asian teachers almost never group children according to ability, but do form heterogeneous groupings to give children experience working in small groups.

Individualization of Instruction. Pursuing the same logic, if children are better educated in homogeneous groups than in heterogeneous ones, then they should be even better served by one-on-one instruction in which the teacher works with an individual child. Tailoring instructional programs to individual levels of performance is considered highly desirable by American teachers and parents. Asian teachers see individual tutoring as only a supplement to whole-class instruction, useful for helping a child who is behind catch up but not as a method of instruction that could form the center of an educational program.

Emphasis on Small Classes. The average number of students in a class differs greatly between American and Asian schools. The classrooms in our study contained an average of 49 students in Taipei, 40 in Sendai (Japan), and only 22 in Minneapolis (Stevenson & Stigler, 1992). Yet still, the American teachers we interviewed believed that classes even smaller than 22 would significantly improve the quality of education in their schools. Interestingly, Japanese teachers actually believe that smaller classes threaten the quality of educational experiences, though they do think that smaller classes might make the teacher's life a bit easier (Tobin, Wu, & Davidson, 1989).

The American focus on individual differences is evident as well in our more formal observations of classroom organization in Japan, Taiwan, and the United States. Figure 5.2, for example, reports the percentage of academic instructional

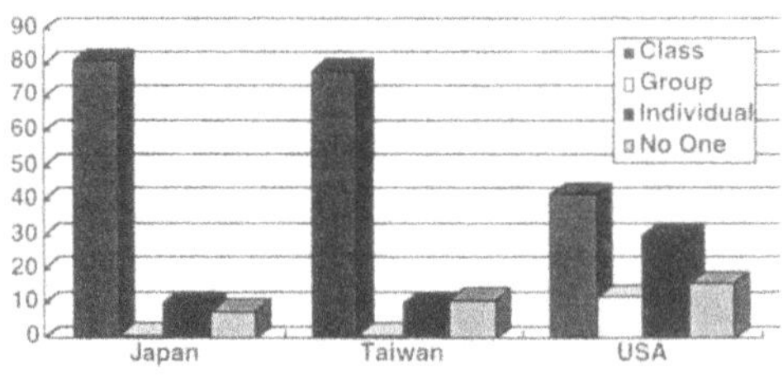

FIG. 5.2. Percentage of time teachers spend working with whole class, small group, individual student, or no one (from coding of teachers).

time teachers in each country spend working with the whole class, a small group, an individual student, or no one (Stevenson & Stigler, 1992). Asian teachers spend roughly 80% of their time working with the whole class, compared with approximately 40% for American teachers. American teachers, in contrast, spend approximately 30% of their class time working with individual students, far more than their Asian counterparts.

It is interesting to examine the consequences for students of these differences in classroom organization. In Fig. 5.3 we present data from student observations in which we coded who was the leader of the student's activity: Was it the teacher, or was the child working alone unsupervised? American students, even in first grade, actually spend more time working alone without supervision than they do working in an activity that is led by the teacher. It makes sense that this would occur: After all, while American teachers are working with individual students one-on-one, what are the rest of the students doing?

We must question whether a few minutes alone with the teacher is worth more than many hours being taught by the teacher as a member of a group. But our purpose here is not to debate the positive and negative consequences of these different educational practices. Our goal is simply to point out that much of what differs between Asian and American schools derives from basic assumptions about learning and ability. As one colleague has suggested, the American teacher is like a maypole with a string radiating out to each student in her class. Because she is trying to individualize instruction for each student she must work hard to assess each student's progress, a formidable task in a room with 20 to 30 children. The strings, as it were, keep getting tangled, and the teacher's job at times seems overwhelming.

The Japanese teacher appears more relaxed for she has only one string that connects her to the whole class. Although Japanese teachers believe that there exist individual differences among students, they do not believe these differences are sufficiently important to warrant individual diagnosis or instruction in most instances. Individual differences are dealt with in very different ways by Ameri-

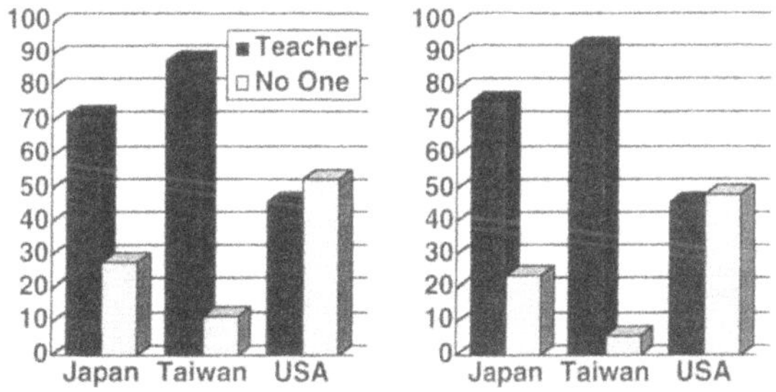

FIG. 5.3. Percentage of time students' activities led by teacher vs. no one (from coding of students).

can and Japanese teachers. Whereas American teachers appear to assume that the existence of individual differences implies that it would be preferable to divide and teach children separately, Japanese teachers see individual differences as a characteristic of the group that should be taken into account when designing instruction. If, for example, one believed in a theory that some children learn better from pictures, others from words, one could use this information in different ways. The American teacher might look for a test to differentiate children on this dimension, then design instruction that would play to each child's strengths. The Japanese teacher would more likely say, "Yes, how interesting. I must be sure to include both pictures and words in my lessons."

Finally, these basic assumptions about learning lead Asian and American teachers to perceive their roles quite differently. In an earlier study (Stevenson & Stigler, 1992) we asked teachers in Beijing (China) and Chicago to identify the most important attribute for a good teacher to have. We gave them five choices and asked them to choose the most important: the ability to explain things clearly, sensitivity to individual differences, enthusiasm, patience, and high standards. Their responses are presented in Fig. 5.4. As we might expect by now, Chinese teachers overwhelmingly selected the ability to explain things clearly, a choice selected by only 10% of American teachers. The number one choice of American teachers was sensitivity to individual differences.

Processes of Instruction in Japanese and American Classrooms

Having described fundamental differences in the way schooling is organized we turn now to a description of the processes of instruction that unfold in Japanese and American classrooms. What we find in this regard often surprises American mathematics educators: Japanese teachers combine their emphasis on whole class instruction with an emphasis on student thinking and problem solving during the lesson, a combination that at first blush appears contradictory to many mathematics educators. In fact, Japanese instruction leads us to question the common pairing of constructivist views of learning with highly individualized approaches to teaching. It is not at all clear that the latter follows from the former. Indeed, perhaps it is the genuine belief in children's active construction of knowledge

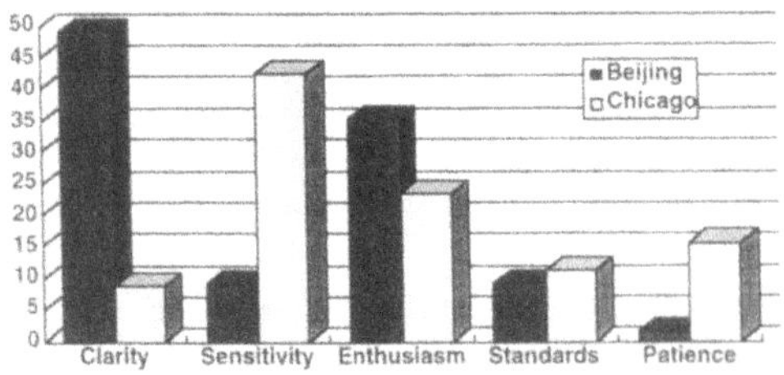

FIG. 5.4. Most important attribute of a good teacher: Beijing and Chicago.

that allows Japanese teachers to be comfortable teaching to the whole class. The same instructional input will be used by different students in different ways, depending on their current knowledge and motivations.

In general, our observations convince us that American and Japanese teachers have very different goals for their lessons. American lessons appear designed to produce a certain performance or problem solution, to teach students how to solve a particular class of mathematical problems. Japanese lessons, in contrast, appear aimed at facilitating thinking and sense-making among the students. In our view, at least four characteristics of Japanese lessons encourage Japanese students to engage in a process of sense-making during instruction. Lesson structure, classroom discourse, the role of the teacher, and the pace of instruction all differ markedly between Japanese and American lessons in ways that might lead Japanese and American students to process instruction in different ways. In the following sections we describe how Japanese and American lessons differ on each of these dimensions. We draw on our most recent data, videotapes of Japanese and American teachers teaching similar topics. More details about our methods can be found in Stigler et al. (in press).

Lesson Structure

Anyone who has tried to describe instruction in a systematic way knows how complex and daunting the task can be. Without denying the complexities, it still is possible to identify different scripts or patterns of instruction that characterize Japanese and American lessons. Most of the American lessons we videotaped start with a development section in which the teacher introduces and explains a concept or skill. Often the teacher works through an example problem step-by-step with the class, calling on invidual students to produce each succeeding step in the solution. After this development section students are given practice problems to work on their own. During this time, the teacher walks from student to student providing help to those who need it.

Japanese lessons work almost in reverse of this. Most of the Japanese lessons we have observed begin with students working on their own or in small groups on a problem that the teacher has posed. After they have struggled with the problem on their own for 10 to 15 min, the whole class reconvenes and students come one by one to the board to present their solutions. Various solutions are presented, not all of them necessarily correct. This is followed by a general discussion, which often leads to the conclusion that the teacher has planned.

These different scripts are examplified in the videotapes of Japanese and American teachers that we have collected. In the following sections we describe one Japanese and one American fifth-grade lesson on how to find the area of a triangle. Although there is much variation within each culture on the teaching of this topic, the differences are obvious. The two lessons we have selected to describe are representative of the Japanese and American lessons that we have

TABLE 5.1
Overview of the American and Japanese Lessons on Finding the Area of a Triangle

Segment	*Length*	*Description*
American Lesson		
1	1.0 mins	Review concept of perimeter
2	8.0 mins	Area of a rectangle: explanation, formula, and practice problems
3	25.0 mins	Area of a triangle: explanation, formula, and practice problems
4	11.0 mins	Students begin homework assignment, teacher walks around and helps
TOTAL	*45.0 mins*	
Japanese Lesson		
1	3.5 mins	Presentation of the problem
2	14.5 mins	Students attempting to solve the problem on their own
3	29.0 mins	Class discussion about the solutions that students came up with, leading up to the general formula
4	5.0 mins	Doing further practice problems from the textbook (students working on their own)
TOTAL	*52.0 mins*	

From Stigler, Fernandez, and Yoshida, in press.

captured in our tapes. An overview of the two lessons is presented in Table 5.1. (Table 5.1 and the accompanying description are largely taken from Stigler et al., in press).

An American Lesson. The American teacher begins the lesson by reviewing the concept of perimeter: What does it mean, how do you find it? He then makes the transition into area:

> So we dealt with perimeter. Today, we are going to deal with area and we are going to deal with the area of two things, we are going to deal with the area of a rectangle and the area of a triangle. Area is how much space is inside a flat shape.

The rest of the lesson is divided into three segments (see Table 5.1), one on the area of a rectangle, one on the area of a triangle, and finally a period of seatwork.

The segment on area of a rectangle starts with the teacher holding up a series of rectangles that have been divided into square units. As he holds each one up he asks the students to tell him the area, which they figure by counting the squares. After several of these, the teacher asks the students for a formula: "Now find me a mathematical way of doing it so that I don't have to count all the time; Brian?"

Brian responds: "Times the width times the length." The teacher writes the formula on the board, A = l × w, and then gives the students two practice problems that require them to multiply the length times the width to get the area.

The teacher then moves on to the area of a triangle:

> Now, let's take off some of this (erases board) and see if we can go on to our next thing, which is, we want to find the area of a triangle. We are going to start out with the same thing, we are going to start out and talk about when we find the area of a triangle we are still finding units, square units like this (holds up a small square). Well here is a triangle (holds up triangle with grid drawn in) and we have units. Now when you get to triangles what's the problem? Sue?

The "problem" the teacher is referring to is that square units are difficult to count with a triangle because they don't fit exactly over the area. Having pointed out this problem the teacher then introduces a solution, giving a demonstration that involves fitting two precut right triangles together to make a rectangle, and showing that the area of each triangle is half the area of the resulting rectangle. The demonstration itself is accomplished quickly, within a matter of seconds, and there is virtually no response—either questions or discussion—on the part of the students. The teacher gives a second demonstration in which he cuts one of the triangles in two and places the pieces adjacent to the other triangle to make a rectangle. Again, he receives no feedback from the students. He then tells the students the formula for the area of a triangle, A = 1/2 × b × h.

After giving them the formula, the teacher poses three problems and has the students apply the formula. He then starts them on the assignment.

A Japanese Lesson. The Japanese lesson can be divided into four segments (see Table 5.1): presentation of the problem; students attempting to to solve the problem on their own; class discussion about the solutions that students came up with; and students working alone on further practice problems from the textbook. This sequence of activities is prototypical of the Japanese lessons we have observed. The teacher almost always begins the class by posing a problem, and the rest of the lesson is oriented toward understanding and solving that problem.

In this lesson, the teacher begins by asking students to name the kinds of triangles they have studied. As they name them—right, equilateral, isosceles, etc.—the teacher puts the corresponding shapes cut out of paper on the blackboard. She then says: "We have various kinds of triangles on the board, and today I would like you to think about how to find out the area of a triangle." She hands out to each student sheets of paper that are printed with outline drawings of the various kinds of triangles. She instructs the students not to find the area of the shapes, but just to think about what would be the best way to find the area. She suggests to the students that they can cut, fold, and draw.

Students then spend 14.5 min working on the problem on their own, during which time the teacher circulates, mostly observing what the students are doing. Students are actively engaged at this point, and though they are not formally divided into groups there is a great deal of dicussion and interaction among students seated in proximity to each other. At the end of this time the teacher reconvenes the whole-class discussion by asking a student to go to the board and explain her method for finding the area of a right triangle.

For the next 29 min a succession of students—picked by the teacher to represent a variety of problem solutions—go to the board to explain their methods for finding the areas of the various kinds of triangles. All of the students use cutout shapes and chalk drawings to explain their approaches.

After each student explains his solution the teacher and the rest of the class discuss the viability of the solution. The teacher then, in collaboration with the students, writes a formula on the board that summarizes the student's solution, for example, "base × height / 2." A total of 9 students present solutions. At the end, the teacher directs attention to the formulas on the board and asks the students if they notice any kind of pattern. A spirited discussion ensues in which students observe and then confirm that the different informal formulas that resulted from the different solutions are really the same across the solutions, regardless of the kind of triangle involved. In the final 5 min of the lesson students use the formula to solve some problems in their textbook.

Classroom Discourse.

Given these differences in lesson structure, it is not suprising that very different patterns of discourse occur during Japanese and American lessons. In Japanese classrooms the prevalent form of discourse is the discussion. In American classrooms it is the recitation: short questions and answers designed to lead the students through a planned path to understanding. Japanese teachers ask questions in order to induce thinking. They ask students to describe alternative solutions, explain them, and justify them in the face of questions from peers. American teachers ask questions in order to control the direction in which the lesson moves. Many American questions are designed to elicit a particular response that the teacher must get in order to move the lesson along. One teacher in our sample started her lesson by asking, "A fraction is what? What is a fraction?" She was met with blank looks, and continued to provide hints before finally filling in the answer herself, "A comparison. A fraction is a comparison." To us this might only be one of many possible answers, and probably not even a very likely one. To this teacher it was the answer she needed to lead into her lesson.

We have begun to validate these observations by applying objective codes to the lessons we have on videotape. In one preliminary analysis (Stigler, Fernandez, & Yoshida, in press) we coded four lessons for the types of questions that teachers ask. Two of the lessons dealt with area of a triangle, and two with the concept of equivalent fractions. One of each pair was Japanese and the other, American.

We found four different kinds of questions:

1. *Name/identify* questions are those where the teacher asks a student to name an answer without asking for any explanation of how the answer was found. Questions like "What kind of triangles have we studied so far," or "What is the length on this shape" would fall into this category.

2. *Calculate* questions are those where the teacher asks for the solution to an explicitly stated calculation. Questions like "So to find the area we do 9 times 12 which is?" or "What is 90 divided by 2?" would fall in this category.

3. *Explain how or why* are questions where the teacher asks for an explanation for answers given or procedures carried out. Questions like "How did you find the area of this triangle?" or "Why is the area here 17?" would fall in this category.

4. *Check status* are questions where the teacher is trying to monitor what everyone else is thinking or doing. Questions like "Who agrees?," "How many people found this?" or "Is anyone confused?" fall into this category.

In Fig. 5.5 we have graphed the percentages of questions in each lesson that fall into each of the four categories. The two Japanese lessons are represented in the left panel, the American lessons in the right one.

It is interesting to note how similar the graphs look between the two lessons within each culture, but how different they look across the two cultures. In both American lessons the most frequently asked type of question was name/identify, followed by calculate and then explain. In the Japanese lessons the most frequent type of question was explain, followed by check status. Neither of these two

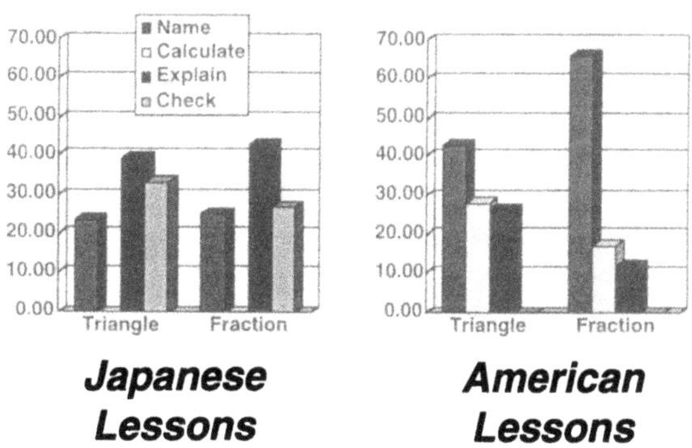

FIG. 5.5. Types of questions asked by Japanese and American teachers.

Japanese teachers asked a calculate question, and neither of the American teachers asked a check status question.

Because Japanese teachers ask their students to explain their ideas so frequently, it is not surprising to find that Japanese students talk proportionally more during mathematics class than do their American counterparts. In our preliminary study of four lessons we have coded amount of student talk in two ways, the results of which are presented in Fig. 5.6.

In panel (a) is graphed the percentage of total words spoken during public discourse that come from students (as opposed to the teacher). By public discourse we mean talk that is intended for everyone to hear as opposed to private conversations between teacher and students or among students. Approximately twice as much student talk is observed in the Japanese class discussions as in the American discussions, across both the triangle and fraction lessons. Panel (b) shows the average number of words spoken by individual students during teacher-student exchanges. (When a teacher asks a question and then calls on an individual student to answer, everything from the initiating question through the last utterance of the student is considered part of a single teacher–student exchange.) Clearly, Japanese students talk more during these exchanges than do American students.

Role of the Teacher.

Significantly, the discourse in Japanese classrooms appears to resemble that among professional mathematicians more than does the discourse in American classrooms: students make conjectures, explanations, and justifications to support their mathematical ideas. Truth is determined by the persuasiveness of the argument, by what makes sense, not by the judgment of the teacher. This leads us to our next point: The role of the teacher differs markedly between the Japanese and American classrooms we have studied. In American classrooms the teacher is the authority, the arbiter of right and wrong. Japanese teachers are very

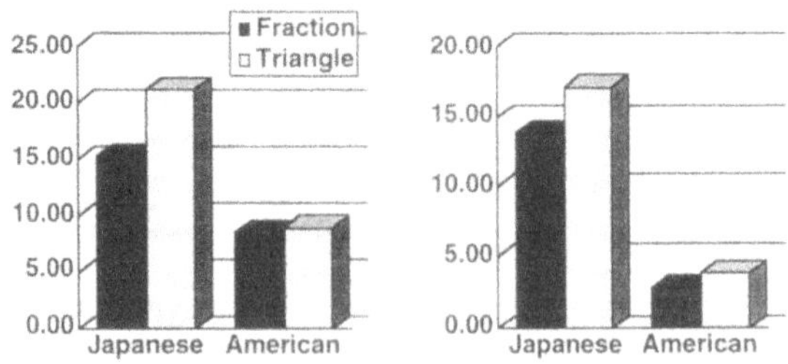

FIG. 5.6. Quantity of student talk: (left) Percent of total words spoken during public discourse that were spoken by students; (right) average number of words spoken by individual students during a teacher-student exchange.

reluctant to play this role and often go to great lengths to avoid telling students directly whether their answer are correct or not.

American teachers try hard to keep errors out of the mathematics classroom, and especially out of the public discourse. This may be because they are afraid that students will remember the wrong answers, a notion that probably can be traced to behaviorist theories of learning. Or they may be concerned that allowing children to err in public would damage their self-esteem. For whatever reason, American teachers tend to quickly correct mistakes when they do occur, and almost never ask children who have incorrect answers to problems to display their solutions to the class. The teacher becomes the focus of authority in such a classroom, with students judging the adequacy of their thinking based on the teacher's response.

Japanese teachers take a very different approach to errors. Instead of seeing errors as indicating lack of ability or potential on the part of the student, Japanese teachers see errors as a natural part of the learning process and as important sources of information about children's mathematical thinking. They believe that discussion of incorrect solutions can play an important role in children's developing conceptual understanding of mathematics. And, most importantly, they believe that giving students the freedom to err is the only way to have them take responsibility for their own mathematical thinking; to believe that they have the power to reason themselves about the correctness of a problem solution.

Pace of Instruction.

The fourth characteristic of instruction that we believe encourages thinking and sense-making in Japanese students is the pace at which it proceeds. As we have noted elsewhere (Stigler & Perry, 1988), Japanese lessons appear to proceed at a very slow pace. This slow pace, combined with rich instructional input, sets up the conditions for student thinking during instruction.

What, exactly, about Japanese instruction leads to the perception that it is so slow-paced? To some extent it must be the organization of the lesson. As noted earlier, Japanese lessons almost always begin with a single problem, the solution to which becomes the focus of the entire lesson. This concentration on a single problem lends coherence to the lesson, and allows a thorough exploration of the problem. Students in American lessons work many more problems than do their Japanese counterparts, and come to emphasize quantity rather than quality of solutions.

The fact that Japanese students talk more during the lesson than do their American counterparts must also slow down the pace of the lesson. Children tend to talk more slowly than adults: They are less articulate and often stop to search for the next word, especially when struggling to describe something as complex as a new mathematical concept. And Japanese teachers appear to wait longer than American teachers for students to compose their answers, though we have not yet measured and compared these times.

Thinking in classrooms takes time. In the American lesson described before little time was set aside for students to ponder the derivation of the formula for finding the area of a triangle. When the teacher did the demonstration with the two cut-out triangles it happened quickly. The students were expected to follow the demonstration, but not given enough time to discover the relation for themselves. In the Japanese lesson, students spent the entire time thinking about and discussing how to derive the formula for finding the area of a triangle. The expectation was that the derivation would take time for students to construct, and would not be understood by students in a momentary flash of insight.

The Sense-Making Hypothesis

We hypothesize that these differences in structure, discourse, teacher's role, and pace lead Japanese students to process lessons differently than American students. In particular, we believe that these characteristics of Japanese instruction convey to students that they should engage in a process of sense-making. Whereas American students may process instruction with the goal of learning to do the problems that will be assigned, we believe that Japanese students seek, as well, to understand the mathematics that is being discussed in the lesson.

We believe that these characteristics of instruction facilitate sense-making in several ways. First, devoting a major part of each lesson to students' explanations of their thinking means that the production and evaluation of explanations are central tasks for Japanese students during instruction. When students work on a problem with the knowledge that they will be asked to explain their ideas to others, they work with a goal of understanding, for unless they understand they will not be able to construct an explanation. When the teacher refuses to be the arbiter of right and wrong, refuses to be the authority in the classroom, students are forced to decide for themselves what makes sense and so take on this responsibility. And, the slower pace of Japanese lessons encourages students to reflect on whether what is said makes sense to them.

Together, these factors create a culture of sense-making in the Japanese classroom. But can we actually document these differences in the ways lessons are processed by Japanese and American students? This is the question we turn to next.

PROCESSES OF LEARNING FROM INSTRUCTION

We have identified several dimensions along which Japanese and American lessons differ and we have speculated that these differences are meaningful from the point of view of student learning. But can we find empirical evidence to support this speculation? This is the frustration of cross-cultural research: Ultimately it leaves us with little beyond simple correlations.

Recently we have begun to develop a program of research in which we attempt to relate students' learning to characteristics of classroom instruction. In the rest of this chapter we illustrate our approach, first by presenting the theoretical framework that guides our research, and then by discussing some illustrative empirical studies that we have recently completed.

Learning From Instruction: A Theoretical Framework

Although we do not yet have a complete theory of how children learn from instruction, we do have some preliminary ideas.[1] Children participating in a mathematics lesson construct a mental representation of the events that make up the lesson. Then, based on this representation, they learn (or not) the content of the lesson.

What kind of lesson representation might best facilitate learning? A child could, for example, choose to represent the events in a lesson in as much detail as possible. If the topic of the lesson were subtraction with regrouping, this child might encode all the different pairs of numbers to be subtracted, the colors of the manipulatives used, and the names of the students who were called on.

However, it is likely that this level of detail is not the key to understanding. A more useful representation might be one that focuses on the logical connections between the events that occur in the lesson. Events carried out in lessons are usually linked together in the context of the teacher's goals. In order for students to fully take advantage of a lesson they must see that it consists of a set of events that the teacher has put together to form a coherent whole.

Many factors are likely to affect students' ability to represent lessons as sets of interrelated events. Key among these factors are the following three:

1. *Characteristics of the lesson itself.* Lessons vary with respect to how clearly they convey the relationships that the teacher intends to convey. For example, if a lesson unfolds at a very fast pace, children might not have enough time to understand how different events are related. Similarly these relationships might be harder to perceive if the teacher does not explain the goal of each activity, but rather leaves it for the students to infer.

The design of some lessons makes it difficult for students to infer links among events. For example, some lessons focus on mathematical procedures but contain little in the way of conceptual information. In such lessons students may lack the knowledge that would enable them to link events together, except as sequential steps in a procedure. Such links will probably be weak because they often will be perceived as arbitrary. Lessons that omit conceptual information lack the glue needed to form a rich web of relationships among lesson events.

---

[1]A more lengthy description of our framework can be found in Fernandez, Yoshida, and Stigler, 1992.

Lessons can also vary in the degree to which the events that take place in them are meant to be related to begin with. It is not uncommon for teachers to provide variety, for example, of topics or materials, at the expense of a coherently structured lesson. Stigler and Perry (1988) describe a lesson in which children learned about measurement, then addition, and finally telling time. Although such a lesson might hold students' attention, the number of meaningful connections that can be made between lesson events is more limited than in lessons that are designed to form a well integrated whole.

2. *Goals and expectations.* Students' processing of a lesson will be guided by their goals and by their expectations or schemas for what is happening in the classroom. The extent to which students process instruction by trying to make it cohere in their minds is likely to depend on whether their goal is to understand the concept being discussed, or just to learn how to do the problems on the worksheet. Often, the students' goals are a reflection of the teachers' goals, as manifested in the tasks teachers pose and the ways in which they choose to evaluate students' learning. But students may have other goals as well, such as to monitor social interactions that transpire in the course of classroom instruction. It is possible that monitoring social interactions can deter from students' ability to focus on making sense of the instruction. Students' beliefs about the domain of instruction can also affect how coherently they represent a lesson. For example, the extent to which students see mathematics as an arbitrary domain, as opposed to one that is supposed to make sense, will affect how they process a mathematics lesson. If students expect two succeeding activities to be logically related to each other, then they may try to figure out what the relationship is; if they don't expect a relationship then they probably won't bother.

3. *Prior knowledge relevant to the content of the lesson.* The sense that students are able to make of instruction will also be affected by their prior knowledge of mathematics. Students who have the requisite knowledge will easily infer the relationship between two concepts the teacher juxtaposes in a single lesson. Students without this knowledge may have no idea why these particular two concepts are being covered in a single lesson.

Learning From Instruction: Empirical Studies

The theoretical framework we have outlined helps us to think about the ways that Japanese and American teaching practices might differentially affect student learning. Specifically, it seems plausible that Japanese instruction might better support students' efforts to form a coherent representation of the events that compose a lesson. But what kind of empirical evidence can we muster to validate the above framework? A search of the literature provides us with little help. There are many studies that relate characteristics of instruction to global measures of achievement such as residualized gain scores at the end of the year (e.g., Good, Grouws, & Ebmeier, 1983), but these studies account for little variance and generally make no mention of the intervening level of analysis, that is, how students process and represent classroom events. There also are no studies that measure students' on-line processing of classroom instruction.

In our recent research we have attempted to explore how students learn from classroom instruction. Thus far we have done two types of studies; in the remainder of this chapter we will present an example of each type. In all of our studies we use videotapes of classroom instruction, and study students' processing of the instruction on the videotapes. In the first type of study we have constructed different versions of a videotaped lesson in order to study the effects of various lesson characteristics on student processing. In the second type of study we have used a single videotaped lesson and compared how students who differ, either in their prior knowledge or in their expectations, process the lesson. For example, we can study how Japanese and American students differ in their processing of the same lesson.

Our on-line measures of processing have included a wide range of standard cognitive science measures such as recognition memory, recall, importance ratings, and so fourth.

Example One: Effects of Japanese- and American-Style Lessons on Students' Sense-Making Orientation (Fernandez, 1994)

In this section we describe a study by Fernandez (1994) that was designed to evaluate the hypothesis that Japanese-style instruction, more so than American-style instruction, encourages students to make sense of lesson events as they unfold. The basic design was as follows: two lessons, one Japanese style and one American style, were designed, taught, videotaped, and edited for presentation. Subjects were randomly assigned to view one of the two lessons. Learning of the content of the lessons was measured using pre- and posttests. Processing of instruction was measured using an on-line recognition task and a think-aloud task.

The reader will by now be wondering how Fernandez measured "sense-making." Let us put off a description of the processing measure for now, and begin by describing the two lessons that were compared, the experimental procedure, and the results of the pre- and posttesting.

The Two Lessons. One lesson was designed to be similar to Japanese lessons as we described them earlier; the other, to American lessons. More specifically, these lessons were designed to vary with respect to their structure, their discourse, and their pace. We do not claim that the lessons are prototypical of Japanese and American lessons. They are inspired by our cross-cultural comparison and were created to vary in ways hypothesized to affect students' sense-making orientation.

The lessons were adapted from an actual Japanese lesson that we had captured on videotape. Both lessons dealt with the same topic, solving word problems with two unknowns, and used the same materials. Both lessons began in the same way and ended in the same way, and both lasted the same amount of time. The teacher was the same for both lessons (Fernandez), as were the students, fifth-graders who were paid to work as "actors" for the occasion.

An example of the type of problem dealt with in the two lessons, along with the materials students were given to use in solving the problems, is displayed in Fig. 5.7. In the problem shown, students use two strips of paper to represent the numbers of boys and girls in the class. Because the problem states that there are more boys than girls, the longer strip is used to represent the boys. The difference between the numbers of boys and girls (six) is represented by the difference in length between the two strips. Represented in this way, the problem can be solved in several ways. The most common procedure is to subtract six from the total number of children in the class in order to make the two strips the same length. Once identical strips are obtained, the remaining quantity can be divided by two in order to get the number of girls. The number of boys can then be found by adding six to the number of girls.

What differed between the two lessons was instructional style. In the Japanese-style lesson students struggled with the problem on their own, then presented their ideas for how to solve the problem to the whole class. One problem provided the focus for the Japanese-style lesson, but three different solution strategies were presented by the students. In the American-style lesson the teacher demonstrated a single solution strategy step-by-step, but then, in recitation style, applied the strategy to solving three problems.

Analysis of the resulting videotapes revealed that in terms of discourse the two lessons differed in much the same way that Japanese lessons differ from American lessons. In the Japanese-style tape, 42% of the teacher's questions asked for explanations compared to only 1% in the American-style tape. Students accounted for 31% of the talk in the Japanese-style tape but only 10% in the American-style tape. Also, when students were asked to rate the pace of the lessons they rated the Japanese-style lesson as significantly slower than the American-style one.

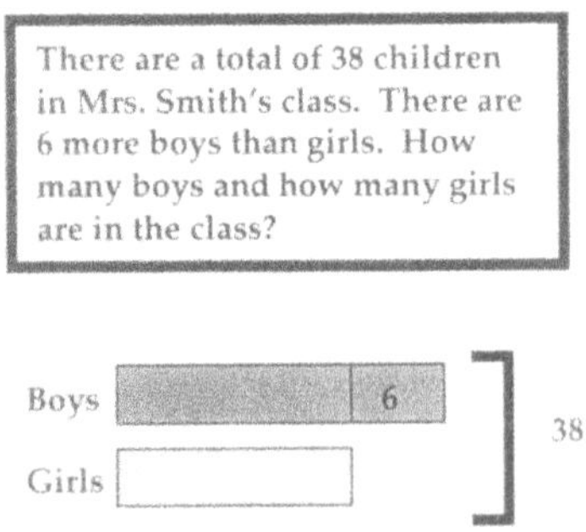

FIG. 5.7. Content of the two lessons.

Experimental Procedure. 100 fifth-grade American students participated in the study. Half the students were randomly assigned to view the Japanese-style lesson, half the American-style lesson. Within each of these groups half the students were tested with an on-line recognition measure and half with a think-aloud measure.

The procedure for all groups of students is represented in Fig. 5.8. All students started with a pretest consisting of one problem of the sort presented in the videotapes. They then viewed one of the two lessons. Each student was given the same materials students used in the videotape—strips of paper, pencil, and scratch paper—and was instructed to watch the tape as though he or she was a student in the class. After viewing the lesson each was given a posttest to assess problem-solving performance. This test consisted of two problems similar to those taught in the videotaped lessons.

After the posttest students were shown another clip of videotape which was common across all experimental conditions. In this section of tape the teacher went through several more practice problems as a continuation of the lesson videotapes. The content of this common tape was procedural: The teacher simply walked students through solutions to three problems. The purpose of this common tape was to provide a setting in which to collect the on-line measures of processing. The hypothesis was that processing of this common tape would be affected by the kind of instruction students watched during the lesson. Students who saw the Japanese-style lesson were predicted to try harder to "make sense" of the instruction in the common tape than students who saw the American-style lesson.

Results on Pre- and Posttests. Before we describe the on-line measures let us first report on students' general reaction to the experiment and performance on the pre- and posttests.

In general students became very involved in watching the videotaped lessons, and took seriously their assigned roles as participants in the lesson. They also

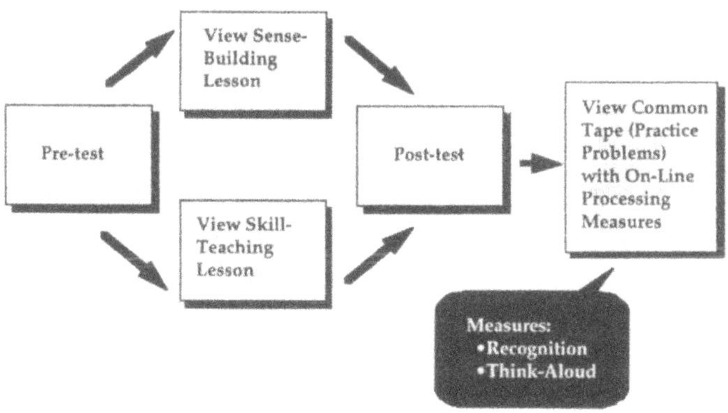

FIG. 5.8. Overview of experimental procedure.

learned from the instruction, as evidenced by their pre- and posttest performance. Sixty percent of all students who could not solve the pretest problem correctly were able to solve the posttest problem. However, the degree of improvement differed across the two experimental conditions. Forty percent of the students who watched the Japanese-style lesson learned to reproduce the problem-solving procedures presented in the videotapes, compared with 63% of those who watched the American-style lesson. Given the emphasis on repeated practice of a single procedure in the American-style lesson, it is not surprising that students who viewed this lesson had more success in acquiring this procedure. But did acquisition of the procedure necessarily imply acquisition of conceptual understanding as well?

The On-Line Recognition Measure. The time has come to describe the on-line recognition measure that Fernandez used to indicate students' sensemaking orientation. What does it mean to try to make sense of a lesson? We believe that sense making involves attempting to link together the different events that compose a lesson into a coherent mental representation. As a lesson proceeds, a student who is trying to make sense of a lesson will try to understand how the event that just took place is related to events that occurred previously in the lesson.

An example from the lessons used by Fernandez illustrates this idea. Suppose the teacher in the videotape is working with the class on the problem presented in Fig. 5.9. At some point, as she reads the problem, she points out that there are more boys than girls. Later she draws rectangles on the board to represent the strips of paper that the students are using to work on the problem, and still later she says, "Let's label this strip 'boys' . . . " We would propose that a student

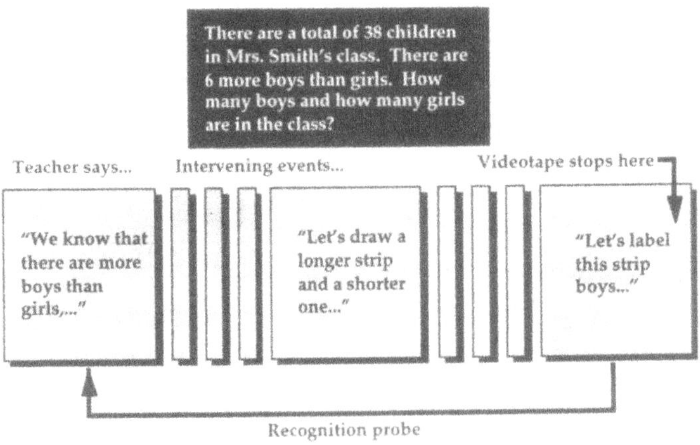

FIG. 5.9. Overview of the on-line recognition task.

engaged in trying to make sense of the lesson would, upon hearing this latter statement, activate the information that there are more boys than girls, presented earlier in the lesson and thus link these two events together in his mind. It would not be possible to understand why the longer strip was being labelled "boys" unless one also remembered that there were more boys than girls in Mrs. Smith's class.

The on-line recognition task was based on this idea. As subjects watched the common part of the videotape, the VCR, which was under computer control, stopped at 24 preset points. Each stopping point was carefully chosen to be at a time when subjects could conceivably be linking back to previously presented information (as in Fig. 5.9). Just as the tape stopped, subjects heard a statement through a speaker and were asked to judge whether the statement was something actually said in the videotape or not. Fourteen of the statements were actually said in the videotape, and were just the statements that subjects should be activating if trying to make sense of the lesson. Ten of the statements were foils which were never said in the videotape.

Fernandez' prediction was that students trying to make sense of the common videotape would recognize the target statements faster than subjects who were not. Interestingly, subjects who viewed the Japanese-style lesson achieved significantly faster recognition times than subjects who viewed the American-style lesson, lending support to the idea that experiencing Japanese-style instruction would facilitate a sense-making orientation on the part of students.

The Final Twist: A Delay Condition. Although this finding is consistent with Fernandez' hypothesis, one could imagine alternative explanations for the faster recognition performance of students in the Japanese-style group. Even with random assignment of subjects to condition there still could be group differences that existed prior to the treatment. Perhaps the Japanese-style group happened to be more computer-literate and thus faster to the space bar!

In order to rule out such alternatives, and to strengthen her claim that subjects who viewed the Japanese-style lesson were actually engaged in the activation of previously presented information, Fernandez added one additional twist to her design. For half the subjects, probe statements were presented immediately as the videotape stopped at each point (immediate condition). For the other half, probes were not presented until 350 msec after the tape had stopped (delay condition). The logic of this new manipulation was as follows: If students were actively engaged in activating previously presented information, the delay should actually speed up their recognition. If students were not engaged in this process, then the delay should not speed up their recognition, and might even slow it down a little as the probed statement receeded in time. Thus, Fernandez was predicting a lesson by delay interaction, with the delay facilitating the recognition of students who viewed the Japanese-style lesson but not that of students who viewed the American-style lesson.

The results are presented in Fig. 5.10. Interestingly, the lesson by delay interaction was statistically significant and in exactly the direction that Fernandez had predicted. Even in the context of such a brief experimental intervention, students who experienced Japanese-style instruction were more likely to be engaged in sense making than were students who experienced the American-style instruction.

Converging Evidence From Think-Aloud Protocols. Converging evidence for this interpretation comes from a different on-line measure, the think-aloud task. In this task, a separate group of subjects viewed the same common videotape as did the subjects in the recognition task. As they viewed the tape it stopped 17 times, at the same points where target probes were presented in the recognition task. This time, however, subjects were asked to think out loud about their understanding of the lesson. The experimenter, they were told, had not seen the earlier lesson but had only come in for the common tape. Their task was to tell the experimenter, each time the tape stopped, "everything someone would need to know to understand what the teacher is saying."

Everything each subject said at each stopping point was transcribed and coded by Fernandez in two ways. First, she coded whether or not subjects spontaneously generated the probe statement that was paired with each stopping point. For example, if the tape was stopped as in Fig. 5.9, Fernandez coded whether or not subjects included in their explanations the idea that there were more boys than girls. Including this statement would indicate that subjects were actively trying to make sense of the stopping point in relation to relevant information presented previously in the tape. The second coding focused on the quality of explanations generated by each subject.

As evident in Fig. 5.11, subjects who viewed the Japanese-style lesson scored higher in both coding systems than those who viewed the American-style lesson. These results provide strong converging evidence that students were affected by

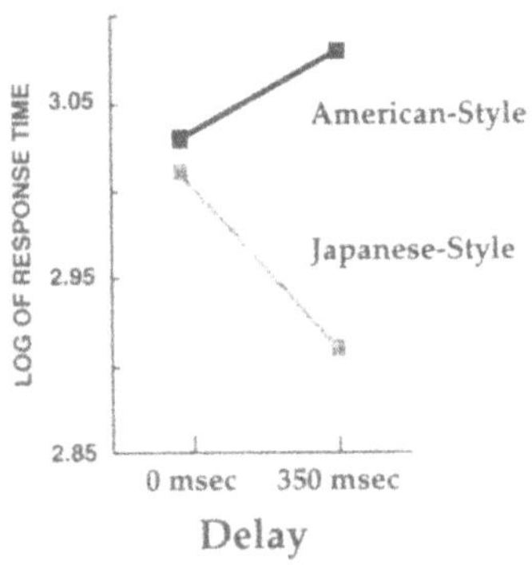

FIG. 5.10. Recognition performance by lesson and delay.

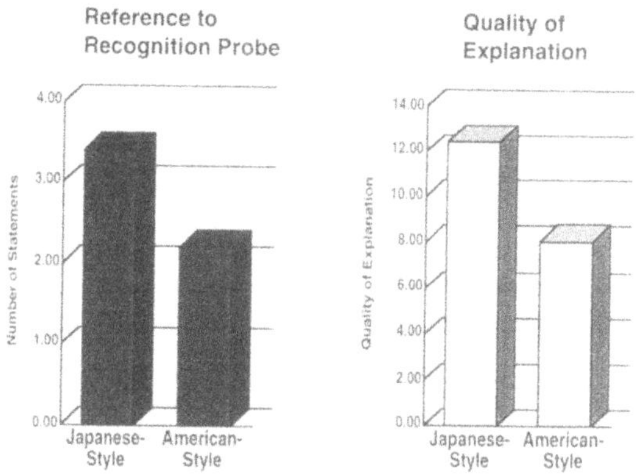

FIG. 5.11. Results from coding of think-aloud protocols.

viewing the Japanese lesson in just the way Fernandez had predicted. Even after such a brief exposure, subjects who viewed the Japanese-style lesson appeared to process the common tape differently from those subjects who viewed the American-style lesson, seeking to understand the lesson by relating each event to earlier events that were provided the necessary context for understanding.

Example Two: Japanese and American Students' Processing of the Same Lesson (Yoshida, Fernandez, & Stigler, 1993)

Fernandez found these differences in processing after very brief exposure to the two instructional approaches. The question arises: What would the effects be of repeated exposure to these different types of instruction over a period of months or even years? In other words, how might Japanese and American students come to differ in the way they process, and seek to process, classroom instruction? We have conducted a study that sheds some light on this question and we briefly describe its central finding here. (A more detailed description can be found in Yoshida, et al., 1993).

In this study we took the Japanese lesson that inspired the lessons used in the study described above, and constructed two versions, one in Japanese and the other in English. These two versions of the same lesson were shown to Japanese and American fourth graders and to American sixth graders. After viewing the lesson each group of students was given a recognition test for statements made during the lesson. In contrast to the Fernandez study, students in this study were tested at the end of the lesson instead of during the lesson. Half the statements were actually made in the lesson; half were foils. In addition, half the statements were relevant to the content of the lesson (e.g., "This part represents the six more boys than girls) and half were irrelevant (e.g., "Don't forget to put your paper clip in the upper left-hand corner of your papers"). The rationale was that recognition memory should be an indicator of what subjects treated as central or peripheral to the lesson as they processed it. Students trying to make sense of the lesson should treat relevant and irrelevant statements differently: Relevant statements should be easily integrated into a coherent representation of the lesson whereas irrelevant statements should remain peripheral to this representation.

The findings are presented in Fig. 5.12. As is evident in the left-hand panel of the figure, Japanese and American fourth graders were equally successful recognizing statements relevant to the content of the lesson, but differed greatly in their performance on the irrelevant statements. American students were just as successful with irrelevant statements as they were with the relevant ones. Performance of the Japanese students, in contrast, dropped markedly for the irrelevant statements and in fact did not differ from chance.

Are these differences truly due to different educational experiences or are they due to knowledge? We know from prior work that Japanese fourth graders know far more mathematics than their American counterparts (Stevenson & Stigler, 1992). Could the difference in recognition be due to the fact that Japanese students understand the mathematics of the lesson more deeply than do the American students, as opposed to reflecting differences in how these two groups of subjects chose to process the lesson? We assessed this possibility by testing a group of American sixth graders whose educational experiences were American but whose mathematical knowledge could be expected to be more on a par with the Japanese fourth graders.

The results are displayed in the right-hand panel of Fig. 5.12. Although their overall recognition performance is higher than that of the Japanese and American fourth graders, the pattern of performance for the American sixth graders was exactly like that of the American fourth graders, suggesting that the difference observed between American and Japanese fourth graders was due to culture, not mathematical knowledge.

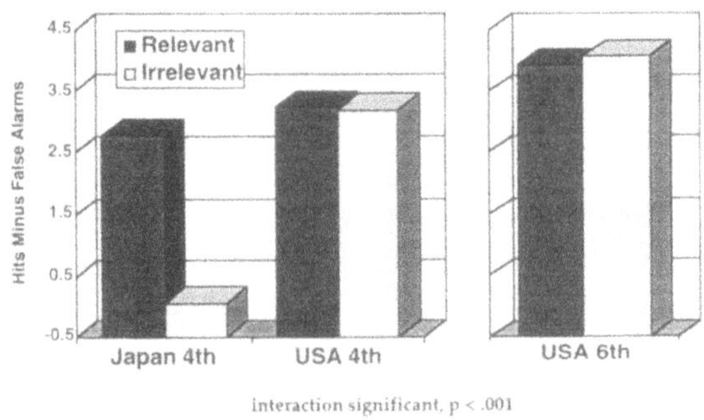

FIG. 5.12. Recognition performance by lesson and delay.

CONCLUSION

At this point we shall conclude this brief overview of our research. Let us recap the three general points we hope to have made in this chapter.

First, we hope to have illustrated the value that cross-cultural comparisons can have in our quest to understand the dimensions along which instruction might vary. Restricting our studies to U. S. classrooms limits our thinking about the range of variables that might affect learning and increases the risk of focusing on false dichotomies—for example, rote vs. understanding—that do not necessarily describe actual variations in classroom teaching. Because most U. S. mathematics teachers appear to follow some variant of a "direct instruction" approach to teaching, studies that compare the results of different styles of teaching within the United States are, in effect, comparing apples to slightly better apples, but not apples to oranges. Using critiques of direct instruction rather than comparisons with alternative instructional systems leads us to compare real fruit with its imagined opposite, a kind of fruit that does not really exist.

Second, we have raised the important, but neglected, question of how children actually construct knowledge from classroom instruction. We have laid out the theoretical framework that guides our inquiry, and pointed out what we believe to be the key questions in our quest to understand how students process instruction. Thinking about and researching these processes is essential if we are to make progress in our understanding of the relationship between teaching and learning. Descriptions of instruction that do not refer to how students learn can easily appear arbitrary; descriptions of learning that ignore instruction risk ecological invalidity.

Finally, we hope that we have demonstrated that comparative research need not be an end in itself but can be a fertile source of hypotheses for experimental investigation. By combining cross-cultural and experimental approaches we can gain new insights into the mechanisms of learning and the role that cultural environments play in learning.

ACKNOWLEDGMENTS

Much of the research reported in the first part of this chapter was conducted in collaboration with Harold Stevenson and colleagues at the University of Michigan. The remainder of the chapter draws on work resulting from a collaborative research project with our Japanese colleagues, Giyoo Hatano, Shizuko Amaiwa, and Eiji Morita. The project is funded, in part, by the Spencer Foundation and by grant number RED-9350004 from the National Science Foundation.

REFERENCES

Brophy, J., & Good, T. L. (1986). Teacher behavior and student achievement. In M. C. Wittrock (Ed.), *Handbook of research on teaching* (pp. 328–375). New York: Macmillan.

Carpenter, T. P., Moser, J. M., & Romberg, T. A. (1982). *Addition and subtraction: A cognitive perspective*. Hillsdale, NJ: Lawrence Erlbaum Associates.

Dunkin, M., & Biddle, B. (1974). *The study of teaching*. New York: Holt, Rinehart & Winston.

Fernandez, C. (1994). *Students' comprehension processes during mathematics instruction*. Unpublished doctoral dissertation, University of Chicago.

Fernandez, C., Yoshida, M., & Stigler, J. W. (1992). Learning mathematics from classroom instruction: On relating lessons to pupils' interpretations. *Journal of the Learning Sciences, 2*(4), 333–365.

Ginsburg, H. A. (1983). *The development of mathematical thinking*. New York: Academic Press.

Good, T., Grouws, D., & Ebmeier, M. (1983). *Active mathematics teaching*. New York: Longman Press.

Graham, P. A. (1992). *S. O. S.: Sustain our schools*. New York: Hill and Wang.

Stevenson, H. W., Lee, S. Y., & Stigler, J. W. (1986). Mathematics achievement of Chinese, Japanese, and American children. *Science, 231*, 693–699.

Stevenson, H. W., & Stigler, J. W. (1992). *The learning gap: Why our schools are failing and what we can learn from Japanese and Chinese education*. New York: Summit Books.

Stigler, J. W., Fernandez, C., & Yoshida, M. (in press). Traditions of school mathematics in Japanese and American elementary classrooms. In P. Nesher, L. P. Steffe, P. Cobb, G. Goldin, & B. Greer (Eds.), *Theories of mathematical learning*. Hillsdale, NJ: Lawrence Erlbaum Associates.

Stigler, J. W., Lee, S. Y., & Stevenson, H. W. (1987). Mathematics classrooms in Japan, Taiwan and the United States. *Child Development, 58*, 1272–1285.

Stigler, J. W., & Perry, M. (1988). Mathematics learning in Japanese, Chinese, and American classrooms. In G. Saxe & M. Gearhart (Eds.), *Children's mathematics*. San Francisco: Jossey-Bass.

Tobin, J., Wu, D. Y., & Davidson, D. (1989). *Preschool in three cultures*. New Haven, CT: Yale University Press.

Yoshida, M., Fernandez, C., & Stigler, J. W. (1993). Japanese and American students' differential recognition of teachers' statements during a mathematics lesson. *Journal of Educational Psychology, 85*(4), 1–8.

6 Mathematics Achievement of American Students: First in the World by the Year 2000?

Harold W. Stevenson
University of Michigan

In 1989, the 50 Governors of the United States convened in Charlottesville, Virginia, to define a set of national goals that would guide educational progress during the 1990s. Joined by President Bush, they announced a set of five goals; several years later two more goals were added. The goals dealt with the preparation of children for school, citizenship, high school completion, adult literacy, teacher education, parental participation, and safe schools. A particular goal that I discuss is the one that proposed "By the year 2000, United States students will be first in the world in mathematics and science achievement."

My discussion relies on a series of studies that our research group at the University of Michigan has conducted during the past 15 years. In these studies we have compared the performance of American students from kindergarten through eleventh grade with the performance of their counterparts in East Asia. We selected East Asian students for comparison because Chinese and Japanese students have led the world in several comparative studies of mathematics achievement (e.g., McKnight et al., 1989). It is these students, among others, that Americans must outperform if they are to achieve the status of the world's best students in mathematics by the end of this decade.

Questions About Comparative Research

Before one embarks on projects in comparative research in psychology and education, some methodological problems must be faced. Of critical importance are sampling of subjects and preparation of materials. I will describe how we responded to these problems before presenting the results of the studies.

Sampling. It is impossible for ordinary researchers to include nationally representative samples of students when they undertake comparative studies of academic achievement. To do so would require budgets of many millions of dollars—a level of support that is rarely attainable for psychological studies. An alternative and less costly strategy is to select comparable sites in the various countries and then to obtain representative samples of individuals in each site. This is the approach we have taken by conducting our research in large metropolitan areas.

In all of our studies we have included suburban schools as well those in the central parts of the cities in an effort to provide appropriate representations of the areas. For convenience we refer to cities, but it should be kept in mind that we have actually included whole metropolitan areas.

For our first studies we chose Minneapolis as the U.S. research site. Knowing that Minnesota rates high in the educational achievement of its students, we assumed that if Minnesota students failed to demonstrate high levels of academic achievement, students from many other states would also be unlikely to do so. Within the Minneapolis metropolitan area we selected a representative sample of elementary schools, including average schools and some of the best and least successful schools. After obtaining the cooperation of school authorities, we randomly selected two first-grade and two fifth-grade classrooms from each school and then randomly selected 6 boys and 6 girls from each classroom as our target subjects. The same general procedure was followed in studies of kindergarten children and of eleventh graders.

On the basis of our personal experience and on the advice of Japanese researchers, we selected Sendai, a city several hundred kilometers northeast of Tokyo, as the Japanese area most comparable to Minneapolis. Taipei was chosen as the Chinese city because it was the only large Chinese-speaking area available to us other than Hong Kong, a city that represents an unusual mixture of East Asian and European cultures. Later, we were able to conduct studies in the metropolitan areas of Beijing, Chicago, and Fairfax County, a large area in Virginia adjacent to Washington, DC.

Many characteristics of the cities must be considered before it is appropriate to make cross-cultural comparisons of children's academic achievement. Among the most important of these are the availability of education to all children, the chronological ages of children at the various grade levels, the organization of the academic year, and the degree of interest of school authorities, teachers, and parents in cooperating in research. With few limitations, cross-cultural comparability among the cultures was attained. Universal elementary education exists in all of the cities, children enter school at approximately the same ages, tests and interviews can be conducted at the same time in the academic year, and school authorities, parents, and teachers were cooperative. Only at the high school level is there a divergence in the organization of education among the cities. In contrast to the all-purpose high schools in the United States, a hierarchical system of education exists in Chinese and Japanese high schools, such that students are assigned either to academic or vocational high schools on the basis of scores on high school entrance tests. Similar percentages of students enter high school in all the cities except Beijing, where a large number of students leave school and enter the labor force after completing ninth grade.

Construction of Materials. It is not difficult to translate tests and questionnaires written in one language into other languages, and this has been a common practice in many cross-cultural studies in psychology. Unfortunately, this practice is not defensible on several grounds. First, translated tests are not fair when members of the second culture have had no experience with the kinds of materials contained in the test. Second, words in one language sometimes do not have clear equivalents in a second language. This is a special problem in psychology, where many concepts are of American and European origin and terms in these languages do not have a close match in languages in other parts of the world. For example, our Chinese colleagues, although skilled in English, had difficulty understanding the meaning of the term *tension pattern*. Although direct translation into Chinese words could be made, it was impossible to find Chinese words that conveyed the same meaning as the original English words. Consequently, we could not ask directly about tension patterns in our interviews.

We believe we solved these problems by including bilingual Chinese and Japanese colleagues in all our discussions dealing with the tests and interviews used in the studies. For the achievement tests in mathematics, we compiled files containing every mathematical concept and operation appearing in the textbooks used in each location. Knowing when the concepts and operations were introduced and by tapping only those appearing in all the textbooks, we were able to develop reliable and culturally fair tests. Items for interviews were devised simultaneously in all three languages. Rather than relying on translation and back-translation, members of the group constructed items in their own language and brought their suggestions before the whole research group. Discussions were then held to assess whether or not items of very similar meaning and nuance could be composed in all three languages. If we decided this was not the case, the item was not included in the interview. Although this procedure is laborious and requires participation of psychologists who are fluent in two of the languages, it is likely to produce culturally fair, linguistically comparable research instruments.

Instruments

Mathematics Tests. The mathematics test given to first and fifth graders had 54 items arranged in increasing order of difficulty. Some items required only computation; others required the application of mathematical principles to word problems. Tests were administered in one-on-one fashion and the children could use paper and pencil. The eleventh-grade mathematics test contained 46 items covering a broad range of problems. This test was administered to groups and a 40-min time limit was imposed. No multiple-choice items were included; all questions on both tests were open-ended.

Interviews and Questionnaires. Interviews were held with first and fifth graders and their mothers. All eleventh graders responded to questionnaires, and subsamples of these students were also interviewed. Mothers of students in these subsamples were also given questionnaires and were interviewed. These interviews and questionnaires included open-ended questions, rating scales, and multiple-choice items. Because it was difficult to schedule interviews with fathers, we asked fathers to complete a questionnaire. Samples at each age level were large, ranging in size from several hundred in each location in the case of elementary school children to over a thousand in each location in the case of high school students.

Classroom Observations. Observations of mathematics classes were made at first and fifth grade. They were of two types: time-sampling observations in which the observer was asked to check whether or not a specified type of behavior occurred during short observational periods, and narrative observations in which an observer recorded everything that took place in each first- and fifth-grade classroom during four randomly chosen mathematics lessons.

Academic Achievement

Two frequency distributions display the results for fifth and eleventh graders. In Fig. 6.1 it is evident that students in Taipei greatly outperformed students in Min-

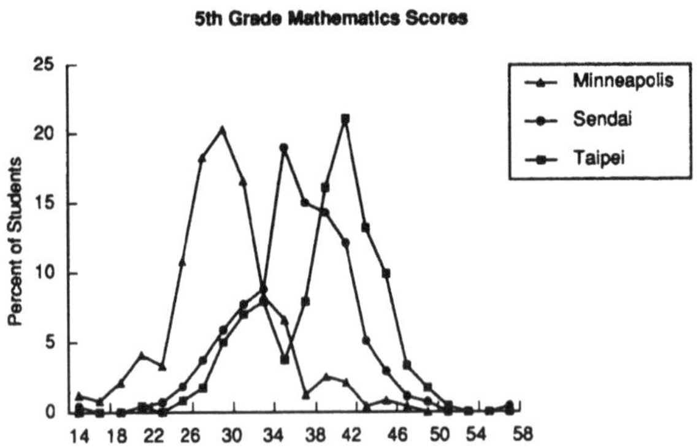

FIG. 6.1. Frequency distributions of fifth graders'scores on the test of mathematics achievement.

neapolis; in fact, few students in Taipei received scores below the average of the scores in Minneapolis. Differences between the scores of students in Sendai and Minneapolis were nearly as great.

Large differences also appeared at eleventh grade. The distribution of scores for students in Taipei was bimodal, as is evident in Fig. 6.2. The higher scores represent the students who were attending academic high schools; the lower scores were primarily those of students in vocational schools. The modal score for American students was much closer to that of Chinese students in vocational than in academically oriented high schools. Students in Sendai also outperformed their eleventh grade American peers. The most remarkable performance occurred in Beijing, where some students actually received perfect scores on the test. Although it is not appropriate to compare the average students in Beijing with the average students in Minneapolis because of the selectivity of students attending any type of high school in Beijing, comparisons of top performers in each city are appropriate.

The quotation of average scores is dismissed by some critics with the argument that it is the performance of the best American students that is important, and that top American students are competitive with top students in other countries. After all, they argue, American universities attract students from all over the world and the United States greatly exceeds other countries in producing Nobel Prize winners. The distributions of scores just described make it extremely unlikely that any support would be found for such an argument, and a direct test destroys it. Because the number of subjects in each location is large, it is possible to select the top 10% of students in each location from kindergarten, first, fifth, and eleventh grades. The average scores of the 10% of students who cluster about the mean for each location can also be obtained for each grade level. When this is done, it is evident (see Fig. 6.3) that among both top and average students, the

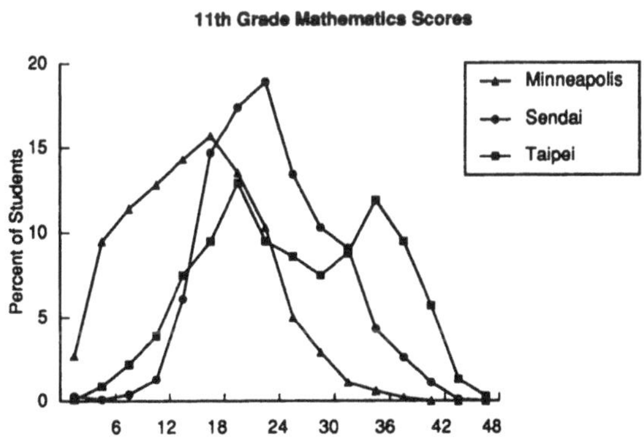

FIG. 6 2. Frequency distributions of eleventh graders' scores on the test of mathematics achievement.

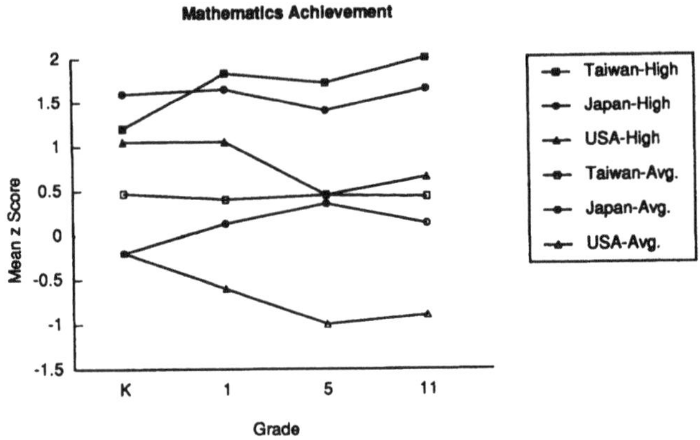

FIG. 6.3. Mean standard scores (*z* scores) for the mathematics test of groups of kindergarten, first-, fifth-, and eleventh grade students who received high (top 10%) and average (middle 10%) scores on the mathematics test.

average scores of the Chinese and Japanese students at all grade levels exceed those of the American students. In fact, at both fifth and eleventh grades the scores of the top American students approximate those of the *average* Chinese and Japanese students.

Another argument sometimes proposed is that Chinese and Japanese students do well on mathematics tests because they are good at memorizing facts and procedures, while the strength of American students lies in their creativity in solving novel problems. We found no evidence to support this argument. We categorized problems given to eleventh graders according to the aspect of mathematics being tested. The percentage of correct responses declined consistently in all locations as successive items dealt with increasingly difficult problems in various realms of mathematics. In all categories, from arithmetic through advanced mathematics, the percentage of American students who answered correctly was below the percentages of Chinese and Japanese students who did so (see Fig. 6.4).

Some assert that poor scores by American students must be improving as a result of the great attention being paid to educational reform in the United States during the 1980s. We were able to evaluate this possibility in 1990 by testing fifth graders in Minneapolis, Taipei, and Sendai in the same elementary schools we had visited in 1980 and comparing their scores to the 1980 test results. The trends established in 1980 were maintained throughout the decade: The average scores of the American fifth graders were consistently below those of the Chinese and Japanese students. The average Japanese—American difference in 1980 was 8 problems; in 1990 it was 7 problems. The comparable Chinese—American differences were 6 and 9 problems. In short, we found some improvement in the

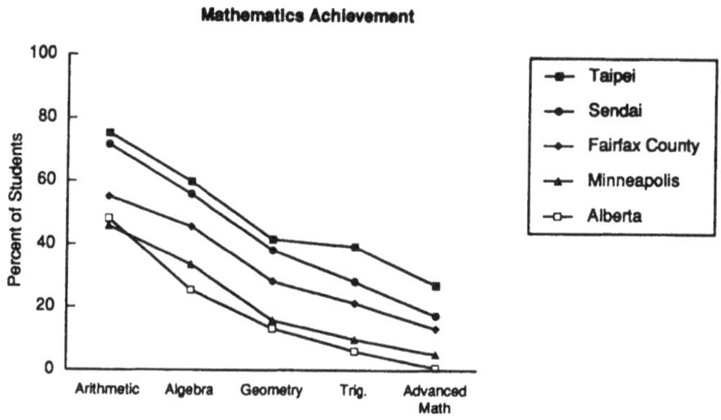

FIG. 6.4. Mean percent correct responses in five mathematical domains.

scores of the Chinese fifth graders during the decade, steady superiority on the part of the Japanese students, and consistently lower scores by the American students.

Whatever comparisons we made, no evidence was found to support the likelihood that American students will outperform their East Asian peers by the end of the 1990s. It is hard to imagine what could be done to improve the scores of American students to the degree necessary to be among the top students in worldwide comparisons.

The fact that U.S. students from kindergarten through high school are not competitive with their Chinese and Japanese peers leads us to ask "Why not?" Because differences in scores appear in the premathematics test given to kindergarten children as well as in the tests given during elementary and high school, one must look beyond the classroom for explanations. Although some of the effects may be attributable to differences in schooling and teaching practices, cultural differences in beliefs, attitudes, and the students' daily home life must also be involved.

The remainder of this chapter describes some of the variables that have been discussed in efforts to explain the gap that exists between the performance of American and East Asian students. Two of the most important variables are intelligence and motivation.

Intelligence and Mathematics

One of the first hypotheses often suggested to explain the remarkable performance of the East Asian students is that they are brighter than American students. Our search of the literature revealed no evidence to support this proposal. Lynn (1982), for example, reported higher IQs for Japanese than for American children on the Wechsler Intelligence Scale for Children (WISC), calculated the

IQs on the basis of the IQ scores Japanese children would obtain if they were computed according to the American standardization sample. A critical flaw in the design of this study precluded any comparisons of this kind: The two standardization groups were not selected in comparable fashions. Lynn attempted to compare Japanese urban children, selected without consideration of their socioeconomic status, with a broadly representative sample of American students. Equally serious criticisms can be waged against other studies purporting to present evidence in favor of superior levels of intellectual functioning on the part of East Asian students.

The only study of which we are aware that included a test constructed specifically for comparison of intellectual functioning of American and East Asian students and also included samples of subjects selected in a comparable fashion in each location is one that we conducted (Stevenson, Stigler, Lee, Lucker, Kitamura, & Hsu, 1985). The test contained subscales patterned after those of the WISC and other commonly used intelligence tests . Although students from each culture displayed strength in various subtests, their overall scores were very similar. Attempts to explain differences in academic achievement by reference to differences in intelligence has little support, therefore, in the published literature.

Motivation

A basic variable involved in learning is motivation, which is assumed to influence attention, willingness to practice, the effectiveness of reward, and other psychological processes. Higher levels of academic achievement should occur, therefore, when students are highly motivated to learn school subjects.

Obtaining direct measures of motivational level is difficult, but inferences about motivation can be made from several types of data. For example, we can ask students a question such as the following: "Let's say that there is a wizard who will let you make a wish about anything you want. What would you want?" When we asked this question of fifth graders in Chicago, only 10% mentioned anything about education, but more than twice as many mentioned wanting money or things. In Beijing, nearly 70% mentioned education, such as wanting to make good grades or to go to college. This example, along with many others, suggest that motivation for education is stronger among Beijing than among Chicago children.

Satisfaction. Another factor influencing motivation is the individual's current level of satisfaction. High satisfaction should reflect low motivation for change. Parents and students who say they are very satisfied with the students' current level of performance apparently see little reason for the student to study more intensely or to spend more time in other ways on school work. When we asked mothers of eleventh graders whether they were dissatisfied, satisfied, or very satisfied with their child's current level of academic achievement, we found remarkably high degrees of satisfaction among American mothers. One-third said they were "very satisfied" with their child's academic achievement; only 10% of the Chinese and 2% of the Japanese mothers made this judgment. Fathers also expressed high degrees of satisfaction: 37% of the Minneapolis fathers, compared to 8% of the Taipei and 6% of the Sendai fathers said they were "very satisfied." Degrees of dissatisfaction were much higher among Chinese and Japanese than among American mothers.

High levels of parental satisfaction were evident not only at eleventh grade, but were found among mothers of American first- and fifth-graders as well (Stevenson, Lee, Chen, Stigler, Hsu, & Kitamura, 1990). We have posed this question to three different cohorts of mothers of fifth graders between 1980 and 1990. Approximately 40% of the American mothers said they were "very satisfied" with their child's performance in school (Stevenson, Chen, & Lee, 1993). Only around 10% of the American mothers said they were "dissatisfied." The responses of the Chinese and Japanese mothers followed the same pattern of high dissatisfaction and low levels of satisfaction found among mothers of eleventh graders.

Although parents may express high degrees of satisfaction, their children may not share these evaluations of their performance. However, like their parents, relatively few American eleventh graders expressed dissatisfaction. Less than half as many American as Chinese and Japanese eleventh graders indicated that they were dissatisfied (see Fig. 6.5).

It seems reasonable to conclude from these data that American students are less highly motivated than are Chinese or Japanese students to improve their academic performance. Other indices also indicate lower motivation on the part of American students, such as their spending less time in study, being absent from school more frequently, and displaying lower levels of attentiveness in class. Data are available for each of these variables, as discussed next.

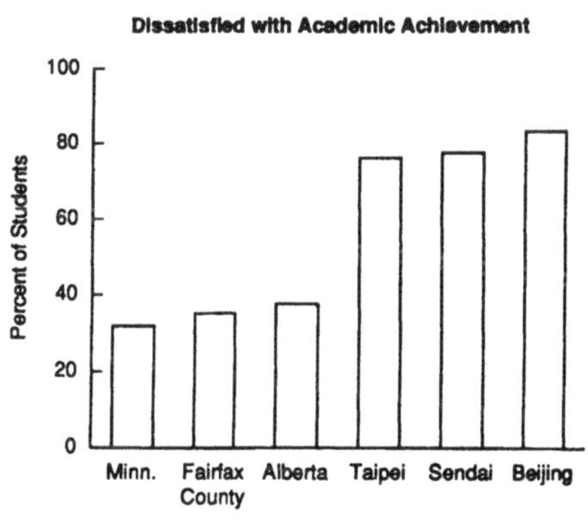

FIG. 6.5. Percentage of eleventh graders who indicated they were dissatisfied with their academic achievement.

Indices of Low Motivation. Estimates of the time students spent studying outside of school were available from the mothers of first- and fifth- graders and from the eleventh-grade students themselves. In all comparisons, the average for American students was lower than that for their East Asian peers. The respective means for Minneapolis, Taipei, and Sendai at first grade were 1.2, 8.2, and 3.9 hours per week; at fifth grade they were, respectively, 4.2, 12.9, and 6.0 hours. The same order of difference appeared at eleventh grade; the American, Chinese, and Japanese students reported spending averages of 10.1, 16.6, and 11.4 hours studying after school.

Absence from school occurred more frequently among American than among Chinese students. Estimates of the daily rate of absence was 2.7% in the Minneapolis elementary schools included in our sample and a remarkably low 0.1% in the sample of schools in Taipei. The highest rate of absence was in Sendai: 3.8%. Among the eleventh graders, Minneapolis students reported being absent over twice as often during the previous semester as students in Taipei and Sendai: an average of 4.5 days compared to 2.0 and 1.8 days.

Finally, the time-sampling observations made in the elementary schools make it possible to determine the percentage of time the target subjects in each classroom were judged to be attending to the teacher or to the task defined by the teacher. Attention was high in Taipei, Sendai, and Beijing among both the first and fifth graders; children were judged to be attending between 80% and 90% of the time. In Chicago, both first and fifth graders appeared to be attentive less than 65% of the time.

These various indices reflect what appears to be lower motivation on the part of American students for academic achievement. The lower motivation appears to be derived in part from the high levels of satisfaction with the students' current levels of academic achievement expressed by the American students and their parents. The high levels of satisfaction appear, in turn, to result from lower standards for academic achievement. Both anecdotal evidence and interview data support this assumption.

Standards. Many American parents complain that it is impossible for them to obtain much information about their children's progress from the report cards children bring home. In most elementary schools only two types of evaluations are made: "satisfactory" and "needs improvement." The progress of most students is judged to be satisfactory; thus it should not be surprising that mothers expressed such strong satisfaction with their children's performance. The grading system becomes more informative after students enter high school and should help parents gain a clearer idea of how their children are performing. Nevertheless, the parents' positive attitudes persist.

There is another reason why Americans may be less clear about academic standards than are parents in other countries. Chinese and Japanese schools follow a national curriculum that describes what students are expected to study each semester of each grade. East Asian parents are able, therefore, to evaluate how closely the performance of their child approximates the standards described in the national curriculum. American parents have no set of standards to which they can refer; thus it is very difficult to determine whether their child is progressing at the expected rate. This may change in the coming years, but thus far only the reports issued by the National Council of Teachers of Mathematics (1989, 1991) provide such guidelines.

Data from our interviews with mothers also point to lower standards on the part of American parents. To obtain an indication of the standards mothers used for judging whether their child was doing well in school, we presented them with the following situation: "Let's say there is a math test in which there are 100 points. The average score is 70. What score do you think your child will get?" We then asked, "What score would you be satisfied with?" The degree of difference between the two scores should reflect the standards held by the mothers. Two interesting findings emerged: First, American mothers expressed unusually high expectations for what their children could accomplish, and second, it appeared to be much easier to satisfy American than East Asian mothers. (The findings are not limited to mothers, for the same conclusions can be drawn from the results obtained from fathers and from the students when this situation was posed to them.)

American mothers of fifth graders and of high school students indicated, on the average, that they expected their children would obtain scores approximately 10 points higher than the score defined as average for the test (Stevenson, et al., 1993). The average score Japanese and Chinese mothers expected their children would make tended to be closer to the defined average of 70. In responding to the second question, American mothers said they would be satisfied if their child received a score close to the score they expected their child would receive. Japanese and Chinese mothers, in contrast, said they would be satisfied only if their child received a score roughly 10 points higher than the one they expected for their child.

Effort and Ability. The reluctance of American students to spend time studying is influenced by factors other than their satisfaction with their current levels of achievement. Students must believe in the efficacy of studying as an important avenue to excellence. There is little need to convince aspiring American athletes and musicians of the importance of practice in developing skill. Students are willing to spend long hours on the playing fields or in practice rooms and they realize that improvement is extremely unlikely unless they do this. Attitudes change when academic work is involved. Although both students and parents acknowledge that practice is important, they suggest that other factors greatly alter the effects of practice. One of these factors is innate ability.

A common finding in comparative studies of academic achievement is the greater emphasis given to studying by Japanese than by American students and the greater emphasis given to innate ability by American than by Japanese students (e.g., Azuma, Kashiwagi, & Hess, 1981; Stevenson, Lee, et al., 1990). The emphasis on hard work in East Asia is in line with long-held tenets of Confucian philosophy that emphasize the importance of hard work as the route to success. Why Americans, who also have a long tradition of stressing the importance of hard work as a route to success, should give so much attention to innate ability is not clear. Neither group denies the importance of both effort and ability, but Americans are more likely than Japanese to assume that highly able students do not need to exert much effort in order to succeed and that some students of low ability are unlikely to succeed, regardless of how diligently they study.

The East Asian attitude is illustrated in the following example. A colleague asked a small group of elementary school teachers in Taipei which academic subject they most liked to teach. On the basis of earlier interviews, she knew that the answer would be mathematics. "But why mathematics?" she asked. "Because there are such large individual differences," was the reply. When the teachers were asked why the presence of large individual differences should influence their choice of subject, they answered, "Because it is so challenging and rewarding to bring all of the children up." The assumption was that all children, if they were taught well and studied hard, would be able to master the subject.

An emphasis on studying was not confined to the elementary school. For example, we told the eleventh graders, "Here are some factors that may influence students' performance in mathematics: a good teacher, innate intelligence, home environment, and studying hard. Which do you think is the most important factor?" Chinese and Japanese students chose "studying hard" nearly three times as frequently as the American students who, in contrast, were nearly three times as likely as the Chinese and Japanese students to choose "a good teacher" (see Fig 6.6).

Motivational factors obviously play an important role in determining students' levels of academic achievement. When standards are high, satisfaction is difficult to attain. When standards are low and the importance of studying is not emphasized, motivation for studying and for working diligently at academic tasks is also likely to be low. At least part of the differences in the academic achievement of American and East Asian students can be attributed to these factors.

Allocation of Time

If large amounts of time are spent on other daily activities, studying is bound to suffer. This is clearly the case for American students. American eleventh graders, for example, reported that they devoted more time to activities such as jobs, dating, and socializing with friends than did the Chinese and Japanese students. They also reported that these activities interfered with their academic studies.

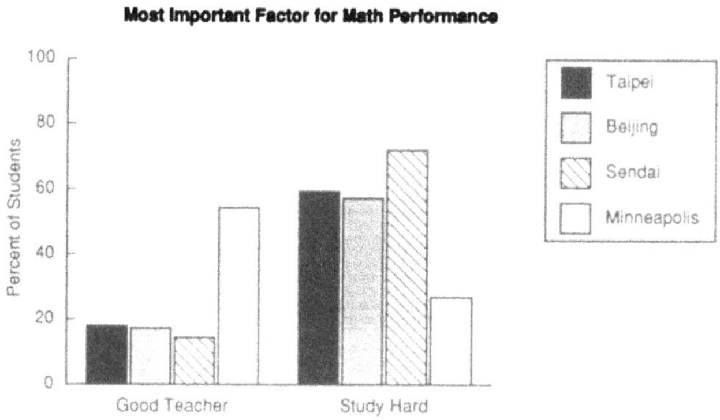

FIG. 6.6. Percentage of eleventh graders who chose "good teacher" and "studying hard" as the most important factors in academic achievement.

Minneapolis eleventh graders reported spending an average of 12 hours a week working at outside jobs; the averages in Sendai and Taipei were 2.8 and 2.0 hours. Similarly, American students spent much more time dating than Chinese and Japanese students: the averages were 4.7 versus 0.9 and 1.1 hours a week, respectively. Finally, American students spent more time with their friends than did Chinese and Japanese students; the averages were 18.4 versus 8.8 and 12.4 hours. Even at fifth grade American children were reported by their mothers to spend more time in play each week than Chinese and Japanese children. The averages were 20.2 hours versus 8.1 and 14.1 hours. A similar trend was evident at first grade; the corresponding averages were 22.1 hours versus 12.5 and 21.8 hours.

Before giving undue emphasis to the time spent in social interaction, it should be pointed out that East Asian students have many more opportunities for interacting with their peers at school than do American students. East Asian schools have more frequent recesses, longer lunch periods, and wider programs of extracurricular activities, all of which offer opportunities for social interaction. Possibilities for interaction with peers are also enhanced by the common practice of Chinese and Japanese students to study with their friends after school. By combining socializing with studying, they may have less need for additional social interaction than the American students, who create a greater separation between the two activities.

The students' impressions that jobs and social interactions interfered with their academic achievement were supported when correlations between the two sets of variables were computed. Correlations between achievement scores and time spent with friends were consistently and significantly negative (Fuligni & Stevenson, 1995). Statistically significant negative correlations were also obtained in all three locations between scores on the mathematics test and time spent working. (The small amounts of time Chinese and Japanese students spent dating precluded the computation of meaningful correlations for this variable.)

Further insight into the basis of the strength of East Asian students' performance comes, therefore, from analyses of the ways students spend their time. Common sense suggests that students are less likely to do well in school when they spend much of their out-of-school time engaged in nonacademic activities, and as we have seen earlier, less time studying.

Teaching

Children's experiences at school, especially those related to the knowledge and skill of the teacher, exert another important influence on academic achievement. Teachers who provide lively, interesting, well organized lessons are likely to gain the students' attention and to arouse their interest in the subject being taught. But preparing and presenting such lessons requires time and energy. Japanese and Chinese educators acknowledge this and provide teachers with the conditions necessary to prepare effective lessons. In contrast to American teachers, who must be in front of a class nearly all of the time they are at school, East Asian teachers seldom spend more than 60% of their time at school teaching. The remainder of their day at school is spent working with other teachers on the construction of lessons, working closely with individual students, preparing lessons by themselves, correcting papers, and pursuing other requirements of good teaching (Lee, Graham, & Stevenson, in press; Stevenson, Stigler, Lucker, Lee, Hsu, & Kitamura, 1987).

The contrast between the daily schedule of East Asian and American teachers was illustrated dramatically in a recent conversation I had with a group of elementary school teachers in Beijing. I told them that I wanted to be sure that my information about the teaching responsibilities of Beijing teachers was correct. "As I understand it," I said, "teachers in Beijing teach only two to three hours a day unless they are homeroom teachers, when they may teach four hours a day. In high school, teachers are responsible for only two lessons a day." "No," they replied, "that is not correct." When I asked what was wrong, they explained, "When we have a new teacher we often assign the teacher only *one* hour of lessons a day during the first year. There is so much to learn, so great a need to prepare lessons that only one class a day seems sufficient."

Teaching schedules that seem luxurious to American teachers are possible primarily because the size of classes is much larger in East Asia: approximately 50 students in each Chinese elementary classroom and 40 in each Japanese classroom. Despite the large number of students in the classroom, therefore, the ratio of students to teachers is about the same in Chinese and Japanese schools as it is in American schools. The lone teacher in an American classroom teaches nearly all the time he or she is at school; the East Asian teacher is at school all day, but only part of the day is in front of a class teaching.

A Lesson. Each class period in East Asian classrooms is constructed around the concept of a meaningful lesson. The goal for each lesson is to present coherent, integrated information about a specific concept or topic. During the beginning of each lesson students are oriented to the purpose or themes of the lesson and an effort is made to place the information in a meaningful context. The latter step was taken much more frequently in the classrooms of Beijing, Sendai, and Taipei than in Chicago (see Fig. 6.7). Chinese and Japanese teachers frequently began each lesson with some type of problem that was meaningful either in terms of the students' everyday experiences or as an application of the concepts they were learning. American teachers were observed to do this in only a quarter of the lessons.

One of the most common ways of insuring that mathematical concepts will be meaningful to children is to embed the concepts in word problems. By being forced to apply the concepts to everyday problems, children gain an understanding of how mathematics is relevant to real-life situations. By fifth grade, the most frequent use of word problems was by Japanese teachers, who included them in 86% of the lessons. They were least popular with American teachers, who used them in only 14% of the lessons.

Whole-Class Instruction. Once the teacher begins the discussion of the lesson, differences in the teaching style of East Asian and American teachers become clear. Because of the large number of students in each class, reliance is placed primarily upon whole-class instruction. This does not mean that the teacher spends the period lecturing. Rather, the teacher acts as a skilled, in-

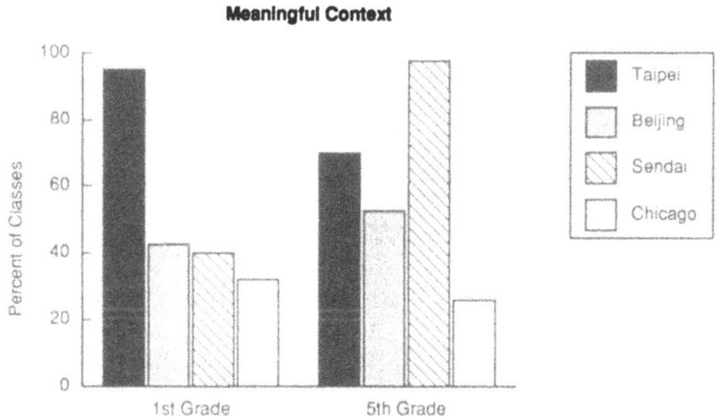

FIG. 6.7. Percentage of classes in which lesson was placed in meaningful context.

formed guide who is available for assistance, and relies frequently on students to produce the information necessary for proceeding through the lesson. In applying this interactive mode of instruction Chinese and Japanese teachers frequently call on students to explain their solutions to a problem and then call on other students to evaluate the relevance and effectiveness of the solutions just discussed. Knowing that the teacher might call upon them at any time, students pay close attention throughout the lesson.

Because of the large number of students in each class and the modest amount of space available in each classroom, the class is seldom divided into small groups. This means that some technique other than grouping children by ability must be adopted in order to meet the needs of slow and fast learners. The technique used by East Asian teachers is to organize each class period into several sequences consisting of instruction, practice, and feedback (see Fig. 6.8). During one sequence students may be asked to solve a problem involving the concepts or operations that have just been introduced. The teacher then asks several of the children to write their solutions on the blackboard. After the effectiveness of the different solutions has been evaluated, a new sequence is begun. Now the teacher passes out drawings of trees and asks the children to think about ways in which the height of trees that depart in various degrees from the vertical could be determined. Several children are called on to explain their ideas and the class discusses their feasibility. This style of teaching is much more characteristic of East Asian than of American teachers, who are more likely to divide the lesson into two parts: a period of instruction followed by seatwork.

By ending the class period with seatwork, students frequently leave the class not knowing whether they have solved their practice problems correctly. In nearly half of the lessons, American fifth graders, for example, left their mathematics classes without having received any feedback about their seatwork. Seatwork exercises used in American classrooms appeared generally to be the most unproductive use of children's time; not only did the students frequently fail to

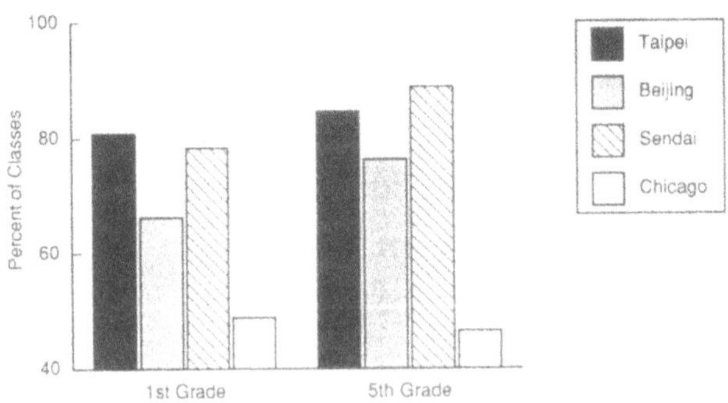

FIG. 6.8. Percentage of classes following the pattern of instruction, practice, and feedback.

receive feedback, the seatwork materials were often poorly integrated with the rest of the lesson and failed to provide children with more than repetitive practice.

A final example involving procedural and conceptual information illustrates the kinds of differences in teaching that are found in East Asian and American schools. Procedural information consists of information about the steps necessary to solve the problem. Conceptual information leads to an understanding of the conceptual basis of a problem. If a lesson contains only conceptual information the students may have a good understanding of a problem but little understanding of how to find an answer. Similarly, if the lesson contains only procedural information the students may know how to solve the problem at hand but be unable to apply it to other problems involving the same concepts. As might be expected, a high percentage of lessons contained procedural information. Where differences appeared was in the percentage of lessons that included conceptual information (see Fig. 6.9). Over half of the Chinese and Japanese lessons, but only a quarter of the American lessons contained conceptual information.

The preceding examples give a brief indication of how teaching practices may influence students' understanding of mathematics. Few persons would dispute the usefulness of beginning a lesson with a description of its goals and purposes, giving students examples of how the lesson has meaningful applications, varying the types of problems and exercises within each lesson, providing frequent opportunities for practice and feedback, and presenting conceptual as well as procedural information. When these and other teaching practices commonly found in East Asian classrooms are described to American teachers they typically reply that this is exactly what *they* do. This is undoubtedly true. However, according to the formal observations just described and to informal observations made during visits to classrooms, American teachers appear to apply these teaching strategies far less frequently than their Chinese and Japanese counterparts.

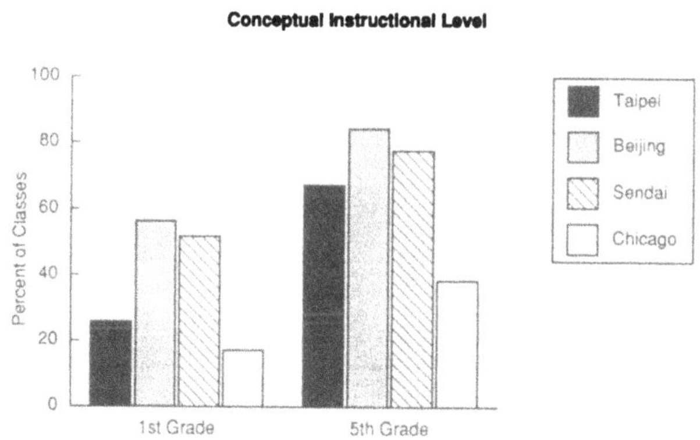

FIG. 6.9. Percentage of classes which included conceptual information.

Teachers' Lives. Before these data are viewed as an indictment of American teachers, it is important to remember the constraints under which American teachers work. They do not have the time to organize the kinds of lessons that most would like to teach and must spend their nights and weekends developing their lessons by themselves. This is more burdensome and generally less productive than if time were allocated during the regular working day for teachers to collaborate with each other and to share teaching techniques and materials that have been especially effective.

American teachers face other obstacles that East Asian teachers seldom encounter. For example, their teaching is frequently interrupted. Announcements over the public address system and the appearance of someone collecting milk money make it difficult to maintain continuity in teaching a lesson. By fifth grade, some type of interruption occurred in nearly half of the lessons during which an observer was present in the American classrooms (see Fig. 6.10). Interruptions practically never occurred in Beijing, Taipei, or Sendai classrooms. These and other factors, such as the ethnic, linguistic, and racial diversity found in American schools, the greater number of dysfunctional families, and problems in discipline, make teaching in American schools a much more arduous process than that faced by East Asian teachers.

CONCLUSION

This overview of some of our findings gives a clear negative answer to the question of whether American students can be first in the world in mathematics by the year 2000. But a negative answer does not mean that this could not ultimately be the case. The fact that the greatest number of gold medals in the 1994 Mathematics Olympiad was received by Americans indicates that Ameri-

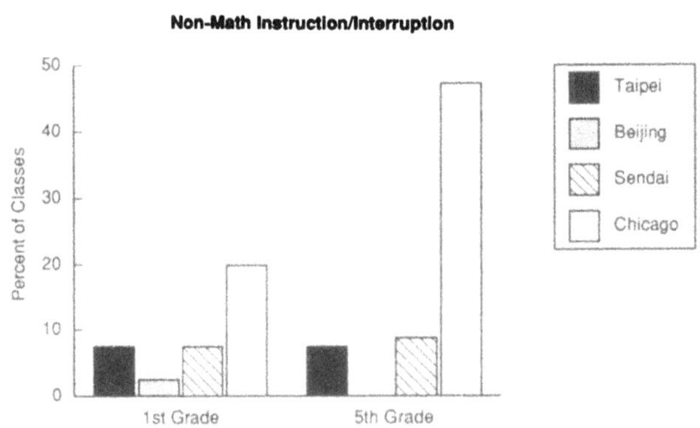

FIG. 6.10. Percentage of classes in which there was an interruption or nonmathematical discussion.

can students are capable of very high levels of performance. Unfortunately, these students are exceptions. We found little evidence of this degree of competence among representative samples of American high school students selected from the three large metropolitan areas included in our studies.

When we looked at factors at home and at school that might explain some of the differences in students' achievement in mathematics we found no esoteric, complex reasons for the superiority of Asian students. The results point to the possibility that the scores of American students could be greatly improved if American parents can be persuaded that the gap in performance between the majority of our students and students in China, Japan, and Taiwan has meaningful implications for their children's future; if American students can be convinced of the utility of studying for persons of all levels of ability; and if school authorities can be induced to provide teachers with opportunities for improving the quality of their teaching.

REFERENCES

Azuma, H., Kashiwagi, K. , & Hess, R. (1981). *Hahaoya no taido koudo to kodomo no chiteki hattatsu* [The effect of mother's attitude and behavior on the cognitive development of the child]. Tokyo: University of Tokyo Press.

Fuligni, A. J., & Stevenson, H. W. (1995). Time-use and academic achievement among Chinese, Japanese, and American high school students. *Child Development, 66,* 830–842.

Lee, S. Y., Graham, T., & Stevenson, H. W. (in press). Teachers and teaching: Elementary schools in Japan and the United States. In T. Rohlen & G. LeTendre (Eds.), *Teaching and learning in Japan.* New York: Cambridge University Press.

Lynn, R. (1982). IQ in Japan and the United States shows a growing disparity. *Nature, 297,* 222–223.

McKnight, C. C., Crosswhite, F. J., Dossey, J. A., Kifer, E., Swafford, J. O., Travers, K. J., & Cooney, T. J. (1987). *The underachieving curriculum: Assessing U. S. school mathematics from an international perspective.* Champaign, IL: Stipes.

National Council of Teachers of Mathematics. (1989). *Curriculum and evaluation standards for school mathematics.* Reston, VA: National Council of Teachers of Mathematics.

National Council of Teachers of Mathematics. (1991). *Professional standards for teaching mathematics.* Reston, VA: National Council of Teachers of Mathematics.

Stevenson, H. W., Chen, C., & Lee, S. Y. (1993). Mathematics achievement of Chinese, Japanese, and American children: Ten years later. *Science, 259,* 53–58.

Stevenson, H. W. , Lee, S. Y., Chen, C., Stigler, J. W., Hsu, C. C., & Kitamura, S. (1990). Contexts of achievement. *Monographs of the Society for Research in Child Development, 55* (1–2, Serial No. 221).

Stevenson, H. W., Stigler, J. W., Lee, S. Y., Lucker, G. W., Kitamura, S., & Hsu, C. C. (1985). Cognitive performance and academic achievement of Japanese, Chinese, and American children. *Child Development, 56,* 718–734.

Stevenson, H. W., Stigler, J. W., Lucker, G. W., Lee, S.Y., Hsu, C. C., & Kitamura, S. (1987). Classroom behavior and achievement of Japanese, Chinese, and American children. In R. Glaser (Ed.), *Advances in instructional psychology* (pp. 153–204). Hillsdale NJ: Lawrence Erlbaum Associates.

7 Research and Reform for U.S. Mathematics Education: What Counts? A Commentary on Stevenson, Stigler and Fernandez, and Resnick

Kathleen E. Kremer
Emma K. Adam
Shane R. Jimerson
Institute of Child Development
University of Minnesota

The 1980s brought an increased awareness among political and educational sectors of the impoverished mathematical skills of many Americans. In part, this heightened awareness was stimulated by representatives from United States industries, who argued that a poorly educated populace was weakening this country's ability to compete in the global market. As evidence, industrialists pointed to large-scale international studies (e.g., McKnight et al., 1987; Stevenson, Lee, & Stigler, 1986) in which it was consistently reported that American children perform worse on mathematical examinations than children from virtually all other industrialized countries; this gap was especially evident when comparing American and East Asian children. Of further concern was a decline in scores through the 1970s and early 1980s on several national indices of mathematical achievement, such as the Scholastic Achievement Test and the National Assessment of Educational Progress (Jones, 1988; Mullis et al., 1994). This situation resulted in numerous proposals regarding how mathematics education in the United States should be reformed. These proposals included a set of national standards suggested by the National Council of Teachers of Mathematics (1989) and various novel teaching and assessment methods (e.g., Lampert, 1986; Katims, Nash, & Tocci, 1993; Simmons & Resnick, 1993). In addition, broader changes to the educational system were tried by various states, such as increasing the amount of time children attended school, expanding the amount of money allocated to education, and raising high school graduation and teacher qualification requirements (Finn & Rebarber, 1992; Murphy, 1992).

Within the last few years, several signs of progress have emerged. For example, the average score on the mathematics section of the National Assessment of Educational Progress (NAEP) has risen (Mullis et al., 1994). More high school seniors also have been completing Algebra II (from 37% in 1978 to 45% in 1992) and have been enrolling in advanced mathematics classes, such as precalculus and calculus (from 6% in 1978 to 10% in 1992; Mullis et al., 1994). Nevertheless, these advances seem minor when compared with the much larger body of evidence that our nation is having continued difficulty educating students in mathematics. First, American children's understanding of this subject remains among the worst of all the industrialized countries surveyed (National Education Goals Panel, 1994). In fact, the gap between what East Asian children and American children know about mathematics may be increasing (Stevenson, Chen, & Lee, 1993). Second, the highest level of mathematical achievement that many American students ultimately reach is quite low. For example, on the 1992 NAEP test, only 20% of the eighth-grade students and 50% of the twelfth-grade students demonstrated mastery of problems involving fractions or decimals; only 6% of the twelfth-grade students could consistently solve algebraic and geometric problems. Furthermore, the rise in NAEP scores has not been accompanied by an increase in the percentage of students mastering the most advanced topics assessed by this test, such as high school algebra. Such results have led NAEP officials to estimate that over 60% of the students in the three grades surveyed (fourth, eighth, and twelfth) possess at best a partial mastery of the knowledge and the skills needed for proficient work at their grade level (Mullis, Dossey, Owen, & Phillips, 1983). Third, the gap between the mathematical achievement of European Americans and of most minority groups remains substantial (Mullis et al., 1983; National Education Goals Panel, 1994). These trends, among others, cast doubt on the feasibility of the 1989 National Educational Goal established by President Bush and the Governors of having United States students rank first in the world in mathematics by the year 2000.

This situation is of concern not simply because our nation's economic productivity and ability to compete in international markets depends on the skills of its workers; tasks requiring mathematical knowledge are ubiquitous in the lives of most adults. They include balancing a checkbook, completing an order form, and determining which bus to take in order to arrive at a destination by a specific time. This use of mathematics has sometimes been referred to as "quantitative literacy" (Kirsch, Jungeblut, Jenkins, & Kolstad, 1993). It involves, in addition to basic computational skills, the ability to extract relevant information from printed documents and to know which mathematical operations to apply in order to achieve a given goal. Although most people have acquired the ability to add, multiply, divide, and subtract whole numbers by the time they graduate from high school (Mullis et al., 1993), many adults seem to have a limited understanding of how to use these abilities in written contexts. Kirsch et al. (1993) reported that 31% of young adults had difficulty solving problems in which they had to extract two numbers from a document and then infer which mathematical operation to use in response to questions such as "how many are there?" or "what is the difference?" Such a problem might require the reader to find two prices in a table and determine the amount of money that would be saved by selecting the cheaper item. In addition, 96% of the young adults had trouble solving conditional problems requiring the integration of information from several parts of a document, such as determining how much a four credit class with a lab would cost if a student registered on time and was not a senior citizen. Such limitations would be expected to interfere with a person's ability to function effectively and autonomously in society, regardless of that person's occupation.

Furthermore, the mathematical education of our nation's children is important because achievement in this domain may influence an individual's occupational prospects. A certain level of mathematical knowledge is required for many careers, including those in technology, sales, finance, and research. People lacking such knowledge are limited in the kinds of jobs that they are initially qualified to accept and in their opportunities for promotion. The relation between mathematical skills and job prospects is likely to become even more important in the future, given that between the years of 1990 and 2005, openings for technological jobs are expected to increase at eight times the rate as those for relatively unskilled work involving labor and operations (Kirsch, Jungeblut, & Campbell, 1992). In addition, mathematics remains a substantial component of standardized exams (e.g., the Scholastic Aptitude Test, the American College Test, the Graduate Record Examination) used in determining admissions to American colleges and universities. A failure to master the mathematical skills assessed on such tests may limit a person's ability to receive the quality of education and academic credentials needed even for jobs that do not require mathematical skills. Thus a focus on mathematical education is clearly warranted.

COMMON ASSUMPTIONS ABOUT MATHEMATICAL REFORM

The chapters by Stevenson, Stigler and Fernandez, and Resnick in this volume represent several innovative ways in which psychologists have addressed the problem of low mathematical achievement among American students. The authors share some assumptions about the nature of the problem and the steps that should be taken in order to rectify it. These assumptions include:

Assumption 1: Children in the United States are Not Reaching Their Potential in Mathematics

Stevenson (this volume) reports that East Asian and American children receive similar overall scores on batteries of general cognitive tasks. He has also reported

(Stevenson et al., 1993; Stevenson & Stigler, 1992) that American children perform at least as well as (and sometimes better than) their East Asian counterparts on tests of facts that are typically not taught in school, such as "why people can't live under water" and "what we mean by inflation when we talk about a country's economy." These results have led Stevenson to claim that East Asian students' superior performance in mathematics is not due to greater aptitude or superior intelligence in general. This claim is important because it suggests that the difficulty many American children have with mathematics is not inevitable. The assumption that American children's mathematical skills can be improved motivates a search for intervention techniques, such as those proposed by Stigler and Fernandez and Resnick. The idea that American children are not reaching their potential in math is also evident in Resnick's comparison of children's poor performance at solving written problems in the classroom (what she labels "school math") with their frequent success at solving these same problems in the context of everyday tasks outside of school (or "street math").

Assumption 2: One Reason Many American Children Have Difficulty With Mathematics is Because of How It is Currently Taught in School

Mathematics instruction in the United States traditionally has consisted of the teacher demonstrating various mathematical procedures without an extensive discussion of the rationale behind each step. In addition, the memorization of numerical facts (such as multiplication and division tables) has been emphasized. Thus mathematics has often been taught simply as a combination of facts and skills rather than as a sense-making activity (Resnick, 1989; Stigler & Fernandez, this volume). The chapters by Stevenson and by Stigler and Fernandez highlight other characteristics that typify mathematical instruction in the United States. For instance, they report that American teachers do not incorporate many opportunities in their lessons for extended student interaction with the teacher or with other students. Problems are solved at a quick pace and are infrequently embedded in meaningful contexts. The lesson tends to be followed by extended, independent seat work during which the teacher aids individual students or prepares future lessons. Resnick raises some possible consequences of these factors for children's acquisition of and application of mathematics knowledge. For example, the emphasis on teaching procedural knowledge that is divorced from conceptual knowledge may lead to incorrect or "buggy" algorithms (Brown & VanLehn, 1982), which are systematic transformations of correct rules that children sometimes use when solving mathematical equations. Children rarely use these incorrect algorithms outside of the classroom when they are dealing with meaningful problems. This emphasis on procedural knowledge may also be responsible for students' inflexibility when applying mathematical knowledge to somewhat novel situations, such as to certain kinds of word problems (Riley & Greeno, 1988). Stigler and Fernandez (this volume) add that lessons structured in the foregoing manner may result in students having difficulty abstracting relevant from irrelevant information.

Assumption 3: Educational Reform in the United States Should Include Changes in Methods of Mathematics Instruction

Stigler and Fernandez and Resnick examine the effects of altering various elements of traditional classroom practices on mathematical achievement. The results of their research suggest that the following instructional changes may improve mathematical achievement: (a) structuring lessons around quantitative problems embedded in meaningful context, (b) having students attempt to solve these problems in collaborative groups, (c) discussing as a class the various solutions derived by groups of students, (d) encouraging multiple answers and the view of mathematics as an open-ended problem solving activity, and (e) using different materials and formats to represent each problem. Although Resnick relies on Vygotksy's sociocultural theory to justify her suggestions whereas Stigler and Fernandez appeal to constructivism, these authors reach very similar conclusions because their theoretical approaches share several core assumptions. For example, both theories assume that children are active learners and that social interaction is an important agent for cognitive development. These core assumptions are not evident in the American teaching practice of having students listen to a teacher's lecture on mathematics and then practice what they have learned through independent seat work.

Assumption 4: Scientific Research is Essential for Determining the Directions Educational Reform Should Take

Although all of the authors use research to explore the problem of low mathematical achievement among American children, they adopt very different approaches. Stevenson documents the magnitude of the problem by comparing what American and East Asian children know about various topics within this domain. In addition, he identifies several factors that differ between both cultures and thus may be responsible for the gap in mathematical achievement that exists between them. These factors include the choice of instructional methods and other school practices, the societal beliefs about what determines academic achievement, and the presence or absence of national standards in various subjects; Stevenson's research is descriptive and exploratory. Like Stevenson, Stigler and Fernandez present some exploratory research, describing how East Asian and American teachers use different techniques when giving a lesson in mathematics. They also experimentally manipulate characteristics of the lesson and of the student in order to examine their effects on the ability to make sense of the presentation. Thus, unlike Stevenson, Stigler and Fernandez attempt to establish whether their various hypothesized factors are causally related to mathematical achievement. These researchers, however, limit their materials to short, videotaped lessons on a few, simple topics in mathematics. In contrast, Resnick implements her suggestions for instructional change in an actual classroom for the duration of the school year (although only one lesson is outlined in her chapter) and relates this manipulation to students' subsequent performance on standardized mathematical exams. Her research consists of school-based intervention and evaluation.

Many of the suggestions for reform that Stevenson, Stigler and Fernandez, and Resnick derive from their research are not entirely novel. Practices such as encouraging active learning and small group collaboration, extensively exploring a few problems rather than having students memorize many facts, focusing on process rather than content, and linking class material to out-of-class situations have periodically been proposed, implemented, and later abandoned in American education, only to reemerge several decades later. For example, these practices can be found in the writings of Dewey, which had an especially strong impact on education during the earlier part of this century (Murray, 1992). This cyclic nature of reform applies to other aspects of education as well. It can be seen in decisions about whether to teach only traditional subjects or to offer additional "practical" classes (such as vocational technology or home economics), and in decisions about centralizing or decentralizing authority within the educational system (Cuban, 1990).

Broad educational reform movements in the United States have often been initiated by pressure from various political and special interest groups and the media in response to national crises rather than in response to educational research (Cuban, 1990). What the authors of these three chapters add to recurring discussions of educational reform are scientific data that can help policymakers and educators decide more objectively what direction future attempts at reform should take. Although the benefit of research may be obvious within academia, it is sometimes viewed as a luxury in other sectors of American society. This attitude is reflected in dwindling governmental funds for educational research within recent years. For instance, only .11% of the Head Start budget in 1989 was devoted to research activities in comparison with 2.5% of the budget in 1974 (Zigler & Styfco, 1994). This cut-back occurred despite a need for research on how this program can be implemented more effectively and on its long-term effects on noncognitive factors, such as physical and social development. Policymakers and educators must be convinced of the benefits of systematic research in order to ensure that reform attempts are grounded solidly in fact instead of in "fad."

DIRECTIONS OF FUTURE RESEARCH

The work presented in the chapters by Stevenson, Stigler and Fernandez, and Resnick has the potential to influence the direction of future reform for mathematics education. Nevertheless, additional research that replicates, refines, and expands this work could make their suggestions even more compelling. What follows are four, broad suggestions for the directions that this additional research should take.

Suggestion 1: Establish Whether Various Factors are Causally Related to Mathematical Achievement

Using cross-cultural comparisons of the United States and East Asia, Stevenson and Stigler and Fernandez identify various attitudes, values, teaching techniques, and other school practices that they believe may partially account for why American children are performing more poorly than East Asian children in mathematics. Based on their research, they offer a number of suggestions for remedying this situation. Their suggestions generally involve altering the American educational system and cultural beliefs to resemble those of East Asia. These suggestions include increasing class sizes to allow teachers to spend more time preparing for lessons, providing children with more breaks during the school day, eliminating tracking, raising academic standards, and teaching children the importance of hard work in achieving goals (Stevenson & Stigler, 1992). In general, however, they have not yet established whether the cultural differences that they believe are important are merely associated with or are actually causing the performance differences. Thus more research is needed before prematurely making conclusions about the nature of the relation between these variables and outcomes in mathematics.

For example, future research might explore the extent to which cross-cultural differences in students' beliefs about the nature of intelligence actually contribute to differences in academic achievement. Recall that Stevenson and Stigler and Fernandez report that American children believe innate abilities play a greater role in determining school performance than do East Asian children. From this finding, the authors conclude that American children will be less likely to persevere when faced with academic challenges than East Asians because they will to a greater extent attribute their difficulty to a lack of ability and think that extra work will prove fruitless. At first glance, this conclusion seems warranted. American students move on to the next question more quickly when presented with difficult problems on timed tests than do East Asian students (Stevenson & Stigler, 1992). Furthermore, individual differences in beliefs about the nature of intelligence have been shown to affect academic performance within the United States. For instance, Dweck and her colleagues (Bempechat, London, & Dweck, 1991; Dweck & Leggett, 1988) have reported that children who view intelligence as a stable trait are more likely to avoid challenges, perform worse when faced with obstacles, attribute failure to personal inadequacies, and feel anxious than children who view intelligence as controllable and capable of being improved. However, Dweck preselected her subjects to represent two extreme viewpoints. She predicted that children who hold more balanced views of intelligence (i.e., believe it to be moderately changeable) will actually be the most adaptive because they will try hard when faced with a moderate challenge but not waste time attacking problems that are clearly beyond their reach (Dweck & Leggett, 1988). In the data reported by Stevenson and Stigler and Fernandez, this optimal pattern of believing equally in the importance of innate ability and in effort seems to resemble more closely the view held by Americans than that of the East Asians. Therefore it is not clear from the present data that the cultural patterns of beliefs described by Stevenson and Stigler and Fernandez actually account for the achievement differences. It is possible that the cultural differences in this area are not large enough to be causing the academic gap, given that neither East Asians nor Americans consider innate ability or effort to be the sole determinant of achievement. Other factors, such as differences in level of motivation and the valuing of education, may instead be largely responsible for American children giving up more quickly when academically challenged.

As a next step, experimental research is needed to provide more convincing evidence of the existence of causal relations; this research will not be easy to conduct. The relation between various factors and mathematical achievement is likely to be affected by the context in which it is embedded (Pellegrini & Stanic, 1993); thus causal links demonstrated in one culture will not necessarily hold true for other cultures. These causal relations may also differ across age groups (Super & Harkness, 1986). Consequently, practices that are effective within the context of Japanese culture (e.g., large class sizes) will not necessarily work as well in an American setting, and practices that help preschoolers learn may be less effective or no longer necessary with older children. Despite these difficulties, the search for causal factors will be crucial for the creation of effective intervention programs.

The need to establish causality also extends to the evaluation of mathematical intervention programs and other attempts at educational reform. It is not sufficient simply to demonstrate that such efforts result in students performing better in mathematics than they had prior to implementation. Rather, resear·hers should also explore which components within the intervention program are actually responsible for its success, and whether this success instead can be accounted for by other factors.

The need for such research becomes evident when comparing the efforts by Stigler and Fernandez and Resnick to raise mathematical competency by altering how Americans typically teach. Both sets of authors report success with their method, although they define success in different ways. Resnick reports that her year-long program resulted in scores on a standardized mathematics exam increasing from the thirtieth percentile to above the eightieth percentile; this improvement is especially impressive given that her population consisted of disadvantaged inner-city youth. Stigler and Fernandez claim that students who viewed a Japanese-style mathematics lesson later recognized this information more quickly or remembered it better than those who saw an American-style lesson, and thus were more actively trying to make sense of the content. However, Resnick's instructional methods seem to differ on two of the three factors (i.e., classroom discussion and pacing) that Stigler and Fernandez use to define their Japanese-style lesson. An examination of the classroom dialog that Resnick provides (see Fig. 4.6 of her chapter) reveals a much more rapid exchange between teacher and pupils than that typically found in Japan. The teacher is asking many directed questions in Resnick's lesson that require very short responses (e.g., "How many are here?"; "How did you count that?") instead of allowing students to explain at length how they solved a given problem as they presumably do in the Japanese lesson. She also frequently revoices or repeats what students say. These apparent differences in instructional methods reflect diverging assumptions that the authors hold about the ideal role of the teacher. Resnick believes that teachers should direct and scaffold classroom conversation; Stigler and Fernandez claim that this conversation should be student-directed. It will be important to determine if the reported success of both methods of instruction is due to the few specific targeted elements that they do share (e.g., an increase in time devoted to single problems and class discussions in comparison with typical American lessons) or to some other common factor (e.g., increasing students' attention to the material) that was not intentionally manipulated. The success of these programs could also be due to factors other than the instructional design, such as the use of teachers who had been involved in the creation of the study and are highly motivated to demonstrate the success of their intervention techniques. Further research would determine whether the outcomes reported by Resnick and by Stigler and Fernandez are maintained when these techniques are applied by new teachers in new situations.

The need to determine whether it is the intervention program rather than other factors that is responsible for improved outcomes seems obvious. Less apparent is the importance of determining which specific elements of a program are causing gains in academic achievement once the effectiveness of the program has been established. Occasionally the argument is made that if a program seems to be working, it does not really matter which part of it is causing the success. Proponents of this argument claim that due to limited research funds, it is more important to find new programs that work than it is to "tinker with" or "fine-tune" those whose efficacy has been established. However, due to limited funds allocated to schools (Kozol, 1991) and the few hours that American teachers have to prepare lessons (Stevenson & Stigler, 1992), it is important not to add ineffectual elements to school reform that would unnecessarily raise the cost (in terms of both money and time) of educating children. In addition, this kind of research is important because it can guide the creation of new intervention programs, both by highlighting the elements that may be most effective, and by clarifying current theories of cognition and instructional design. A thorough understanding of successful interventions will help inform theory, and improved theories will result in even better interventions.

Identifying which aspects of the intervention are causally related to the outcome tells little if the meaning of the outcome that is measured is unclear. The first experiment reported in the chapter by Stigler and Fernandez illustrates this point. In this study, the authors want to establish that students process information more actively and coherently after viewing a Japanese-style lesson as opposed to an American-style lesson. They assume that more active processing of the lesson information is associated with better learning and results in improved achievement. Quality of processing was assessed using three measures: speed of recognizing specific statements contained in the lesson and both quality and quantity of probed recall for this material. These measures seemed to favor those who viewed the Japanese-style lesson. These students recognized lesson content more quickly, recalled more information, and provided "higher quality" responses. Yet it is unclear to what extent these measures actually reflect how well the students learned the lessons, given that those in the American-style condition actually performed better on the post-test mathematical quiz than those in the Japanese-style condition. Success at solving relevant mathematics problems following instruction on that topic may more adequately reflect the ability of students to make sense of a lesson than more ambiguous process measures involving reaction time or recall. Although the conclusions of Stigler and Fernandez may nevertheless prove warranted, this example points to the need to consider the validity of measures. This task can be accomplished by providing converging measures for each variable of interest.

Suggestion 2: Expand Research on Teaching Practices to New Domains and Populations

Expand to New Domains. American children have difficulty with many academic subjects other than mathematics. International studies consistently rank the scientific understanding of American students as among the worst of industrialized countries (e.g., Lapointe, Mead, & Phillips, 1989; National Education Goals Panel, 1994). In addition, although scores on subtests of the National Assessment of Educational Progress have risen slightly over the past few years, the average level of achievement for each subject remains somewhat limited (Mullis et al., 1994). The 1992 assessment revealed that approximately half of the 17-year-olds had not acquired much specific knowledge about science. Sixty-four percent of these students could not write detailed essays, and 57% had difficulty comprehending lengthy reading passages.

Such statistics have not gone unnoticed. Along with the previously mentioned mathematics goal, increasing the rate of literacy and becoming first in the world in science by the year 2000 were selected as 1989 National Educational Goals. Many of the efforts aimed at reforming mathematics education, such as the establishment of grade-level standards, are also being applied currently to other subjects (e.g., by the American Association for the Advancement of Science, 1993).

Given the need for educational reform in these other subject areas and the apparent success of the teaching methods proposed by Stigler and Fernandez and Resnick in their chapters, it seems prudent to explore whether these methods are applicable to areas outside of mathematics. Resnick suggests that mathematics may be a "privileged" domain (and thus particularly appropriate to her teaching methods) for at least two reasons. First, young children begin school having already acquired a rich knowledge in this area, including principles for counting (R. Gelman & Gallistel, 1978) and an understanding of relations among quantities (Resnick, 1992). Second, for the most part, the logical relations learned early in this domain are maintained at higher levels of mathematics (Resnick, 1992). Thus children's early mathematical knowledge does not seem to require radical restructuring in subsequent years. It is likely that the success of the instructional proposals by Stigler and Fernandez and Resnick depends on these two qualities of mathematics knowledge. For example, teaching students primarily by having them derive solutions to problems in collaborative groups and then reach a class consensus on the correct answers may require a certain level of prior sophistication with the area being explored and an absence of incorrect beliefs that have to be unlearned and are resistant to change.

To some extent, several other domains taught in school may share this privileged status with mathematics. Many psychologists now believe that by 3- to 4-years-of-age, children acquire fundamental frameworks in such areas as physics, psychology, and biology (for a review of this literature, see Wellman & S. Gelman, 1992). That is, they develop a core, coherently-organized understanding of the ontological entities and general causal mechanisms encompassed by each of these domains. These frameworks, or skeletal principles, then facilitate the learning of additional, detailed information (R. Gelman, 1991). As a result, children know a lot about certain domains by the time that they begin elementary school. For example, young children already have acquired a somewhat sophisticated understanding of the animate-inanimate distinction. They realize that animate objects alone can self-initiate movement (Massey & R. Gelman, 1988), think and feel emotions (R. Gelman, Spelke, & Meck, 1983), grow (Rosengren, S. Gelman, Kalish, & McCormick, 1991) and possess unique insides essential to their identity (S. Gelman & Wellman, 1991). They also have begun to understand some specific biological processes, such as inheritance (Springer & Keil, 1989). In these cases where children do come to the classroom with preexisting knowledge of a domain, teachers may be able to apply the instructional methods that Stigler and Fernandez and Resnick have suggested (e.g. expecting children to create and reflect on solutions) with only minor modifications.

In some other domains, however, children may have little prior experience and limited conceptual knowledge that is directly relevant (e.g., history). Furthermore, for certain topics within privileged domains, students' core beliefs may conflict with an advanced understanding of the topic in question. For instance, R. Gelman and Meck (1992) have suggested that children have difficulty with fractions in the classroom because they tend to overextend counting principles to this case. This misapplication can result in such errors as judging reciprocals with larger denominators as being "more" than those with smaller denominators (e.g., 1/20 versus 1/10). As another example, students tend to believe that "no movement occurs without a force" rather than the Newtonian principle of "no acceleration without a force" (Carey, 1986). These errors seem resistant to change. In such cases, children may require new teaching methods (for example, the use of analogies) rather than methods which build directly on their existing knowledge of the domain being taught. Yet other aspects of the authors' proposals may still be relevant, such as the need to actively engage the class in the lesson materials and the need to scaffold student learning.

Expand to New Populations. It cannot be assumed that a particular teaching method that has proven efficacious with one age group will work well with another. Therefore it will be important for Stigler and Fernandez and Resnick to evaluate the effects of their teaching methods on various age groups and to be prepared to modify them accordingly. Granted, some experts (e.g., Chi & Ceci, 1987) believe that it is the acquisition of domain-specific knowledge independent of age that primarily leads to future cognitive development. If this is the case, then teaching methods may only need to be modified depending on how much prior knowledge the learner has in the area that is to be taught. However if, as other experts believe (e.g., Case, 1985; Sternberg, 1989), domain-general processes are at least partially responsible for cognitive development, then the age of the learner needs to be taken into account. For example, young children may not have the metacognitive skills to analyze problems or to reflect on their own and others' errors in the manner required by Stigler and Fernandez and Resnick. The systematic expansion of research to examine the effects of these teaching methods on new age groups will answer these questions.

Finally, future research should explore how the teaching methods proposed by Stigler and Fernandez and Resnick need to be modified in order to accommodate different groups of children, such as those with learning disabilities or other mild handicaps. Although over two million students currently are identified as learning disabled (Bateman, 1992), this population tends to be underserved by educators, researchers, and policymakers. The special needs of learning-disabled students frequently are not considered when deciding on the direction that educational reform should take. These students also tend to be excluded from or their data are not reported separately on national and state assessments of educational achievement (National Center on Educational Outcomes, 1992). Thus important data are lacking for this population which could aid reform efforts. Given that learning disabled students may come to the classroom with limited background knowledge, cognitive strategies, and metacognitive awareness (Montague & Applegate, 1993), it seems reasonable to assume that such students may benefit from a different combination of instructional methods than their nondisabled peers. Learning disabled students may lack the skills needed to benefit from instruction that is primarily student-directed. Instead, they may learn more when teachers model cognitive processes and then extensively guide their attempts at practicing them while only gradually withdrawing this support (Hutchinson, 1993). Keeping in mind the needs of special populations may be especially important for educational reform in the United States because, unlike Japanese students, American students do not have tutoring services widely available after school if they should fall behind in their course work. Furthermore, these students have the most to lose by the adoption of inadequate teaching methods (Mercer, Harris, & Miller, 1993).

Suggestion 3: Consider Broad Societal Factors More Extensively

Conducting rigorous scientific research almost inevitably requires focusing on a limited aspect of a problem. A full understanding and solution, however, often needs a broader frame of reference. In choosing to study instructional practices, Stevenson, Stigler and Fernandez, and Resnick are forced to ignore a wide range of other factors that may equally well account for the performance differences between East Asian and American students. Before concluding that instructional change is essential for improving the mathematics achievement of American students, Stevenson, Resnick, and Stigler and Fernandez must consider more fully the broader societal context in which classrooms, teachers, and students are embedded. That is, they must take a systems perspective (Sameroff, 1983), examining the multiple and interacting layers of influence in each culture that could be contributing to this educational problem.

Stevenson makes it clear in his chapter that he does not believe teaching practices to be entirely responsible for the performance gap between Americans and East Asians. He states: "Although some of the effects may be attributable to differences in schooling and teaching practices, cultural differences in beliefs, attitudes and the students' daily life at home must also be involved" (this volume, p. 137). Both Stevenson and Stigler and Fernandez point out what they think some of these cultural differences in attitudes might be. They note in the United States a belief in the importance of individual differences and a stronger tendency to attribute performance to innate ability than do East Asian students. In contrast, East Asians emphasize the similarities among students and are more likely than

American students to attribute performance to effort. Such attributions are thought to relate to students' motivations and academic achievement. Stevenson also briefly mentions some other contextual differences that may make teaching a more difficult job in the United States, and thus may influence how much students learn in the classroom: the greater ethnic, linguistic, and racial diversity of classrooms, the larger number of dysfunctional families, and the more frequent problems with discipline.

Other researchers interested in explaining students' academic performance within the United States have identified a large number of factors beyond the classroom context that influence academic performance. As Brooks-Gunn, Guo, and Furstenberg (1993) point out: "The antecedents of educational attainment have been studied using a variety of disciplines and conceptual models . . . Sets of antecedents include family factors, contexts other than the family, and individual characteristics" (p. 272). They list a number of family factors that have been studied in relation to achievement: (a) the family economic situation, including actual income and resource allocation, (b) socialization practices, including specific parenting practices, beliefs about parenting, and the modeling of behavior, and (c) relationship factors, such as family structure and father absence. Among the factors outside the family, they list the influence of: (a) the peer group, such as the effect of interacting with peers who have a limited commitment to education, (b) the neighborhood, which affects the level of exposure to negative influences, such as drugs and crime, or to positive influences, such as working adults, and (c) school factors, such as resources and quality of teaching. In terms of individual characteristics, they note that general cognitive ability and motivation are associated with school performance, but that these variables themselves are influenced by familial, school and peer factors (Brooks-Gunn et al., 1993). Note that these researchers see school factors as only one component in an intricate system of factors influencing academic performance.

Classrooms in the United States and in East Asia are embedded in very different societal contexts. What features of the United States context beyond the classroom may help explain the relatively poor mathematics performance of its students? These factors can be divided into those affecting the United States population as a whole, and those that primarily affect minority subgroups within this country.

Factors Affecting the U.S. Population as a Whole. It is estimated that over 20% of American children under the age of 18 live in poverty (Children's Defense Fund, 1994). Along with poverty frequently comes hunger, inadequate housing, and limited health care. Increasing numbers of American children are the victims of violence. According the Children's Defense Fund (1994), homicide is now the third leading cause of death among children 5- to 14-years-old and the second leading cause of death among youths ages 10- to 24-years. Many other children who are not the direct victims of violence either witness such events or live in fear of them. Increasing reports of child abuse and neglect confirm that danger is not only found outside of the home. Many American children live in single-parent families without the benefit of the financial and emotional support of two adults (Children's Defense Fund, 1994) or experience the emotional turmoil of parental divorces and remarriages. Children bring these circumstances and experiences with them to school. It is clear that hunger, sickness, sadness, anger and fear may detract from their attention and motivation levels in the classroom, regardless of the structure of the lesson. Some of these variables that can undermine educational readiness in the United States may be present to a lesser degree in East Asian countries. Certainly Japan comes out ahead of the United States on many key economic and health variables for children (UNICEF, 1993).

Other contextual variables may contribute to the academic gap primarily in secondary school. In both America and East Asian countries, children are bombarded by media images that encourage them to become consumers. Only in America, however, do approximately two-thirds of all high school juniors and seniors hold jobs in order to afford the products and activities that they have come to desire (Steinberg, Fegley, & Dornbusch, 1993). The number of hours students work in high school has been positively associated with later dropout and negatively associated with a number of educational outcomes, including scores on standardized tests (Marsh, 1991). This gap in achievement may be further widened by the different incentives which each country offers students for performing well in school. College-bound students in both regions are rewarded for their scholastic achievements with access to more prestigious colleges and enhanced employment opportunities. Greater differences emerge, however, when comparing the large groups of American and East Asian students who decide to enter the workplace directly after high school. For American students not going on to college, there is little if any correspondence between their high school grades and the types of jobs or salaries they receive (Hamilton & Hamilton, 1994; Rosenbaum, 1991). As a result, once students have made the decision not to go on to college, little incentive remains for them to perform to their fullest in high school. Many students are merely biding their time until they can get their high school diploma, which is about the only academic qualification many employers request (Rosenbaum, 1991). In comparison, high school grades appear to have large effects on initial job placement in Japan (Rosenbaum & Kariya, 1989, 1991). The authors note that this factor makes job allocations highly predictable in Japan, reinforces the schools' disciplinary control over students, and creates strong incentives to achieve in school even after the option to pursue higher education is eliminated (Rosenbaum & Kariya, 1991). Thus the differential performance of Japanese and American students (especially in high school) may be at least partially due to differences in the incentive structures for performance in the two countries.

Factors Affecting Minority Groups Within the United States. Even more than for students of the majority culture in the United States, the performance of particular racial and ethnic groups in this nation is challenged by obstacles both within and outside the classroom. Although clearly considerable variability exists within any group, the performance of many students from minority groups may be compromised due to differences in language or in styles of communication and interaction that do not blend with the mainstream classroom culture (Tharp, 1989). In addition, many minority students are subjected to prejudice and discrimination by their peers, teachers and the world outside the classroom, including the future world of employment (Ogbu, 1986, 1987). Students from these groups may realistically believe that their employment opportunities within mainstream society are limited by their minority status and may subsequently lose their motivation to work hard and excel in their school work.

Students from some cultural groups (e.g., Asian Americans), however, tend to do well despite their minority status (Sue & Okazaki, 1990). It is likely that some groups are discriminated against more than others in such areas as education and job placement. In addition, Ogbu (1986, 1987) points out that it may not be just the objective facts of minority status and discrimination that matter for students' performances, but also their subjective interpretations of their circumstances. Ogbu suggests that minority groups who came to the United States voluntarily with the goal of improving their circumstances (e.g. Asian Americans) may strive hard to conform and perform well within the dominant American culture. Other groups who were incorporated into the country involuntarily and then were subordinated by the dominant culture (e.g. some African Americans and Native Americans) may have much more mixed feelings about "playing the game," or working for self-advancement within the context of the culture that had oppressed them (Ogbu, 1986, 1987). Regardless of whether this particular thesis is correct, it is likely that attitudes towards education are shaped by the way children from minority groups are currently treated in the classroom, by complex interactions between culture and history, and by students' perceptions of all of these factors. These attitudes, in turn, affect minority students' motivations and academic performances.

Although a greater degree of cultural homogeneity is found in Japan, this country is not immune to problems of discrimination and minority group underachievement. According to Ogbu (1986, 1987), lower caste Buraku students in Japan do poorly on measures of literacy, scholastic achievement, intelligence, and high school completion when compared to the dominant Ippan students. In the United States however, the Buraku do as well as other Japanese American students. The fact that certain subgroups of Japanese students achieve better in American than Japanese classrooms and that Asian Americans tend to outperform other groups of American students suggests the importance of factors beyond the classroom in determining performance. A number of such factors have been explored in order to illustrate this point. The purpose here is not so much to argue for the relative merit of any particular explanation of the performance gap but to demonstrate that multiple and interacting factors need to be considered. Focused investigations of a limited number of factors affecting mathematical performance in the United States (such as those carried out by Stevenson, Stigler and Fernandez, and Resnick) are an important and necessary step to understanding this educational problem. However, just as the adoption of blue jeans in Japan is not likely to result in a culture of rugged individualism, it cannot be assumed that the adoption of a single aspect of Japanese culture (e.g., their style of classroom instruction) or other cultures will result in a dramatic change in the motivation and performance of American youth. There are too many other influences, which are both rooted in American history and dependent on its current social and economic circumstances. Stevenson, Resnick, and Stigler and Fernandez are taking the important step of examining what Americans are doing right and wrong as educators, and how they might do it better. While challenging the status quo of teaching in the United States, they will also need to ask how the societal context will support or undermine the instructional changes that they wish to institute. Indeed, some of the broader societal factors mentioned above may have to change first before their recommendations for instructional change will be effective.

Suggestion 4: Consider Potential Barriers to Mathematics Reform

There are a number of practical barriers to implementing classroom reform of the type suggested by Stevenson, Stigler and Fernandez, and Resnick. Although addressing all of these barriers is clearly beyond the scope of an individual researcher, this activity is necessary before effective reform can take place. These considerations include: making reform proposals more specific, examining structural components of the United States educational system which may impede the successful implementation of these proposals, and identifying the costs associated with various reforms.

Specificity of Reform Proposals. In order for educational reform to be successful, proposals must be implemented as intended. Gresham (1989) refers to this issue as "treatment integrity." Frequently, educational researchers offer general suggestions for how teaching practices should be altered. Yet specific instructions or additional training may be needed in order to prevent teachers from interpreting and applying the proposals in a variety of ways consistent with their prior beliefs about how students learn best and what materials should be taught (Tobin, 1987). Such variability could detract from the efficacy of the program.

This consideration applies to the proposals offered by Stigler and Fernandez and Resnick in this volume. For example, Resnick provides several instructional principles that she claims will result in students acquiring a deeper understanding of mathematics (what she labels as "math math"). One of these principles is "talk about mathematics; don't just do arithmetic." This emphasis on discussion may appeal to many teachers. Yet some of the teachers may apply this principle by leading students in a highly structured conversation about mathematics for the entire class period, whereas others may spend this time having students discuss the problem among themselves. Although the recommendations offered by Stigler and Fernandez and Resnick provide direction, further specifics will likely be needed in order for teachers to maintain the integrity of the authors' suggestions.

Structural Constraints of the Education System. Even if specifics are offered, current practices within the American educational system may impede the ability to successfully implement the reform proposals. Some of these potential obstacles are identified by Stevenson and Stigler and Fernandez in this volume. For instance, these authors mention that American teachers are in front of the class several more hours a day than their Japanese counterparts; conversely, the amount of time set aside for lesson preparation in Japan during school hours greatly exceeds that which is available in the United States. If the instructional techniques offered by Stigler and Fernandez and Resnick are to be applied correctly, American teachers will need more time preparing lectures than they now have in order to incorporate all of the elements identified as important by research. Stevenson and Stigler (1992) believe that this additional time can be obtained by increasing class sizes in the United States while reducing the number of courses for which teachers are responsible. They base this conclusion on the success of the Japanese at instructing up to 45 pupils simultaneously (Stevenson, 1991).

Before undertaking any reform, however, additional aspects of the educational system must be fully considered which could affect its success. In this case, larger class sizes in Japan may be possible in part because students who fall behind seem to have outside remediation mechanisms (e.g., after school *juku* programs, tutoring by parents) more readily available to them to substitute for individualized attention from the teacher than do American students. As a result, in order for reform to succeed, further components of the educational system may have to be altered or else new solutions generated if the proposed change is unfeasible or impractical.

Furthermore, structural factors may affect whether various proposals for educational reform are even attempted. Stevenson, Stigler, and Resnick have each noted that national curricula and standards exist in many countries besides those found in East Asia (Resnick & Resnick 1985; Stevenson & Stigler, 1992). In countries in which a single ministry of education controls such instructional decisions, reform can be implemented systematically and simultaneously for the entire populace. In contrast, the educational system of the United States is highly decentralized, with practices and regulations frequently varying by district or by state. Although several organizations such as the National Council of Teachers of

Mathematics (1989) have recently established standards and other proposals intended for national distribution, the trend within the past few years has been towards increased activity at the state level (Finn & Rebarber, 1992). Given the historial mistrust that American citizens have had with this arrangement, an empowering of the federal government with many additional educational decisions seems unlikely. Yet this organization may be needed in order for reform to be applied in all 50 states.

Costs of Educational Reform. Finally, before deciding on which educational reforms to implement, the potential costs of each option must be considered. Beyond the financial expenditures of generating new curricula and retraining instructors, certain American values may need to be compromised if educators are to adopt various practices from other cultures. For example, in mainstream American culture, the individual is emphasized over the group. This value leads to the assumption that children have unique needs and rights that should be respected (Spence, 1985), which is reflected in the prevalent American practice of tracking students. It also is evident in the establishment of special education as a distinct entity in the American educational system where teachers receive special training, separate funds are allocated, and special laws regulate the services. In contrast, the Japanese place all students (except those with moderate or severe mental retardation) in unsegregated classes in elementary school and automatically promote them through the grades (Stevenson, 1991). Elsewhere, Stevenson and Stigler (1992) have suggested that Americans should adopt this practice of not tracking students except for those with major handicaps. Yet this practice conflicts with American values which have strong historical roots. It is unclear whether parents would agree to replace the fairly individualized education that so many children are currently receiving with more generalized instruction.

Clearly educational researchers by themselves cannot be expected to overcome these barriers or even to consider all of them when creating proposals for educational reform. Such activities, however, may be possible through the collaboration with others. From the earliest stages of experimental work, researchers need to be in touch with others involved in various areas of education (e.g., policy makers, administrators, teachers, parents) in order to generate realistic and potentially effective proposals for change. Collaboration will ensure that expertise is provided from multiple domains and will prevent the alienation of important players in the reform process. Otherwise researchers' findings may be seen simply as interesting ideas which serve no functional value for reform.

CONCLUSION

Educational research has the potential to inform future reform movements in mathematics education within the United States. The chapters by Stevenson, Stigler and Fernandez, and Resnick in this volume represent significant contributions to this effort. Stevenson provides convincing evidence that a performance gap in mathematics achievement exists between the United States and other industrialized nations. He also has begun to identify some of the factors that may be contributing to this gap. Resnick has demonstrated the need to build on children's existing skills and knowledge when designing a mathematics curriculum. Stigler and Fernandez have explored the strengths of the East Asian style of mathematics instruction and begun to demonstrate its effectiveness with American students. In this commentary, we have identified assumptions shared by the authors and suggested ways in which each of their contributions might be enhanced and expanded. It is not expected, of course, that Stevenson, Stigler and Fernandez, and Resnick can respond to all of these suggestions personally. Rather, their efforts at providing systematic research grounded in theory and comparison provide a foundation on which other researchers can build. The ideas in these chapters, along with future efforts at mathematics research and reform, should in time assist in reducing the performance gap in mathematics between Americans and people from other countries. Even more importantly, this process should help to improve the mathematics confidence, enjoyment, and understanding of students within this country.

ACKNOWLEDGMENTS

Preparation of this manuscript was partially supported by a National Institute of Child Health and Human Development training grant (HD07151) awarded to the Center for Research in Learning, Perception, and Cognition at the University of Minnesota and by the Social Sciences and Humanities Research Council of Canada. The authors would like to thank Lisa Rohleder, Anne Pick, and Charles A. Nelson for their suggestions and encouragement.

REFERENCES

American Association for the Advancement of Science (1993). *Benchmarks for science literacy: Project 2061*. New York: Oxford University Press.

Bateman, B. (1992). Learning disabilities: The changing landscape. *Journal of Learning Disabilities, 25*(1), 29–36.

Bempechat, J., London, P., & Dweck, C. S. (1991). Children's conceptions of ability in major domains: An interview and experimental study. *Child Study Journal, 21*(1), 11–36.

Brooks-Gunn, J., Guo, G., & Furstenberg, F. F. Jr. (1993). Who drops out of and who continues beyond high school? A 20-year follow-up of black urban youth. *Journal of Research on Adolescence, 3*(3), 271–294.

Brown, J. S., & VanLehn, K. (1982). Towards a generative theory of "bugs." In T. P. Carpenter, J. M. Moser, & T. A. Romberg (Eds.), *Addition and subtraction: A cognitive perspective* (pp. 117–135). Hillsdale, NJ: Lawrence Erlbaum Associates.

Carey, S. (1986). Cognitive science and science education. *American Psychologist, 41*(10), 1123–1130.

Case, R. (1985). *Intellectual development: Birth to adulthood*. New York: Academic Press.

Chi, M. T. H., & Ceci, S. J. (1987). Content knowledge: Its role, representation, and restructuring in memory development. *Advances in Child Development, 20*, 91–142.

Children's Defense Fund (1994). *The state of America's children yearbook 1994*. Washington, DC: Author.

Cuban, L. (1990). Reforming again, again, and again. *Educational Researcher, 19*(1), 3–13.

Dweck, C. S., & Leggett, E. L. (1988). A social-cognitive approach to motivation and personality. *Psychological Review, 95*(2), 256–273.

Finn, C. E., Jr., & Rebarber, T. (1992). The changing politics of education reform. In C. E. Finn, Jr. & T. Rebarber (Eds.), *Education reform in the '90s* (pp. 175–193). New York: Macmillan.

Gelman, R. (1991). Epigenetic foundations of knowledge structures: Initial and transcendent constructions. In S. Carey & R. Gelman (Eds.), *The epigenesis of mind: Essays on biology and cognition* (pp. 293–322). Hillsdale, NJ: Lawrence Erlbaum Associates.

Gelman, R., & Gallistel, C. R. (1978). *The child's understanding of number*. Cambridge, MA: Harvard University Press.

Gelman, R., & Meck, B. (1992). Early principles aid initial but not later conceptions of number. In J. Bideaud, C. Meljac, & J. P. Fischer (Eds.), *Pathways to number: Children's developing numerical abilities* (pp. 171–189). Hillsdale, NJ: Lawrence Erlbaum Associates.

Gelman, R., Spelke, E. S., & Meck, E. (1983). What preschoolers know about animate and inanimate objects. In D. Rogers & J. A. Sloboda (Eds.), *The acquisition of symbolic skills* (pp. 297–324). New York: Plenum.

Gelman, S. A., & Wellman, H. M. (1991). Insides and essences: Early understandings of the nonobvious. *Cognition, 38*, 213–244.

Gresham, F. M. (1989). Assessment of treatment integrity in school consultation and prereferral intervention. *School Psychology Review, 18*(1), 37–50.

Hamilton, S. F., & Hamilton, M. A. (1994). *Opening career paths for youth: What can be done? Who can do it?* Washington, DC: American Youth Policy Forum.

Hutchinson, N. L. (1993). Students with disabilities and mathematics education reform: Let the dialogue begin. *Remedial and Special Education, 14*(6), 20–23.

Jones, L. V. (1988). School achievement trends in mathematics and science, and what can be done to improve them. In E. Z. Rothkopf (Ed.), *Review of research in education, Vol. 15* (pp. 307–341). Washington, DC: American Educational Research Association.

Katims, N., Nash, P., & Tocci, C. M. (1993). Linking instruction and assessment in a middle school mathematics classroom. *Middle School Journal, 25*(2), 28–35.

Kirsch, I. S., Jungeblut, A., & Campbell, A. (1992). *Beyond the school doors: The literacy needs of job seekers served by the U.S. Department of Labor*. Princeton, NJ: Educational Testing Service.

Kirsch, I. S., Jungeblut, A., Jenkins, L., & Kolstad, A. (1993). *Adult literacy in America: A first look at the results of the National Adult Literacy Survey*. Princeton, NJ: Educational Testing Service.

Kozol, J. (1991). *Savage inequalities: Children in America's schools*. New York: Harper Collins.

Lampert, M. (1986). Knowing, doing, and teaching multiplication. *Cognition and Instruction, 3*(4), 305–342.

Lapointe, A. E., Mead, N. A., & Phillips, G. W. (1989). *A world of difference: An international assessment of mathematics and science*. Princeton, NJ: Educational Testing Service.

Marsh, H. W. (1991). Employment during high school: Character building or a subversion of academic goals? *Sociology of Education, 64*, 172–189.

Massey, C. M., & Gelman, R. (1988). Preschoolers' ability to decide whether a photographed unfamiliar object can move itself. *Developmental Psychology, 24*(3), 307–317.

McKnight, C. C., Crosswhite, F. J., Dossey, J. A., Kifer, E., Swafford, J. O., Travers, K. J., &

Cooney, T. J. (1987). *The underachieving curriculum: Assessing U.S. school mathematics from an international perspective.* Champaign, IL: Stipes.
Mercer, C. D., Harris, C. A., & Miller, S. P. (1993). Reforming reforms in mathematics. *Remedial and Special Education, 14*(6), 14–19.
Montague, M., & Applegate, B. (1993). Mathematical problem-solving characteristics of middle-school students with learning disabilities. *The Journal of Special Education, 27*(2), 175–201.
Mullis, I. V. S., Dossey, J. A., Campbell, J. R., Gentile, C. A., O'Sullivan, C., & Latham, A. S. (1994). *NAEP 1992 trends in academic progress* (No. 23-TR01). Princeton, NJ: Educational Testing Service.
Mullis, I. V. S., Dossey, J. A., Owen, E. H., & Phillips, G. W. (1993). *Executive summary of the NAEP 1992 mathematics report card for the nation and the states* (No. 23-ST03). Princeton, NJ: Educational Testing Service.
Murphy, J. (1992). Restructuring America's schools: An overview. In C. E. Finn Jr. & T. Rebarber (Eds.), *Education reform in the '90s* (pp. 3–20). New York: Macmillian.
Murray, F. B. (1992). Restructuring and constructivism: The development of American educational reform. In H. Beilin & P. Pufall (Eds.), *Piaget's theory: Prospects and possibilities* (pp. 287–308). Hillsdale, NJ: Lawrence Erlbaum Associates.
National Center on Educational Outcomes (1992). *Being first in the world in science and mathematics. National Education Goal 4 and students with disabilities* (Brief Report No. 5). Minneapolis, MN: Author.
National Council of Teachers of Mathematics (1989). *Curriculum and evaluation standards for school mathematics.* Reston, VA: Author.
National Education Goals Panel. (1994). *The national goals report: Building a nation of learning.* Washington, DC: Author.
Ogbu, J. U. (1986). The consequences of the American caste system. In U. Neisser (Ed.), *The school achievement of minority children: New perspectives* (pp. 19–56). Hillsdale, NJ: Lawrence Erlbaum Associates.
Ogbu, J. U. (1987). Variability in minority school performance: A problem in search of an explanation. *Anthropology and Education Quarterly, 18,* 312–334.
Pellegrini, A. D., & Stanic, G. M. A. (1993). Locating children's mathematical competence: Application of the developmental niche. *Journal of Applied Developmental Psychology, 14,* 501–520.
Resnick, D. P., & Resnick, L. B. (1985). Standards, curriculum, and performance: A historical and comparative perspective. *Educational Researcher, 14*(4), 5–20.
Resnick, L. B. (1989). Developing mathematical knowledge. *American Psychologist, 44*(2), 162–169.
Resnick, L. B. (1992). From protoquantities to operators: Building mathematical competence on a foundation of everyday knowledge. In G. Leinhardt, R. Putnam, & R. A. Hattrup (Eds.), *Analysis of arithmetic for mathematics teaching* (pp. 373–429). Hillsdale, NJ: Lawrence Erlbaum Associates.
Riley, M. S., & Greeno, J. G. (1988). Developmental analysis of understanding language about quantitites and of solving problems. *Cognition and Instruction, 5*(1), 49–101.
Rosenbaum, J. E. (1991). Are adolescent problems caused by school or society? *Journal of Research on Adolescence, 1*(3), 301–322.
Rosenbaum, J. E., & Kariya, T. (1989). From high school to work: Market and institutional mechanisms in Japan. *American Journal of Sociology, 94*(6), 1334–1365.
Rosenbaum, J. E., & Kariya, T. (1991). Do school achievements affect the early jobs of high school graduates in the United States and Japan? *Sociology of Education, 64,* 78–95.
Rosengren, K. S., Gelman, S. A., Kalish, C. W., & McCormick, M. (1991). As time goes by: Children's early understanding of growth in animals. *Child Development, 62,* 1302–1320.
Sameroff, A. J. (1983). Developmental systems: Contexts and evolution. In P. H. Mussen (Series

Ed.) & W. Kessen (Vol. Ed.), *Handbook of child psychology: Vol. 1. History, theories, and methods* (4th ed., pp. 237–294). New York: Wiley.

Simmons, W., & Resnick, L. (1993). Assessment as the catalyst of school reform. *Educational Leadership, 50*(5), 11–15.

Spence, J. T. (1985). Achievement American style. *American Psychologist, 40*(12), 1285–1295.

Springer, K., & Keil, F. C. (1989). On the development of biologically specific beliefs: The case of inheritance. *Child Development, 60,* 637–648.

Steinberg, L., Fegley, S., & Dornbusch, S. M. (1993). Negative impact of part-time work on adolescent adjustment: Evidence from a longitudinal study. *Developmental Psychology, 29*(2), 171–180.

Sternberg, R. J. (1989). Domain-generality versus domain-specificity: The life and impending death of a false dichotomy. *Merrill-Palmer Quarterly, 35*(1), 115–130.

Stevenson, H. W. (1991). Japanese elementary school education. *Elementary School Journal, 92*(1), 109–120.

Stevenson, H. W., Chen, C., & Lee, S. Y. (1993). Mathematics achievement of Chinese, Japanese, and American children: Ten years later. *Science, 259,* 53–58.

Stevenson, H. W., Lee, S. Y., & Stigler, J. W. (1986). Mathematics achievement of Chinese, Japanese, and American children. *Science, 231,* 693–699.

Stevenson, H. W., & Stigler, J. W. (1992). *The learning gap: Why our schools are failing and what we can learn from Japanese and Chinese education.* New York: Summit.

Sue, S., & Okazaki, S. (1990). Asian-American educational achievements: A phenomenon in search of an explanation. *American Psychologist, 45*(8), 913–920.

Super, C. M., & Harkness, S. (1986). The developmental niche: A conceptualization at the interface of child and culture. *International Journal of Behavioral Development, 9,* 545–569.

Tharp, R. G. (1989). Psychocultural variables and constants: Effects on teaching and learning in schools. *American Psychologist, 44*(2), 349–359.

Tobin, K. (1987). Forces which shape the implemented curriculum in high school science and mathematics. *Teaching and Teacher Education, 3,* 287–298.

UNICEF (1993). *The state of the world's children 1993.* New York: Oxford University Press.

Wellman, H. M., & Gelman, S. A. (1992). Cognitive development: Foundational theories of core domains. *Annual Review of Psychology, 43,* 337–375.

Zigler, E., & Styfco, S. J. (1994). Head Start: Criticisms in a constructive context. *American Psychologist, 49*(2), 127–132.

8 An Evolutionary Approach to Cognition and Learning

William R. Charlesworth
University of Minnesota

This chapter is divided into five sections. First, the case is made that, despite their strong commitment to the genetic determination of phenotypic traits, evolutionary theorists have long recognized that phenotypic variability is also a function of environmentally produced changes in behavior and morphology. Because such changes take place over ontogeny, the study of development entered evolutionary thinking early in its history. Additionally, many in Darwin's time assumed that the various cognitive processes that existed in vertebrate species must have had a significant impact upon individual adaptation and reproduction over the course of evolution. For this reason cognitive processes were viewed as being significantly implicated in the evolutionary process.

In the second section of this chapter, I note how researchers influenced by the synthetic theory of evolution (hereafter STE—a combination of Darwin's theory of natural selection, Mendelian genetics, numerous empirical studies, and mathematical models) came to deal with cognition and learning (brain processes hereafter referred to as CL processes). The majority of early CL researchers failed, however, to address questions most relevant for STE because they did not study CL processes as mediating behavior in natural environmental settings. As a consequence, the question of the functional role CL processes play in natural selection has still not been adequately addressed.

Establishing a satisfactory empirical link between evolutionary theory and CL research has been delayed by various obstacles. Several of these obstacles are discussed in the third section of this chapter. The careless use of concepts, categories, and labels, misleading dichotomies, excessive faith in existing theories of limited generality, and the use of reductionistic methods to deal with complex phenomena are viewed as contributing to this problem. It is also argued that CL processes are so complex and so infinitely generative that most approaches to studying them at present can at best produce results of very limited generality. As a consequence, our current knowledge of CL processes is badly fragmented. While STE can pull some of these fragments together, a purely evolutionary approach, however, is viewed here as not sufficient.

In the fourth section, I argue that even if STE were to be taken seriously, much more is needed to identify and understand CL processes. To begin the quest for the "much more," I suggest we step back from current research paradigms and take a more synoptic view of CL than has traditionally been the case. As a way of operationalizing this view, I offer the "synoptiscope," a simple strategy to expand the domain of CL research. While entailing much more openness and conceptual elasticity than CL researchers may bargain for, use of the synoptiscope, I argue, is necessary if we wish to have a satisfying and coherent theory of CL processes.

In the final section, I note that adopting STE thinking and employing the synoptic approach to CL phenomena will provide convincing reason for the social importance of CL research. The solution to mounting global problems requires a better understanding of CL phenomena since it is human behavior, as mediated by CL processes and their consequences, that constitute the most serious source of such problems. Suggestions are made as to what aspects of CL processes should be studied.

EVOLUTIONARY CONCEPTIONS OF COGNITION, LEARNING, AND DEVELOPMENT

There is no longer any question that evolutionary theory is relevant for all life sciences including the human behavior sciences. It is important, therefore, to abandon the notion that evolutionary theorists are exclusively committed to genetic reductionism and hence reserve no significant place for the causal role environmental factors play in the emergence of behavior. Also, it is well-known that early evolutionary biologists assumed unquestionably that the abilities to cognize, learn, and communicate evolved to give organisms the flexibility to respond adaptively to environmental challenges. As Richards (1987) points out, many major 19th Century evolutionary theorists wrote copiously on "mind" and "habit": Darwin himself published a paper on the psychology and behavior of a developing infant and, at the end of his life, completed a major empirical effort on the "mental power" of earth worms (Darwin, 1877, 1890). For Darwin, as his followers, Galton (1907), Wallace (1891), and Romanes (1898), among others, "mental power" was the product of a brain that aided adaptation. Given differences in heredity (hence differences in brains) such power was distributed in unequal amounts across, as well as within, species.

In the decades following Darwin numerous evolutionary-minded thinkers—

Morgan (1895), Baldwin (1902), later Harlow (1958), Lorenz (1965), Stenhouse (1974), Riedl (1979), Humphrey (1976), Crook (1980) and, more recently, Donald (1991), Plotkin (1993), and Bogdan (1994), accepted as a virtual given that CL processes (more specifically, the abilities to acquire, store, process, retrieve, and apply information) evolved because they made significant contributions to each animal's ability to survive and reproduce. In short, recognition of a vital link between evolution and CL processes is both old and new. The link itself, however, is a long way from being satisfactorily substantiated by empirical research.

Evolution

Darwin's theory of evolution was based on the concept of natural selection acting on populations of living organisms. Populations changed over generations for two interdependent reasons—intrapopulation variation in phenotypes based on hereditary factors and environmental selection factors. New species (species being defined as populations of organisms reproductively isolated from each other) emerged as a result of selection factors acting upon inherited phenotypes. The mechanism of selection was simple: Intact organisms are capable of producing greater numbers of offspring than their environments can tolerate. The vast majority of organisms, however, fail to produce offspring because of countervailing environmental forces (hostile climate conditions, limited space and food, predators, diseases, etc.) that have a direct negative impact on their abilities to adapt and reproduce. Because individual organisms vary amongst themselves genotypically and phenotypically, their capacity to contribute descendants to subsequent generations also vary. As a result of persistent selection, successive populations come to vary sufficiently enough over time to divide into different species.

Heredity

That a part of the nature of organisms was inherited from ancestors was understood as far back as Aristotle. The mechanism of inheritance, however, was not clear until Mendel's (1866) findings became known (belatedly) to the scientific community at the turn of the century. Unaware of Mendel, Darwin struggled with different modes of inheritance including Lamarck's theory, which asserted that certain characteristics acquired during the organism's lifetime were passed on to offspring. Lamarck's hypothesis, while eventually discredited, is often evoked to account for the transmission of culture, an important product of CL processes. The science of heredity and its value in understanding populations changes has accelerated remarkably since the turn of the century. The same has been true for the science of many physical, behavioral, and psychological phenotypes. The science of the environment, however, that selects phenotypes, and their associated genotypes, has not.

Environment

Despite heavy emphasis upon inheritance, early evolutionary biologists gave equal theoretical status to environmental factors—after all, it was environmental factors that select for or against genetic mutations. Malthus' (1798, 1826) work on population and its controls provided Darwin with the key to natural selection. As Malthus convincingly argued, environmental factors play the pivotal role in determining the size and fecundity of populations. Apparently, his argument was so convincing no one tested it empirically. Research on the relationship between phenotypes (especially behavioral phenotypes) and environmental factors never really got underway as one would expect after reading Darwin. Only within recent decades of the ecology revolution have environmental factors begun receiving the systematic empirical attention they deserve (Bowler, 1992).

Resource Economics

STE theorists argue that if a trait is widespread throughout a species it must serve some important adaptive purpose, that is, species members must gain some benefit from it as well as pay some costs for it, the latter usually involving risks to survival or energy expenditure. Like any trait, behavior and its underlying brain mechanisms require energy both for their acquisition and construction as well as for their employment for adaptive purposes. Because energy sources lie in resources located in the outside environment every organism exists in a continuously precarious position. From the time it is created each organism must be able to obtain and defend its energy resources during all phases of its development. That research on resources was omitted from early formulations of the evolution of the "mind" gives added reason to the thesis that Darwin's theory of natural selection really never took serious hold in the psychological sciences (Charlesworth, 1992).

Development

The task of studying genes, environment, and resource-related behavior is complicated by the fact that their interaction generally occurs slowly and often unpredictably over the life span. Darwin recognized that development was the critical temporal dimension during which CL abilities were formed. He also recognized that during such a time interval, many events could happen that would ultimately affect both the process and outcome of natural selection. It was well understood in his time that individuals changed over developmental time for at least two reasons—exogenous (environmental) and endogenous (maturational)—and that such changes accounted for a significant amount of phenotypic variability within populations, variability that could not be directly attributed to genetic variations. The consequences of such changes were targets of natural selection along with directly heritable physical individual differences. Exogenous changes trigged by such factors as pathogens, deficient nutrition, accidents, social isolation, and so forth, could be identified and be shown to produce individual variability in survival and reproduction.

Whereas endogenously induced developmental changes are not as evident as the exogenous, they, too, Darwin felt, must be subject to natural selection. However, he was not sure what mechanisms were involved. In general, integrating ontogeny into the bigger theoretical picture of evolution was a major theoretical problem for Darwin as well as for others who followed him (Gould, 1977). Today, the role of age, development, and life history are receiving special recognition by STE theorists. As Bekoff and Byers (1985) point out, most animal populations are age-structured, hence age must enter significantly into the evolutionary equation—that is, on the genotype x environment side of the equation. But development also exists on the other side of the equation as a phenotypic outcome of genotype x environment interaction. It is this double-duty role of development that complicates the task of incorporating development into the evolutionary picture.

As is now recognized, evolutionary theory is a theory of adaptation, hence STE theorists invariably ask what adaptive function does any existing trait have, development included. It should be noted that the ability to develop, that is, to change from an immature to mature state, is viewed by STE theorists as a distinctive trait distinguishing major animal taxa. The actual process of developing, unlike many other traits, is quite costly: It takes much energy, exposes the organism to risks, and in many species subtracts significantly from reproductive time. Hence, as the theory requires, it must serve some very important functions which, if known, would help us understand why development evolved at all. According to Bonner (1958, 1993), the capacity to develop most likely evolved for a series of related reasons. Increase in animal size (and number of cells) appears to have had adaptive value during early animal evolution, thus supporting a strong trend over phylogenesis toward complex multicellular organisms. Along with more cells came cell differentiation and along with that special means for coordinating cell activity. Such coordination presumably made possible complex behaviors more able to deal with correspondingly complex environments and hence aid organisms that possessed them to exploit new resources. Populations of animals that evolved the ability to develop presumably enjoyed a reproductive advantage over those that remained relatively simple in their structure and function, such an advantage accruing not only from greater complexity but also from additional time to learn about the idiosyncratic environmental features necessary for survival.

Development and CL as Coevolved Adaptations

Given that STE theorists acknowledge the importance of CL and development, we can now ask what is it about their theory that would make them think differently than traditional developmental CL theorists. The facile STE answer to this is that human CL processes and development are evolutionary adaptations that have served our ancestors by aiding them to satisfy basic biological needs for survival and reproduction. CL and developmental processes are grounded neurologically in hard-wired capacities made possible by genetic predispositions found in all intact species' members. In other words, such predispositions are causally responsible for initiating and controlling species-specific embryogenesis that creates the neural substrates that ultimately make human CL processes and development possible. Such genetic predispositions have the ability to do this because they have been correlated over evolution with phenotypic adaptations that have enabled naive species members to survive and reproduce in species-typical environments.

From the STE viewpoint, then, CL and development are not processes that operate against genes and their survival requirements. To the contrary—they are processes that evolved to support genetic requirements by being in the service (usually) of survival and reproduction. *Usually* because animals and human can learn self-destructive habits or develop life styles that endanger survival and make reproduction impossible. Nevertheless, in virtually all species, CL-guided behavior acts like a homeostatic mechanism that enables each individual to maintain an optimal level of need satisfaction in the face of continual environmental challenges. While CL processes operate on an immediate, day-to-day basis, developmental processes, in contrast, perform a much different function over much longer time periods, acting like a long-term expansion mechanism that slowly and irreversibly enlarges the capacities of the organism to adapt to changing environmental conditions.

Brains, CL Processes, and Behavior

The processes of coordinating cell activity and acquiring information about environments have to have a physical site. At this point the brain enters the evolutionary picture—especially when a particular species inhabits an environment that requires that the organism detect, acquire, store, process, and appropriately apply information in order to survive and reproduce. By themselves, however, the brain and its CL processes are adaptively worthless: They need behavior to do the job of surviving and reproducing. The capacity to engage in unlearned behavior patterns (instincts) provided an infrastructure that animals use early in development when CL processes are being acquired. When this infrastructure is inadequate, CL processes take over and confer the necessary modifiability to behavior to make it adaptive. According to STE thinking, then, genes, brains, behavior, and CL processes coevolved and became linked over evolutionary time. As Alcock (1975), points out, "learning mechanisms" are products of a genetic-developmental program, which in turn are products of natural selection. Cognition as a critical feature of these mechanisms enters as a part of the adaptational complex.

Mayr (1974), a major architect of STE thinking, went further to enrich such linkages. He maintains that most vertebrates (especially mammals) inherit two genetic programs (ends of a continuum) that code for at least two types of brain programs—"closed programs" and "open programs." The former generate fixed behaviors, stimulus preferences, and reward mechanisms, an aggregate of features traditionally referred to as instincts. Open programs, in contrast, involve cortical functions that confer greater plasticity to behavior. Such functions make both learning and unlearning possible as well as create CL processes that permit planning and behavioral enactment of plans at an imaginary level. Mayr's thesis, however, went beyond simply rewording the instinct/habit distinction: As a Darwinian, he too brought in the environment. Closed programs are useful in controlling social behavior in species in which each individual has to send and perceive a rigid set of standard social signals. This is necessary for purposes of identifying species' members, sending and receiving species' relevant signals, and engaging in species' relevant cooperative and reproductive behaviors. Unexpected deviations from such expectations about the social environment (due to idiosyncratic learning or cognitive novelties) would clearly jeopardize such interactions. Open programs, in contrast, are brought into operation when species' members are compelled to be flexible in the face of changing physical environments such as finding prey or eluding predators. The capacities to learn and unlearn, to anticipate, evaluate, and to reason are ideal for animals whose resource support resides in complex and changing environments. According to most STE theorists today, humans evolved both programs to a high degree testifying both to their adaptational rigidity in meeting reproductive needs and to their flexibility in providing the means to meet them in complex changing environments. Today, STE theorists have succeeded (conceptually at least) in linking brain, behavior, and varying features of environmental challenges, all critical factors implicated in human evolution. A more unifying theory does not exist.

Human Evolution

The evolution of Homo sapiens constitutes the potentially richest picture of how learning CL processes appeared in the course of evolution in general. In the new and complex niches that emerged after millions of years of early animal and plant evolution, most characterized by increasingly specialized adaptations, a taxa of small altricial (immature at birth) primates appeared. Varying species of the latter were followed by hominids, a bipedal, large-brained offshoot of apes, who in turn were succeeded by genus Homo. Later Homo sapiens, a much cleverer member of the primate order appeared, one characterized by highly developed toolmaking, social structures, and hunting and gathering skills. The environmental conditions surrounding most groups of hunter/gatherers were for the most part Pleistocene—climate extremes, periodic food and water shortages, conditions that stimulated a need for collective group action to gather food, hunt, find shelter, and fight off predators and human competitors. In short, big brains and ontogenetic time to program them were vital to achieve such adaptations. But the programming needed adaptive information and this came in the form of culture.

Culture

For most early STE theorists it was obvious that culture was a major characteristic of humans everywhere. Alfred Russell Wallace (1891), a coconstructor, along with Darwin, of the theory of evolution by natural selection, was especially aware of this. However, most evolutionary theorists of his time paid little empirical attention to culture. It took over a century for STE theorists to begin conceptualizing how to address this question. Dawkins (1976) conceptualizes culture as the other source (besides DNA in the human gene pool) of inherited information passed from one generation to another. As genes are the units of biological transmission, so "memes" (from the Greek *mimeme* imitation) are the units, according to Dawkins, of cultural transmission, such transmission taking place from brain to brain by various means of communication (socialization, instruction, imitation, artifacts, etc.). Biologists like Bonner (1980), interested in animal tool-use and the acquisition of tool behaviors, view animal culture as accounting for local innovations of adaptive behaviors and artifacts. For Bonner, culture demonstrates the existence of tendencies and abilities accounting for the adaptive flexibility long known to exist in natural populations. Such a view is applied by STE theorists to the conceptualization of human culture (e.g., Boyd & Richardson, 1985; Dobzhansky, 1963).

In reference to the enthusiasm of biologists to recognize culture and thereby enable them to forge a long-waited link with human disciplines such as anthropology and psychology, it should be noted that the primary interests of a substantial majority of current STE theorists (see Tooby & Cosmides, 1989 below) are the ultimate factors associated with big primate brains and complex cognitive adaptations. These factors reside in human evolutionary history and in the environmental challenges that shaped such history. Given this, STE theorists ask ultimate (as contrasted with proximate) questions: What precisely were the physical, economic, and social forces that created problem solving abilities, abstract reasoning, counting ability, and language and what was the relationship between these forces and the relatively enormous and rapid expansion characterizing human populations?

Organism/Environment Interaction

The evolutionary interest in big brains, cognition, and learning focuses sharply on organism/environment interaction and the effect of such interaction upon reproductive success. Interestingly, while Darwin insisted that species' CL traits were tied closely to environmental challenges and opportunities, a whole century of intelligence research proceeded with virtually no concern for linking environment and cognitive ability. I made this point earlier (Charlesworth, 1979) as part of an argument that intelligence has traditionally been studied psychometrically, as a study of cognitive abilities, rather than naturalistically, as a study of everyday problem solving or adaptive behavior. The failure to tie CL abilities to environmental conditions is most likely the main reason CL theories and STE developed pretty much independently of each other.

Genetic Determinism

Despite the role STE theorists concede to development and CL processes in producing phenotypic plasticity, they never underestimate the conservative role genes play in ensuring that adaptive phenotypes inevitably appear in intact species members, perform specific functions, and do so generation after generation. Much of the active DNA in genes is assumed to have evolved to be prescriptive, that is, to ensure that specific neurophysiological mechanisms develop in predictable, species-universal and adaptive ways. STE theorists have been working successfully on this assumption. They are less successful, however, in dealing with the emergent processes that produce novel phenotypes during ontogeny. Such processes appear to result from experience and environmental contingency, epigenetic factors not yet successfully incorporated into STE formulations (Gottlieb, 1991).

In summary, then, STE presents us with a dynamic view of life, one that embraces both genetic as well as environmental sources of behavior determination, with instincts as well as habits and thinking as modes of adaptation. Two more specific points can be made about his view as they are represented today in STE research. First, Darwin's theory has become enormously generative of empirical research. Its hypothetico-deductive structure has made it possible to produce numerous testable hypotheses, virtually all of which are potentially falsifiable (Ghiselin, 1969). Such structure has also made it possible for STE to be generalized to other disciplines only casually referred to by Darwin. Current applications of STE are expanding to cover a wide range of phenomena ranging from moral systems (Alexander, 1987) sex and social status (Barkow, 1989; Daly & Wilson, 1978), to social and personality development (MacDonald, 1988), to cognitive algorithms (Barkow, Cosmides, & Tooby, 1992) and psychiatry (McQuire & Troisi, in press). Such efforts attest to the great generativity of STE thinking. The second reason that STE is so impressive is that it has enormous colligative power—that is, it has the power to pull together numerous domains of diverse phenomena in a very persuasive way.

EMPIRICAL ATTEMPTS TO LINK COGNITION AND LEARNING TO EVOLUTION

Many early ethologists and psychologists were influenced by certain aspects of Darwin's theory in their studies of behavior and CL processes. Ethologists focused on proximate mechanisms of perception, learning, and early experience;

psychologists, in contrast, focused on comparing CL processes in different species. Findings from both disciplines contributed greatly to the growing field of behavior research at the time. But their efforts were not in the direction ultimately taken by STE thinking. For the most part during the first 7 or so decades of the 20th century, ethologists and comparative psychologists did not grapple with Darwin's central thesis—namely, that of natural selection and the implications this thesis had for understanding behavior and its function in general and CL processes in particular. Today, things are different. Ethologists and comparative psychologists are aware of more aspects of the implications of natural selection. Also, evolutionary biologists, such as E. O. Wilson (1975), emerging from a rich empirical tradition of animal research have made a dramatic entree (under the label *sociobiology*) into the domain of CL process research. All three disciplines—ethology, comparative psychology, and sociobiology—are addressed briefly here, followed by promising efforts from CL researchers not recognized as being in the STE tradition.

Early Ethology

Early ethologists generally assumed that behavior was under two major classes of control—instinct and experience (learning)—and that various forms of cognitive processes were clearly mediating the latter. This assumption was recognized in their work on fixed action patterns and stimulus releasers as well as in their work on habituation, classical/instrumental conditioning, imitation, imprinting, and insight (Eibl-Eibesfeldt, 1989). As biologists, ethologists also recognized that many species are doubly equipped—first, to behave consistently and adaptively when faced with species-common problems, and second, to behave with flexibility when faced with local, idiosyncratic, and constantly changing problems (Thorpe, 1956). The concepts of facultative (learned, flexible) and obligative (instinctive, rigid) traits is a good example of this. This distinction was clearly acknowledged by early ethologists such as Konrad Lorenz. Contrary to many of his critics, Lorenz (1965) recognized that while most animal species operate on the basis of instincts they are also often capable of learning. His "innate teaching mechanism" conferred upon the individual animal the ability to learn what was locally adaptive without jeopardizing instinctive needs. His work on filial imprinting, in particular, is a classic example of his recognition of the collaborative role rigid gene-constructed mechanisms and environmental stimulation played in constructing adaptive behavior. Lorenz, Tinbergen, and other ethologists went further than comparative psychologists at the time by insisting that both instincts and the ability to alter behavior evolved as a result of the interactions of ancestral populations with environmental conditions. For them, no Lockian tabula rasa could have ever evolved since many environmental features (like predators or the absence of parents as learning models) require instant, unlearned adaptive responses.

The early ethological approach had several limitations, however, as far as CL processes are concerned. Ethology's emphasis upon observing behavior as it occurred under natural conditions kept researchers on the outside of the organism. CL processes could only be inferred from naturally occurring behavior over which the investigator had virtually no control. Controlled experimentation of well-defined variables was necessary. But this could only be legitimately done after extensive reconnaissance observation was done to establish what variables were appropriate to study (Lehner, 1979). As a rule, ethologists traditionally have felt that their first task was to observe, describe, and create a good ethogram (objective, comprehensive, and accurate) of the animal's behavior in its natural habitat. To study CL processes, complex experimentation was recognized as necessary but would have to come after behavior repertoires were identified and classified.

Comparative Psychology

Psychologists at the turn of the century took a different tack than ethologists in their approach to CL processes. Influenced partly by Darwin's interest in species comparison, early psychologists began their efforts by comparing CL processes in various species. For the vast majority of researchers, the ultimate goal was to discover general laws of learning and cognition that would hold for all species with relatively complex nervous systems. The discovery of such laws, it presumably was hoped, would support Darwin's key argument that continuity across species was evidence of descent from a common ancestor. As a consequence of such a research strategy, however, virtually all of the information comparative psychologists collected was on what we now call proximate mechanisms—the immediate conditions surrounding CL processes. The ultimate functions of such mechanisms, that is, the long-term adaptive purposes such mechanisms serve in regulating the organism's relationship with its environment, were neglected. The immediate consequence of this approach for our knowledge of animal behavior was to disconnect the organism and its behavior from its natural environment as well as from its reproductive function; the long-term consequence was to depart a great distance from Darwin and natural selection.

Reasons behind such a strategy are understandable. As many psychologists of their time who were anxious to separate themselves from philosophy and "softer" (clinical and educational) approaches to human behavior, the majority of comparative psychologists decided to conduct their CL research in controlled laboratory settings (Lockard, 1971). Although meeting needs for control (as well as for convenience), this strategy also allowed for deep probing of processes that would never be revealed by field observation. The strategy, of course, not only took the animal out of the picture of everyday natural adaptation, but also betrayed the mistaken belief that CL capacities could best be understood in terms of a phylogenetic scale, that is, in terms of a *scala nature,* the notion that animals can be scaled from simple to complex (on any trait) along some line of evolutionary descent. This notion has plagued early ideas of evolution in general (Hodos & Campbell, 1969).

However, to their credit, comparative psychologists were correct in assuming they could better than anyone else understand the internal organizations of the animals they were studying by using tight experimental and assessment techniques. They succeeded in this respect: Much has been learned about the general principles governing learning and cognition that are accepted today as givens even if not having satisfactory explanatory value (Bolles & Beecher, 1988). That animals would be cognitively organized in their relationships with (or putting it more strongly, because of) their environments may not have been clearly recognized by most comparative psychologists. If they did recognize it, they may have found this relationship too difficult to study.

The long-term consequences of their approach made comparative psychologists specialists—in species, methods, substantive foci, and in the concepts used to deal with them. The end result of their efforts was a number of contrasting reductionist paradigms that answered certain questions and raised many more, some very troubling. If learning was by definition nothing but associations or reinforcement, what about representation or cognitive maps; if only cognitive maps what about motivation; if only insights, what about the functions of need satisfaction: if only in rats and pigeons, what about in monkeys and chimps? Such restriction of focus and definition had operational advantages but were bound to work against achieving a general theory of CL processes. For certain, their efforts drifted very far from Darwin's theory.

Restricting definitions and conditions etc. to meet rigorous research standards also had unintended consequences. For example, by restricting CL processes to learned associations scratched out by experience on a tabula rasa, comparative psychologists inadvertently created a growing body of studies that gradually contradicted the tabula rasa notion. The belief that any animal could be taught virtually anything (within general limitations of course) and reinforced to retain such learning was destroyed by studies that showed this clearly was not the case. For example, Breland and Breland (1961) discovered that even most well-behaved animals were capable of reverting to very inappropriate ancestral behavior patterns if the training conditions somehow did not suit them. An additional shortcoming of such reductionism was that it ignored a very significant fact about animal behavior—namely that, not only does the natural environment influence learning contingencies (by acting directly and continually on the animal), but that animals themselves act on their environments and change them in return. Studying animals in controlled laboratories does not disclose the important phenomena of bidirectional and multivariable causation, nor does it disclose information on how animals react under normal social conditions. The presence, for example, of friendly or hostility conspecifics (all excluded from learning experiments for obvious reasons) can alter behavior immensely.

As a long-term consequence of both early ethological and comparative research paradigms, then, we still do not understand much about how CL processes are implicated in evolution. For theoretical and commonsense reasons we feel certain CL processes are necessary for adaptation. But there are still no convincing empirical data to support the general hypothesis that CL processes specifically make a necessary contribution to any species' survival and reproductive success. As Plotkin (1988) pointed out " . . . without the empiricism there will be no support for the notion that learning has a causal role to play in the process of evolution" (p. 161).

In addition to this shortcoming (after all these years of Darwin), it can be argued that one of the unintended consequences of much of the so-called early "Darwinian" approaches by psychologists to CL processes has been a fragmented and unnatural (as in unrepresentative) view of how animals and humans are altered by experience. This view, it is my contention, has contributed in part to today's sense of disarray and hopelessness about constructing a general satisfying theory of CL phenomena.

Current Ethology

A modern ethologist's interest in animal and human CL processes has at least two major beliefs behind it—first, that, as is the case with anatomical and biological functions in general, there is continuity in cognition over evolutionary time—CL processes must be present in a big-brained species (Darwin would allow no major saltations between species), and second, all phenotypes, including the capacity for behavior and cognition, are present in animals because they have served vital functions during the evolutionary history. An example of a modern cognitive ethologist will be noted here for illustrative purposes.

After working many years on orienting and navigating behavior in birds and bats, Donald Griffin (1976, 1992), an eminent ethologist, became convinced that a strictly parsimonious behaviorist account of their behavior was insufficient. Something more than SR machinery was behind such complex behavior. The simple "machine-in-the-animal" hypothesis has a long history in ethology, having got strong support by Loeb and other early mechanists such as Lloyd Morgan whose parsimony canon had a stranglehold on most research at the time. For decades, the machine hypothesis appeared to have controlled researchers more than the inferred machines controlled the animals they studied. The hypothesis ultimately had to give way to field observations of many species. Primate research, for example, was revolutionized by field observations such as those by Goodall (1986).

Griffin's move from behavior to mind was prompted by the fact that much of what his bats and birds were doing was much too complex to be accounted for in simple stimulus/response terms. As a consequence, he adopted the concept of cognition as the most appropriate way to conceptualize the mediating activity between activity between stimuli and responses. This is hardly new to CL researchers, but it is a big step for a behavior-oriented ethologist. Griffin, however, went one step further and, construed this mediating activity in terms of conscious awareness, a step that in my estimation is unnecessary and can cause big problems for him. Whatever the ultimate outcome of Griffin's particular research orientation, his focus on cognition has helped strengthen the growing link between ethology and CL research (Ristau, 1991).

Sociobiology

While initially studying social behavior and groups, sociobiologists have also turned their attention to CL processes. A major principle in sociobiological reasoning is that social animals, in order to maximize reproductive success, must cooperate with other members of their species. Being able to distinguish between genetic relatives and nonrelatives and act accordingly require relatively complex cognitive operations—for example, memory and recognition of specific individuals, calculation of the costs and benefits of interactions with them, and detection of noncooperators (Hamilton, 1964; Trivers, 1971). Furthermore, many species engage in social interactions that are clearly frequency dependent, that is, the individual must know how and when to employ certain strategies depending on immediate social and physical conditions (Maynard Smith, 1982). Inferring CL processes behind strategic behaviors is the most reasonable inference STE theorists can make to account for them. A recent elaboration on such reasoning is that of Barkow et al. (1992) who ambitiously propose a new field, "evolutionary psychology," its practitioners operating on the assumption that "understanding the process that designed the human mind will advance the discovery of its architecture" (p. 3). Their further aim is to apply this understanding toward what we currently know about culture. The thrust of their approach is mainly functional, namely to use an "evolutionarily derived task analysis to generate hypotheses about the structure of cognitive processes" (p. 11). Given that the human brain evolved when the process of economic adaptation was mainly hunting and gathering, a task analysis of the specifics of such adaptation would be drawn from paleontological data as well as from observations of current hunter gathers. Tasks such as finding food or a mate, parenting, tracking game, cooperating and communicating with others, require complex psychological mechanisms. Because analogs of such tasks presumably can be found in modern life as well, identifying such mechanisms, even though they have been shaped millennia ago, is possible. How these mechanisms function, then, is the primary task of the evolutionary psychologist.

Such an approach is interesting but not totally novel. Functionalism has been around a long time in psychology. What appears to be new is that the evolutionary psychologists views CL mechanisms as the "causal link" between evolution and current behavior. Natural selection, as Tooby and Cosmides (1989) point out, operates on the neural mechanisms that control behavior and consequently on the genetic programs that create such mechanisms during early ontogeny. Focus, therefore, should be on behaviors researchers have reason to believe serve as markers for decision-making algorithms that make adaptive behavior possible. Because it is impossible for the neurosciences at present to provide us with any specific information on the substrates of such cognitive functions as problem solving, abstract reasoning, and planning, researchers should forge links between what they think have been the major adaptational tasks facing our ancestors that required cognition and the mechanisms today that make such cognition possible (see Cosmides, 1989, for an interesting empirical attempt to demonstrate this). Attending to behavior per se (as most ethologists would do), sociobiologists believe, is an error since behavior is highly variable. Focus, instead, should be on the cognitive architecture lying behind the behavior. Humans in particular have been selected to possess that kind of neural architecture that makes them facultative strategists, that is organisms that are preeminently able to adjust their behavior to a wide range of environmental contingencies in order to optimize their survival.

Tooby and Cosmides (1989) also make clear a very important point often ignored by many CL researchers, namely that "behavioral variation is not an embarrassment to evolutionary theory, it is a prediction" (p. 281). Such variation is not only interindividual, but intraindividual as well since human behavior is highly context sensitive. Humans, in other words, have evolved the ability to be context sensitive because their contexts change rapidly at the same time their needs to survive and reproduce remain unchanged and insistent. If such needs are not met, individuals fail to survive.

It is much too early to comment on the prospects for CL research of current STE views. What appears to be a general shortcoming in the approaches of many ethologists and sociobiologists is that they appear to be working ideas that do not easily translate into more functional/behavioral research since it is behavior upon which natural selection operates (Alexander, 1990). That is, they do not concentrate sufficiently on those daily animal/environment interactions that produce functional consequences. Instead, they appear to remain inside the head which, while an obvious way to study cognitive "architecture," compels them to repeat traditional hypothetical postulations of what is there and hope that what they measure is indicative of what animals normally do to survive and how their brains function to achieve it. A recent theoretical effort by Bogdan (1994) on how to approach goal-directed (functional) behavior as an important evolutionary adaptation may help overcome this shortcoming. Such an approach is necessary to test hypotheses linking cognitively guided behavior to actual instances of survival and reproduction. Another possible soft spot in the sociobiologists strategy for CL research has to do with their heavy reliance on conjecture. Conjectures about cognitive demands made on ancestral hunter/gatherers may not produce as many novel insights as expected. Furthermore, some current adaptations (as sociobiologists recognize) may diverge so greatly from true cognitive demands that comparisons between modern humans and their Pleistocene ancestors are no longer reasonable. In their orientation towards STE, both CL ethologists and sociobiologists do not appear, for the most part, to have departed from traditional cognitive mechanism research. This means much of the research they may consider undertaking may have already been attempted under different labels or are in the process of being carried out (as is noted later). Barkow et al. (1992) are aware of this and, in line with the Darwinian tradition which is to aim for conceptual integration across disciplines, agree to learn to "accept with grace the irreplaceable intellectual gifts offered by other fields" (p. 12).

Darwin's Minimal Impact

From all that has just been noted one would expect that the evolutionary approach to understanding learning, development, and cognition has had the potential to jump off to a good empirical start—at least in evolutionary biology circles. This, however, does not seem to be happening. Plotkin (1988) and Tooby and Cosmides (1989) recognize this as do others in other areas of psychology (Costall, 1986; Morss, 1990). A major feature of STE thinking is the critical role played by natural selection, a role that is virtually never addressed in general psychology, particularly in developmental psychology (Charlesworth, 1992). Piaget was much more Lamarckian, and Freud more Haeckelian, than Darwinian. Darwin's effect on cognitive psychology per se is not any different. In discussing the four major views of "the nature and development of human cognitive systems" (plus other approaches), Flavell, Miller, and Miller (1993) report no evidence of any significant role STE in the formation of all four views and approaches. Why this should be the case may simply be due to widespread belief that CL processes have escaped evolutionary selection and hence can not be subject to the same methods of empirical analysis applied to anatomy and behavior.

Exceptions

There are interesting minor exceptions to the general trend of current CL evolutionary research just mentioned that have STE potential. Some are empirically underway and some more suggestive, but not as yet generative of empirical research programs. Scarr (1983) proposes that we consider infant intelligence as a species adaptation, invariant in its general features across all intact species' members, but variable across individuals in its details. This distinction is an important one that underlies much of evolutionary thinking since it parses CL processes into those upon which selection forces apparently do not operate and those upon which it does. In addition to Scarr, others, such as Gigerenzer and Hug (1992), grapple with questions of domain-specific reasoning, social contracts, and cheating. Such efforts epitomize important issues in evolutionary thinking about cognition, its development, and their adaptive significance.

In addition to those just mentioned, there has been a strong focus in research on mental retardation on the role of learning and cognition in individual adaptation, especially as it is measured using naturalistic observation (Sackett, 1978). Such emphasis, however, makes no reference to STE, but does deal with CL proximate factors whose adaptational role in the life of individuals must likely influence survival and reproductive success. Recent and current research on everyday cognitive skills (e.g., Rogoff & Lave, 1984, and Resnick, this volume), is clearly within this category. Research in the area of memory has made recent progress stimulated by Neisser's (1982) insights on the current CL theory. Acknowledging the current discouraging condition of cognitive theorizing, Neisser (1982) makes a cogent plea for studying memory in "natural contexts," enlisting in the process a number of interesting research efforts to support his point. Neisser also recognizes the influence of ethologists in altering modern learning theory by insisting on knowing "how animals really behave in their natural habitats" (p. 10), but points out that "behavior biologists" are still far from agreement on many theoretical issues. Further, on the theme of memory in every day settings, are efforts by Gruneberg, Morris, and Sykes (1988) to report on and stimulate interest in research on the nature and function of memory in practical settings.

The aforementioned research promises new areas of research that will definitely complement that of the ethologists and sociobiologists. Some empirical work has been done in traditional psychology connecting learning and cognition to adaptational success (e.g., years of education), however, such work (to my knowledge) has usually been non-theoretical, nonsystematic, and sporadic. Empirical studies seeking possible connections between learning/cognition and basic biological functions of survival and reproductive success in particular appear virtually nonexistent. Why this may be the case is part of the theme of the next section.

OBSTACLES TO LINKING CL RESEARCH TO EVOLUTIONARY THEORY

Why no empirically productive link developed between CL research and evolutionary thinking, despite a century available to do so, is an interesting question historians of science have to answer. In the present section, two general obstacles to establishing such a link are proposed, one consisting of the way CL researchers have conceptualized their efforts and the reductionistic stance they took to operationalize their concepts, the other consisting of the nature of CL processes themselves. The effects of both are viewed here as greatly responsible for the fact that CL research is fragmented and hence still a long way from developing any semblance of a unified theory.

Concepts, Categories, and Their Labels

Concepts, categories and their labels are indispensable features of *knowing*—without them, creating a body of knowledge is impossible. However, concepts, categories and labels often have a way of mutually reinforcing each other's existence in a misleading way as far as the empirical truth of their referents is concerned. They also have a way of establishing boundaries that separate their empirical referents, and hence their research disciplines, from all others. A few conceptualization problems are addressed here specifically as obstacles to linking CL research to STE thinking. I intentionally chose examples of researchers informed by biology but apparently not by STE; those not informed by biology have just as many such problems.

Many CL researchers frequently use conceptual labels whose meanings simply do not mesh with STE thinking. An example is the concept of *constraints* or *boundaries* on learning. The term, emerging out of empirical findings such as Breland and Breland's (1961) operant conditioning studies, and Garcia, McGowan, and Green (1972) taste aversion studies, refers to the fact that members of a particular species can not learn everything, or learn some very specific things on one trial or during one critical period only, because their learning mechanisms have been constructed in particular way by evolution. The term was frequently evoked to account for the failure of general learning theory to apply its principles to all species capable of learning (Hinde, 1982). The problem with the term *constraints* is that it connotes that any species could learn virtually anything (tabula rasa) if it were not for evolved genetic constraints. Such a connotation, however, is not consistent with STE thinking—different species evolve different needs and perceptual/ cognitive abilities in response to the particular ecological demands made upon them. No more and no less: capacities evolve, not limitations. Constraints (as well as the behavior geneticists' concept of reaction range) exist only in the minds of those who believe that if it were not for them, animals could do much more (or less) than they do. Today, we realize that if we knew our research animals' natural behavior, we would neither view animals as constrained nor as potential tabula rasae upon which experience continually writes new ways of doing things. We would view them as animals whose ancestors have adapted more or less successfully to their environments. We would also not have to view them as research subjects waiting to be taught how to speak or solve complicated problems, thereby closing the gap between them and humans (as Darwin felt was necessary to keep his theory intact).

Other similarly misleading terms are *prepared learning* (Seligman & Hager, 1972) or *privileged learning* (Cary & Gelman, 1991). From the STE point of evolved traits have no teleological properties-they makes no preparations for and confer no privileges upon future use. A trait is simply the consequence of earlier adaptations which evolved under certain recurring environmental conditions. As an adaptation, a trait remains useful as long as such conditions continue. If such conditions fail to continue, the trait is not disappointed. I should note here that biologists had an analogous problem with the concept of preadaptation that was evoked to account for the apparently abrupt appearance of a physical structure, for example, the elephant's trunk apparently began as an olfactory organ which over a rapid period of evolutionary time "became" an organ for manipulating objects. The olfactory organ was first labeled a preadaptation but because of the teleological implications of the term *preadaptation* was replaced with exaption or "exaptation" (Gould & Vrba, 1982).

Although much interesting research has emerged from replacing the traditional classical approach to learning (that there are general laws of learning and all animals possess an equipotentiality to learn—Pavlov, Skinner, Estes) with that of species-specific boundaries and preparednesses, CL research did not (still does not) face up to STE thinking and the methodology that would help operationalize it. The point is that boxing in species' abilities with boundaries will ultimately lead to disappointment since CL abilities provide an ongoing dynamic changing of animal adaptations—but on the animal's terms only. Pushing animals to acquire or demonstrate human CL abilities will provide knowledge less about animal CL processes than about human motivation. The essence of the STE argument is to take species as they are and try to find out why they got that way. Circus owners and television advertisers can try to make them into something else.

Another conceptualizing problem that has plagued much animal CL research is the already-mentioned concept of *scala naturae*, the scale applied often to CL phenotypes like intelligence, for example, that ranges on a continuum from low in amoeba to high in primates (Hodos & Campbell, 1969). Such behavior scaling, although appropriate, perhaps, for ordering DNA, brain size, or some physical trait that can be quantified and scaled, misconstrues the reality of species' differences in behavioral adaptation. Each species evolves its CL behavioral capacities for adaptations in response to its specific ecological niche, not in accordance with an ideal standard shared by all species. The implications for CL research of adopting the scale or rejecting it are not minor. For example, one can either decide to study chimps to understand human CL and its evolution, or one can study hunter gatherers whose current social structures and economies match to at least some extent those of our ancestors in terms of the CL demands required to deal with them. That we share a great portion of our DNA with chimps appears, at first glance, to make them a good comparison species for studying common CL abilities. However, chances are that many specific human CL abilities, stimulus preferences, and perceptual abilities, in particular, are products of different selection pressures than those that chimps had to face for the approximately six million years humans and chimps diverged from a common ancestor. While humans and other primates have many obvious physical and behavioral traits in common, humans and social carnivores also share many behavioral traits such as group hunting skills and social structures which reflect the survival and reproduction demands put upon them by their economic demands. Give this, CL comparisons between humans and social carnivores can be just as important as comparisons between humans and other primates.

Species-specific human CL abilities, especially language ability, appears to have emerged during the Pleistocene when our ancestors were hunter/gatherers and needed them. In light of this it seems reasonable to argue that cognitive scientists interested in the evolutionary origins of human CL processes should best study how present-day humans employ their CL and language abilities to adapt to a hunter-gatherer (as well as modern) conditions rather than solely seek comparisons with other primate species, a long tradition in much comparative psychological research.

Dichotomies

As double conceptualizations, dichotomies can raise serious problems. They may be initially convenient for partitioning an amorphous mass of information, but can quickly turn out to be inadequate when the facts come in. CL researchers have their share of dichotomies— conditioned/unconditioned responses, competence/performance, sensorimotor/operational intelligence, episodic/semantic memory. Such dichotomies usually have a grain of truth to them, but can be misleading if they suggest that the phenomena they refer to are in reality discontinuous, mutually exclusive or, worse yet, in functional opposition to each other. Some may be, some not. Only viewing them within a broader context (a point made in the next section) will decide. It seems a waste of time to insist that a dichotomy is empirically real when the empirical basis that led to creating it is very shallow.

When discrete categories (often the prime result of dichotomizing) are claimed to represent the natural order of things (i.e., when they are reified) and scientists proceed to build an edifice of theory upon such reification intractable problems can arise. A classic example of the category problem in biology is the category of species. As Mayr (1982) points out the concept of species as distinct, mutually exclusive biological entities, made it virtually impossible to conceive of evolution as a process of descent with modification. Only when species were viewed as diverse populations of individuals similar in some ways but different in others was it possible to conceive of speciation occurring—that is, some individuals splitting off from the larger population and gradually forming a different population. When two populations evolve to a point when they are reproductively isolated from each other do they become separate species (reproductive isolation being the acception definition of a species). In arguing this point Mayr makes a strong case against typologizing phenomena that in actuality are not types, but clusters of individuals sharing some traits and not others.

Comparative psychology had a similar problem when it was a common practice to study *the white rat*. As Mayr would ask, Which one? The same can be asked of the terms *the 2-year-old, the preoperational child,* and *left brain thinking*. Ethologists encounter individual animals and seek ways to cluster them behaviorally and anatomically before making generalizations that will allow clustering them into species members. The clustering process, however, cannot terminate in a type. No types exist in the empirical domain: they are invented as tools for thought and communication. Unlike the physical world, the biological world has no clean-cut uniformities, but consists rather of individuals and individual adaptations acting on the basis of laws only partly understood or not yet discovered. Because of this, biologists and psychologists who model their disciplines after the physical sciences are bound to run into difficulties.

Methodological Reductionism

The way phenomena are conceptualized and labeled determine the methods used to study the phenomena. A major problem arises when a particular method is arbitrarily employed to the exclusion of all other methods. The effect of this practice is to produce diminishing returns in generating new connections with other disciplines (or theories) dealing with the same phenomenon. Two major examples of such practices are limiting research solely to psychometric measurement or to experimental testing. Although both methods are obviously important research approaches, their exclusive use reduces CL phenomena to the narrow range of variables only those using the methods can successfully study. The exclusion of other variables not only ultimately limits the generalizability of the results produced by the method, but also creates definitional and priority barriers to other CL research efforts. In short, the effect of "methodological reductionism" (reducing phenomena to prescribed units), alters the significance of the phenomenon in its relations to everything else with which it in reality has contact.

Although reductionism can never be avoided in science the level at which it is employed is decisive depending on the complexity of the phenomenon and the how much is understood of it. Animal behavior is very complex and still relaatively little understood. Ergo, the level of reduction should be limited at first to forming loosely bounded categories based on observation in natural (or semi-restricted) environmental conditions. This has been the time honored approach of ethologists who so far have had great success with it.

CL Processes: Complex and Infinite

If behavior is complex, CL processes (unconstrained by physical limits on movements of muscle and bones), are even more complex, astronomically so. Given such complexity, it is understandable that CL researchers put finite boundaries around the phenomenon of their choice as quickly in their research careers as is professionally acceptable. This can be accomplished a number of ways—a popular one being to focus on precise proximate factors and to frame around them specific questions of causality and development that can be answered relatively quickly. Doing this, of course, is achieved best by ignoring larger problems of function and of the ultimate or evolutionary factors that created the CL mechanisms. Ignoring large issues, though, from the STE point of view means producing a partial description and explanation thereby running a great risk of being unnecessarily parochial or down right erroneous.

Cognition has the intriguing feature of being covert in its operation as well as infinite in it productive capacity. Both features conspire to confound empirical research. The covert feature of cognition is especially frustrating when attempting to make sense of behavior on the basis of observation only. This feature leads to tightening of stimulus control by eliminating naturally occurring conditions. Relying instead on interviews of research subjects only raises other problems. Language is enormously rich in its potential to do anything the speaker wants without disclosing anything about cognitions. One can cognize empirical truths, mathematical laws, as well as myths and falsehoods without disclosing anything reliable or valid to researchers. From the STE point of view, confabulation and guile are complex human adaptations whose function is not to validate or invalidate theories, but to maximize the persons success in social situations (Rue, 1994). The covert and infinitely slippery quality of cognition are two important reasons for the existence of behaviorism.

The problem of the infinite generative capacity of CL processes (including, of course, language) is the most interesting. It has to do basically with the fact that the human nervous system appears capable of unlimited modifiability; it is so complex, so creative, and so generative (compared to anything in the known universe), it has an unrestrainable ability to produce sounds, images, meanings, objects capable of expanding its own activities. Alfred Russell Wallace was impressed with the intellectual abilities of the so-called primitive peoples in various parts of the world with whom he spent much time. His basic thesis was that their intelligence far exceeded the demands made upon their cognitive abilities. Given this, he felt natural selection could not have selected for them, since there were no selection forces at the time to do the job. It was generally known during his time that so-called "savages" invented things that had no utilitarian value as well as possessed the ability to adapt to radically different life styles if forced. Such plasticity on their part in the face of novel challenges must have surely been noticed by Darwin on the Beagle voyage. One of his companions was a Fuegian hostage, Jemmy Button, who was being returned to his native land after three years of forced exile in Europe during which Darwin noted were "sufficient to change savages into, as far as habits go, complete and voluntary Europeans." After "becoming" a European, Button was able to shed his European ways and join his cannibal friends within a year after leaving the Beagle.

Fragmentation of CL Research

The combination of the aforementioned problems has, in my estimation, resulted in a field that is conceptually confused, greatly fragmented and consequently of limited value for those who wish to form a unified theory of CL processes as well as for those who wish to put CL knowledge into socially useful practice. An example of this fragmentation is documented by White (1985) in a survey of seven introductory cognitive psychology text books published between 1979 and 1980. White counted all their references which amounted to over 3,200. Of the 3,200, 19 were cited in all texts; 144 were cited in at least four texts, and 2,620 publications appeared only once in one text. Such lack of overlap could be due to at least two reasons—the authors simply were unaware of most publications outside their domain of expertise, and/or they were aware but found no reason to cite them because they did not fit in within the conceptual framework the authors adopted for their book. Actually, no narrow partisanship need have been involved—only idiosyncratic conceptual barriers could produce such an effect with no special effort on anyone's part.

If text book experts are not agreed on what is important to teach the next generation, one can ask to what extent the experts can justify their major principles and concepts. In the area of cognitive development, a great and interesting variety of perspectives of intellectual development exist at the moment, but no integration of them is (or can?) at present being made. Nor can such perspectives form any plausible links with STE thinking. Perhaps the only integration possible at this time is simply to declare that learning, information processing, cognitive representation and so on are all functionally active in aiding individuals solve problems, that all such CL abilities overlap in some respects but still preserve their insular *modularity,* and that sooner or later there will be sufficient neurological evidence to help clear up the confusion.

Such fragmentation, of course, does not only characterize cognitive psychology: It is also true of psychology in general (Lykken, 1991; Meehl, 1978, 1990) and developmental psychology in particular. After an extensive review of the discipline, Parke, Ornstein, and Rieser (1994) conclude that the field of developmental psychology still lacks an "overarching paradigm" to integrate the vast areas of research findings as well as to "replace the disfavored grand theories" that have influenced the field for so long (p. 64). Such fragmentation becomes apparent daily when researchers are compelled to come up with a string of qualifying statements about what at first seemed clear cut when they started their research. Those who have experienced first hand the birth, growth, and demolition (partial or complete depending upon one's commitments) of our major theories can recognize this. Such a state of affairs is also true in psychiatry which has, for over a century, been plagued by "conceptual pluralism," and "a mosaic of well-entrenched ideological, professional, and economic groups not easily dissuaded from their views" (McQuire & Troisi, in press).

It should be quickly pointed out that deep problems with theories of learning and development were recognized decades ago. Skinner (1950), for example, wondered (for other reasons, of course) whether theories of learning were necessary. Later, Jenkins (1974) expressed similar concerns. Historically, what seems to have happened is that early psychologists built theories and publicized them very successfully even though they were built on shallow empirical foundations. Although their theories have to some extent enriched our field and generated interesting research, they have also turned out to be limited in degree of generalization or misleading. As for the present, I argue we should take them less seriously and get on with the task of expanding the foundation of our empirical research to be much more inclusive of phenomena than has heretofore been the case. A way to do this is the topic of the next section.

THE SYNOPTIC APPROACH: A STEP TO A SOLUTION

As noted earlier, Darwin's theory is persuasive because it successfully synthesizes a very wide range of diverse phenomena. Darwin made it a point to explore all facets of what he was studying by collecting and collating information from a wide variety of sources—journal articles, field observations and experiments, technical reports, travelogues, correspondence, etc.—as well as from a wide range of species. The virtue of this effort was that it opened his theory to numerous avenues of verification as well as of falsification. The success of Darwin's approach was not lost on later students of biology. Decades after Darwin, Niko Tinbergen (1963) urged ethologists to take the broadest view possible of the particular behavior they were interested in. His rule of thumb was to ask four questions of behavior: questions of proximate causation, adaptive function, phylogenetic status, and development. The application of this rule over the past several decades has undoubtedly contributed to the recent plethora of ethology research.

In the present section I urge that an approach in the same direction (but more radical) be adopted. This approach is aimed at expanding the borders of CL phenomena. The fact that CL research is in conceptual disarray and badly fragmented may convince many that a more rigorous tightening of method is necessary, that the field must become more specialized and reductionistic, and that more precisely defined provincial boundaries be established. But the opposite argument can also be made—that the full range of CL phenomena has not been adequately sampled, hence loosening up on methods and opening existing boundaries is now the best strategy-even if it will lead temporarily to confusion and delay the construction of new theories.

To operationalize this argument, two concrete suggestions are offered here. One is that CL researchers forge a better connection with STE. This connection can expand our understanding of the functions of CL processes and the origins of their brain mechanisms, as well as improve our general understanding the role of CL processes of human adaptation. The second suggestion is that CL researchers "step back" from reductionistic analytic methods and take a much more synoptic view of CL phenomena. There is no space to develop in any depth the conceptual and historical reasons why I think this should be done. I discuss some of these reasons in a paper addressing Darwin's ideas and their influence on developmental psychology (Charlesworth, 1994). In addition, I urge ethologists and sociobiologists to take a synoptic view of human adaptation by insisting on obtaining field observational data to test hypotheses linking behavior to actual instances of adaptation (Charlesworth, 1994). As is generally known from recent primate research, field observation has revealed a much wider range of behavioral phenomena than any other approach. For now a brief discussion of the synoptic view is all that is possible.

The Synoptiscope

"Stepping back" can be achieved by using a simple conceptual tool I label here the *synoptiscope*. Unlike physical tools such as microscopes or telescopes, the synoptiscope entails no costs other than search time and some stationery. It consists of two major components, a strong motive to use and stay with it, especially when one's research is in a rut, and five steps:

1. search widely for variables (hereafter V) that are in any way associated with the phenomenon one is interested in (hereafter P),
2. establish the nature of the connections between V's and P as well as between V's and each other,
3. estimate, whenever, possible, the strength of these connections,
4. determine, whenever possible, the amount of P (variance or other measure) accounted for collectively by the V's, and
5. iterate the first four steps until a "satisfactory" picture of P emerges.

Using the synoptiscope often means proceeding haphazardly, taking advantage of a wide range of traditional and nontraditional ways to turn up new V's and establishing their connections to P. It should be emphasized that the process is primarily inductive and essentially atheoretical. Contrary to what many modern philosophers argue, not all observations are theory-laden. If they were, scientists would hardly ever confront unexpected phenomena (they consistently do) and scientific progress would be excruciatingly slow if not impossible (which it is very often not). It should be noted that when facing a new research prospect, ethologists, as noted above, are urged to engage in nontheoretical "reconnaissance observation" to familiarize themselves with the phenomenon of interest (Lehner, 1979). This is often the "most arduous" phase of their research and requires an openness to whatever is "out there." Use of the synoptiscope epitomizes this openness.

In contrast to microscopes and telescopes that are constructed to narrow the visual angle of P thereby eliminating its wider context, the synoptiscope does the opposite—it pulls observers back from P allowing them to view it much more macroscopically. Such a view automatically brings together many V's related to, or constitutive of, P as well as places P into a broader context of other P's with which it may have less obvious connections. Such a view also dispels many simplified ideas we have of most phenomena and also reduces the tendency to reify concepts. The synoptiscope also forces us to check to see if the CL phenomenon of our fancy exists outside of the methodological and theoretical contexts in which it was first discovered.

One effect of the synoptic approach is to undermine tendencies to reduce and categorize phenomena prematurely. It also helps reduce the influence of special interest groups in a particular empirical domain taking over. For example, the approach questions whether it is a good idea to dichotomize causes into situational or dispositional, or to view CL factors in terms of competence or performance factors, to divide performance on the basis of learning styles or of *right brain* vs. *left brain* functions—in short, to conceive and label a phenomenon (for practical or whatever reasons) in such a way that it can not be connected with anything else. The tendency to isolate a phenomenon, label and conceptualize it is very strong. As Kuhn (1970) made clear, scientists attempt to force nature into conceptual boxes many of which one provided by professional education.

At its most challenging, the synoptic approach questions whether analytically reducing P's to deterministic, lineal, and quantitative causal terms (the Galilean method of idealizing phenomena for experimental purposes) is superior to expanding P's as participants in a much more interactive, multivariate, probabilistic world of disparate factors. That such an expansion will lead to syncretism, a pasting together of everything into an arbitrary collage, is a danger, but hardly a great one for those using scientific methods. The likelihood of such an expansion creating improved empirical conditions for a new synthesis is much greater.

Results of the synoptiscopic approach can be presented in the form of a *synoptigram*, a picture of a P and its associated V's. A synoptigram's function is to document the results of synoptiscopic efforts for research purposes. It consists of an as-exhaustive-as-possible collection of disparate pieces of information that for various reasons are, have been, or theoretically should be associated with P. The initial synoptigram gives little preference to any V. Over time and iterations, though, the synoptigram, will grow and/or shrink as the strength of the various associations between the V's and P are established, new V's are added to it, and spurious V's discarded. An example of a well-known P is the common cold. The synoptigram in Fig. 8.1 was constructed out of various sources including an article from the *New York Times*. The large box containing "The Common Cold" is the central phenomenon that needs explanation. The satellite boxes collec-

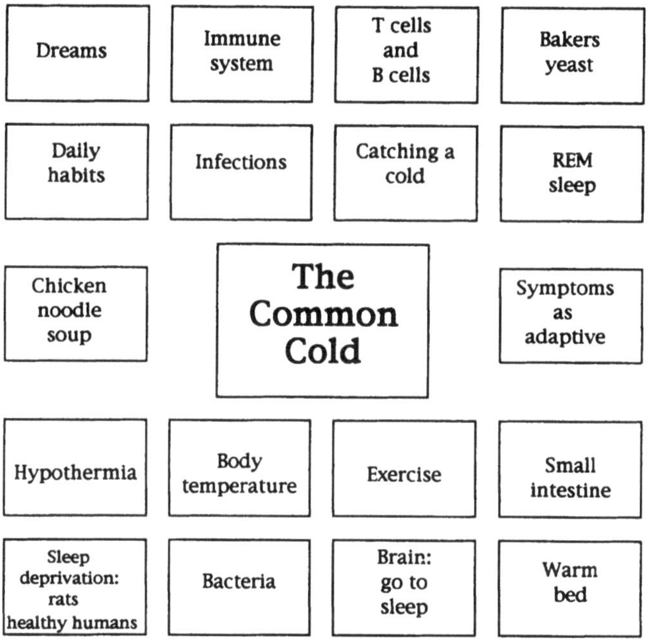

FIG. 8.1. The common cold. "The picture is a model of reality." "The picture consists in the fact that its elements are combined in a definite way." From Wittgenstein (1922) 2.12, 2.14.

tively constitute sources of variables or phenomena associated with the common cold. These sources range from current scientific knowledge of the immune system in general and T and B cells in particular to persistent anecdotal claims about the role of taking hot fluids (chicken noodle soup), to getting rest in a warm bed, or to keeping fit with exercise as ways to avoid or deal with the common cold. That cold symptoms have possible adaptive value originates in current, more elegant sources of ideas such as those associated with Darwinian medicine (Nesse & Williams, 1994).

What is obvious from this synoptigram is that the common cold is a more complex P than traditionally thought and that understanding its nature, origin, and possible function requires a much broader view of it than originally entertained. What should be recognized is that folk knowledge and personal experiences with a cold, along with scientific data, belong (at least initially) in the synoptigram as a possible source of important V's. The length of time fallacious folklore and invalid scientific conclusions remain in the synoptigram is inversely related to the speed with which the synoptigram is expanded—through iteration—the wider and more rapid one looks, the faster falsehoods and spurious connections are discovered.

Major P's will invariably require looking outside one's immediate discipline for relevant V's. CL researchers interested in building a general theory need to look into the domains of anthropology, economics, political science, the humanities, environmental sciences, genetics, and the neurosciences. This is a staggering list but should be expected since many CL processes (problem solving, reasoning, memory, etc.) are very wide ranging P's because they are implicated in most, if not all, human adaptations.

"Sources" synoptigrams are also possible. An example of sources CL researchers should pay attention to are depicted in the synoptigram in Fig. 8.2.

The Sources synoptigram is not mere whimsy: The human condition spans an astronomical number of different behavioral domains and experiences. Not getting access to them is comparable to ignoring certain features of an animal species because one does not know they exist or prejudges them as trivial or irrelevant. An excellent example of researchers who have succeeded in taking the most synoptic methodology humanly possible of birds and their behavior can be found in the work of Peter and Rosemary Grant on Galapagos finches (Weiner, 1994). Their "Sources synoptiscope" includes absorbing all of Darwin's writings, daily conducting hundreds of observations of finch behavior over a 20-year

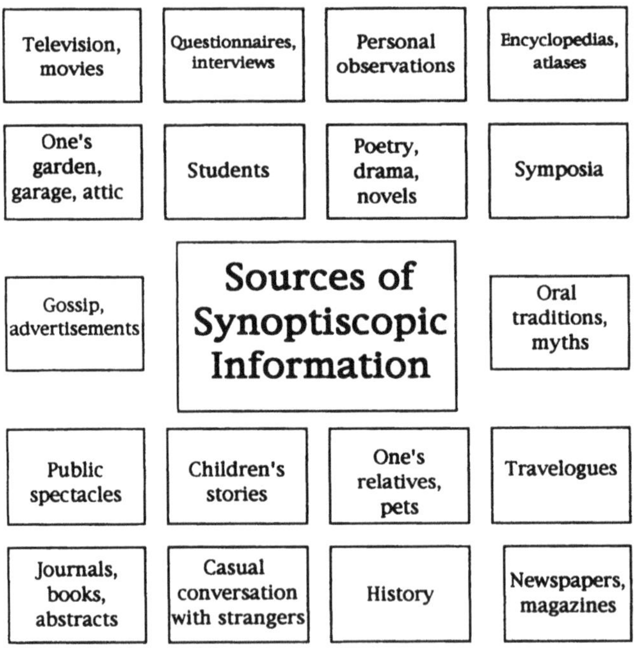

FIG. 8.2. Sources of synoptiscopic information. "Thus the picture is linked with reality; it reaches up to it." "It is like a scale applied to reality." From Wittgenstein (1922) 2.1511, 2.1512.

period, measuring the beak size of thousands of finches to one hundreds of a millimeter, counting and categorizing millions of seeds, measuring rainfall, and x-raying and extracting DNA molecules from finch blood samples. No future understanding of Galapagos finches and their origins and modes of speciation will be adequate without recognition of such a comprehensive achievement. To their great credit, their multimethodological approach driven by their search for the mechanisms of natural selection has created convincing empirical proof that evolution (as Darwin would have predicted) is still taking place.

An example of a synoptigram that has currently energized research in a very productive manner has been one that has emerged from STE thinking. It deals with sexual behavior. The synoptigram depicted in Fig. 8.3 is derived from a

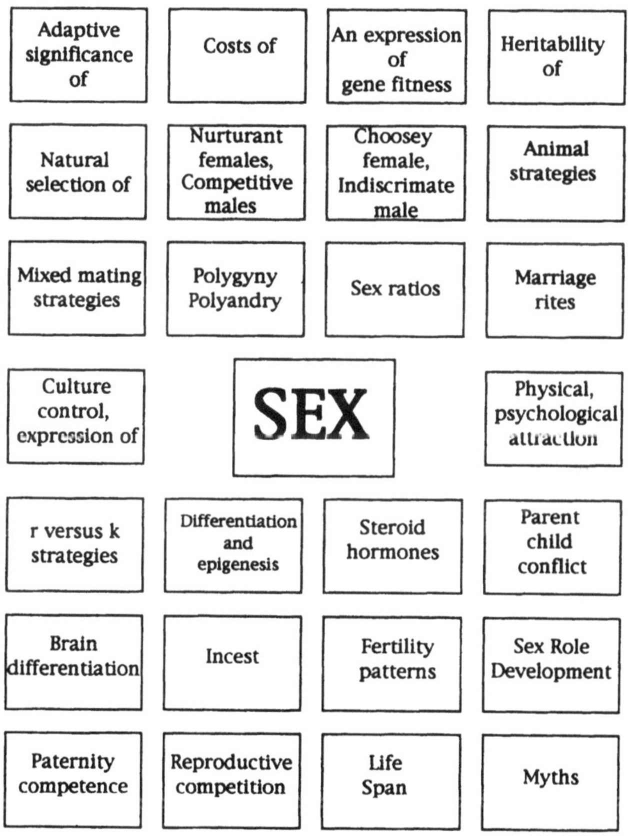

FIG. 8.3. Human sexual behavior. "The picture represents every reality whose form it has." "The picture contains the possibility of the state of affairs of which it represents." From Wittgenstein (1922) 2.171, 2.203.

variety of sources (Daly & Wilson, 1978) and includes the general concepts of r and K reproductive strategies derived from animal population biology. This synoptigram represents recent progress toward a synthesis of the field. No current theory of sex and reproduction can ignore the V's in the synoptigram and their interconnections.

A phenomenon at the heart of much CL research is that of "memory." Fig. 8.4 consists of a synoptigram of memory, one that will in the not too distant future most likely be much more detailed and comprehensive as the result of collaborative efforts between CL scientists, neuroscientists, molecular geneticists, and evolutionary biologists.

Once the first synoptigram is created, the investigator, as noted, can examine more closely the associative links between P and the V's as well as between the V's themselves. Over time, weak or spurious links are eliminated and strong ones retained but always subject to future tests of validation. Further, while primarily an instrument for discovery, the synoptiscope can quickly generate information that serves the functions of verification and falsification. In other

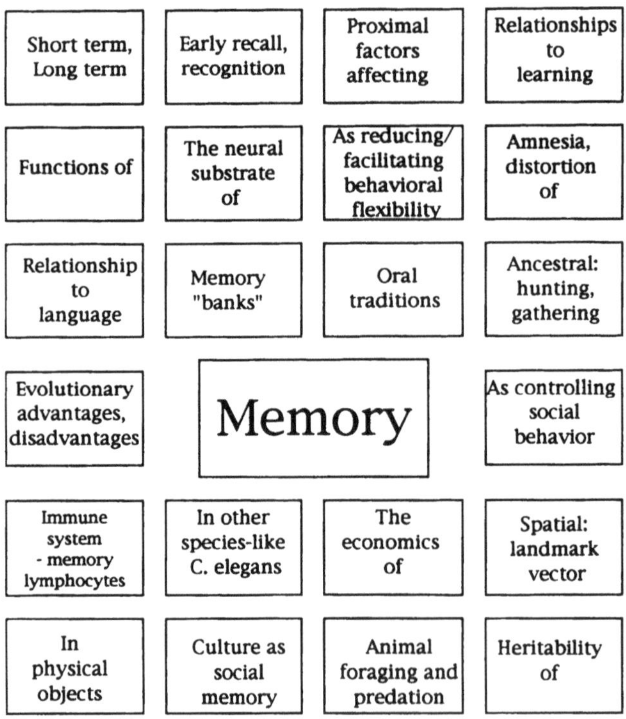

FIG. 8.4. Memory. "The picture agrees with reality or not; it is right or wrong, true or false." From Wittgenstein (1922) 2.21.

words, continual iterations are crucial because they serve three major functions —they eliminate chance V's-such V's will drop out on successive iterations; they corroborate nonchance V's—multiple replications from different sources always add strength to existing connections; and they have the potential for incorporating new V's into the picture.

What the Synoptiscope Is Not

The synoptiscope is not in the strict sense a heuristic since a heuristic is created to solve specific, usually well-defined problems. Instead, the synoptiscope sets conditions for creating problems whose solution, ideally, will ultimately be optimized because of the breadth of the conditions the synoptiscope originally provides the researcher. The synoptiscope is also not a primary tool for construct validation à la Cronbach and Meehl (1955) since a good construct is usually the outcome of a specific activity rather than the initiator of the activity. Similarly, the synoptiscope is not a tool for building dynamic systems models in that it presupposes no boundaries (between one system and another) and (at least initially) has no parameter estimates associated with systems and their associated V's. The synoptiscope merely creates conditions for weaving a wider nomological net of relationships around P than we would normally weave using traditional approaches. Further, the synoptiscope is not another form of contextualism that relativizes or "deconstructs" P to the point of loss of meaning. The synoptiscope is a simple method employed in the belief that the universe, while enormously complex, contains sufficient order to make substantial (if never complete) understanding possible. This includes the universe of immense pluralistic proportions that characterizes humans and their behavior where so many differing cause and effect factors coexist in complex combinations. The synoptiscope commemorates the spirit of the late Paul Feyerabend's (1975) *Against Method*. In his celebration of anarchy, Feyerabend notes that "A scientist who wishes to maximize the empirical content of the views he holds and who wants to understand them as clearly as he possibly can must therefore introduce other views, that is, he must adopt a pluralistic methodology" (p. 30). Even if one does not want to live as anarchically as Feyerabend, it is not reasonable to reject out of hand insights that others (artists, historians, teachers, parents, nurses) outside one's discipline or outside of science itself hold about P but are never consulted.

Finally, as a discovery tool, the synoptiscope per se has no particular theoretical pretensions. Operating on what initially seems reasonable and commonsensical, the synoptiscope has no internal logical structure and therefore generates no hypotheses, at least in the beginning of its formation. Its only weakness is that it may not extend far enough in a particular case. The syntopiscope is associated with divergent thinking but also requires focused attention, notation, and organized recording of what is experienced. Its main task is to supply reliable materials for the construction of theories. A supplemental consequence of its activity is the demolition of hastily conceived hypotheses or theories built on too narrow a conceptual and empirical basis to encompass the phenomena they are purported to explain.

Rationale for the CL Synoptiscope

The rationale behind using the synoptiscope in CL research is simple. In order to develop a comprehensive theory of CL phenomena, one has to seek out all known instances of it. This is especially the case if one wishes to get practical control over CL processes, critically involved in education, psychotherapy, public information, and child rearing.

In traditional CL research much commonplace information on CL has been classified as extraneous noise or chance factors that have to be eliminated or reduced by various methods (large representative samples, control groups, tightly managed test conditions, etc.). Such sanitizing methods are obviously justified in certain subdomains of applied research. For example, it is generally argued that operant conditioning has been both a useful assessment as well as therapeutic tool but only under certain conditions. However, the P's operant researchers focus on are connected to aspects of adaptation (cognitive and linguistic, for example) that are only handled by operant methodology. This limitation ultimately raises problems. A specific example of the limited application of current CL principles to solving educational problems can be found in area of generalization of treatment effects in educational intervention. As Johnston (1979) points out, most educational treatments fail to generalize to natural settings. This fact suggests to some that it might be better to eliminate the distinction between treatment and generalization settings by constructing artificial settings for the educationally disabled where generalization is bound to be more powerful. Even if this were achieved, however, we would still not known what CL principles govern naturally occurring behavior.

Complexity, and CL research

The enormous complexity of the universe of physical objects and life forms has now been "officially" recognized, labeled as *chaos*, and more or less formally established as an object of scientific inquiry guided by complexity theory (Gleick, 1987). This new science has been developed to view chaos in terms of multiple systems, all interacting in some fashion or other, none usefully reducible to traditional scientific analytic methods, all subject, rather, to multidisciplinary inquiry. Whether complexity theory can be productively applied to all research domains remains to be seen. Its relevance for our understanding of CL phenomena, however, is not unimportant. As noted earlier, given the complexity of most P's of major interest, the traditional scientific approach to them has been analytic and hence reductionistic, the ultimate consequence of which has been fragmentation of CL phenomena and a consequent loss in overall comprehension and as well in efficacy of applying CL research to solve problems. The fact that much research in traditional psychology deals with independent stimulus or subject variables that account for relatively small amounts of variance in the dependent variables is evidence of this. Recognition of this state of affairs is not new in psychology. Lykken (1968, 1991) and Meehl (1978), for example, have been aware of this situation for several decades. The awareness of the complexity of human behavior and its multiple determinants and the inadequacy of most research strategies to deal with them plus the fact that nearly everything is correlated with everything else (Meehl's, 1990, "crud" factor), has led to the recognition that a major re-structuring of research methods and data analysis are necessary. A shift from cause to correlation (bivariate, rank, point-biserial, multivariate) and from bivariate to multivariate analyses is seen by Cohen and Cohen (1975), Petrinovich (1981) and others as a concrete way out of the reductionistic trap.

Coherence and Concatentation

As just mentioned, the synoptiscope's immediate goal is to discover V's that are of possible relevance to P and then to establish the strength of their associations with P as well as with other V's. The ultimate outcome of such activity hopefully is discovering a new truth about P, one strengthened by increased coherence (or concatentation) while simultaneously reducing the strength of the crud factor by eliminating "incoherent" variables having minuscule connections with P. Coherence is one of the five traditional criteria for establishing the truth value of a statement (the other four being correspondence, authority, logic, and intuition). According to Runes (1958), coherence theory is a "Theory of knowledge which maintains that truth is a property primarily applicable to any extensive body of consistent propositions and derivately applicable to any one proposition in such a system by virtue of its part in the system" (p. 58). An exponent of the coherence theory of truth, Blanshard (1940, 1965) develops this definition further. He prefaces his discourse of coherence theory by noting that problem solving, as one of our major cognitive activities, is aimed at building "a bridge of intelligent relations" between what we know and what we do not know. . . . "Sometimes this bridge is causal, as when we try to explain disease; sometimes teleological, as when we try to fathom the move of an opponent over the chess board; sometimes geometrical, as in Euclid" (Nagel & Brandt, 1965, p. 145). He goes on to argue that this scientific bridge building is a systematic attempt to connect the unknown to what is already known and constitutes the basis for accepted shared beliefs. Blanshard (1962) also points out that the aim of thought is understanding the nature of things and . . . "by understanding is meant apprehension in a system" (p. 33)—also noting that "Whether any bit of alleged knowledge is true will depend in the first instance on whether it coheres with our system of knowledge as a whole, and the degree of truth possessed by this system will depend in turn on its coherence with that all-inclusive system which is at once the goal of our knowledge and the constitution of the real" (p. 29). He uses systems broadly here: Systems can range from mathematical logic and mechanical models to hierarchical taxonomies to any clustering of similar objects that are *correlated*—a pile of stones is coherent because each stone is correlated with each other, materially and geologically, while a pile of junk is not. The most correlated entities are organisms whose parts and functions tightly cohere as do their evolutionary histories.

Today, we acknowledge that all living things and their physical ecology are also *interrelated*, having multiple associations with each other and their eco-niches. Such ideas are hardly new. In 5th Century BC, Anaxagoras argued that nothing exists by itself but shares connections with everything else. Today it is an ecological given that everything is connected to everything else. Blanshard goes further than others in developing the epistemological warrant for such statements, pitting in the process the coherence theory of truth against the other theories of truth. The degree to which different factors cohere, he argues, constitutes a test of its degree of truthfulness—"Fully coherent knowledge would be knowledge in which every judgment entailed, and was entailed by the rest of the system" (p .146). In psychologists' terms, the degree of intercorrelation determines the level of empirical truth. In developing this idea Blanshard, however, has downplayed the importance of correspondence of ideas to fact. Correspondence to fact is obviously the major criterion of empirical research, hence, we cannot go all the way with Blanshard's argument. All legitimate pieces of the puzzle have to be true, not just parts that fit into a picture. Actually, one could argue that a newly discovered V that is not a fact will ultimately be rejected because it will not be replicated.

The concept of *concatentation*, developed by Reichenbach (1932/1933, 1949), shares a similar meaning with the concept of coherence. In his discussion of the foundations of probability, Reichenbach recognized the imperative of removing the depiction of phenomena from the perspective of a two-valued logic and replacing it with the perspective of probability. Probability suggests multiple approximations to the truth of a phenomenon, each approximation contributing to the system of knowledge that purports to depict the phenomenon accurately and definitively (at that point of history)—"Scientific knowledge represent, therefore, a system of concatenated posits [in the synoptigram, different V's] which has an inner order in terms of the principle of the best posit [in the synoptigram, the set of V's most highly correlated with P]" (p. 319).

The general point being made here is that there already exist attempts to justify the epistemological basis of the synoptiscope as I present it here. Truth can be viewed a number of ways—as a term for an unspecified number of disparate perceptions consistently clustered together, the clustering conceptualized in terms of various as yet unknown principles, or in terms of the kinds of laws demonstrated by physicists under ideal experimental conditions. Given the nature of CL process, the former appears most appropriate for current researchers.

As noted earlier, CL processes are so pervasive within, and constructive, of the human condition, that we are still a long way from obtaining a rough outline of this picture. The relationship of CL phenomena to issues involving application of CL research findings to solving problems of human adaptation makes a synoptic view of CL facts even more crucial. These problems are addressed in the next section.

SOCIAL SIGNIFICANCE OF COGNITION AND LEARNING RESEARCH

For theoretical reasons alone CL processes can stand as a major focus of human STE research. Without doubt, CL processes play a major role in human adaptation: No satisfactory theory of human evolution can ignore them. CL research, additionally, has potential social value as well. Human behaviors controlled by CL processes are responsible for adaptive culture and scientific achievements. Such behaviors can also be maladaptive for there is no longer any question that the major threat to human existence is human behavior. The problem is how to conduct relevant CL research to improve human adaptation as well as reduce this threat. Several steps influenced by STE thinking are offered here to help solve this problem.

Altering attitudes

Major misconceptions about biological theory and research still plague major segments of lay society and the scientific community. Despite current interest in behavior genetics and gender differences and similarities, the public and the great majority of social scientists still need to be encouraged to acknowledge certain biological facts as well as current ideas shared by STE researchers. First, every intact individual contains a brain that has been under a long evolutionary history of construction. While brand new in its current phenotypic expression in each individual, each brain's architecture is ordered by evolved genetic processes to function in ways useful to survival and reproduction. Humans, as we know them today, would not exist if each brain was a tabula rasa that had to be programmed anew at birth. To ignore the brain's evolved functions and individual differences in such functions is to create an incomplete picture of social and cultural phenomena (controlled by CL processes) at best and a misleading one at worse. Brain research has fortunately a rich history and is growing to be a focus of major attention. However, recognition of the human brain and its evolved functions by those working in applied areas such as education has been traditionally absent (Charlesworth, 1994).

The neglect of the brain in applied affairs, unfortunately, appears to be a specific symptom of the more general problem of biophobia within the social sciences and large segments of the public. For example, there are still strong and widespread feelings that evolutionary theory is dangerous for social stability, individual freedom, and religious beliefs (Degler, 1991). Such feelings are built on understandable concerns that cannot be fully addressed here. A major concern is built on the conclusion that STE provides "scientific" support for racism, sexism, and eugenics. This concern is usually in direct response to what Kitcher (1985) labels the danger of "pop" Darwinism, that is, the misuse of STE concepts for various ideological reasons. Such dangers certainly exist, but they exist for any scientific domain that has a good theory. Nuclear physics is a good example.

Second, and more critical, in the history of legitimate moral and ethical concerns about biological science there is virtually no comparable concern for the potential malicious effects of a purely nonbiological view of the determinants of human behavior. A good example is the tabula rasa belief adhered to by many cultural determinists, behavior modifiers, and environmentalists. Policy makers, convinced that everything important about human behavior is taught from birth through conditioning or imitation justify their convictions when such views gain support from scientific findings. Such a conviction is beneficial if such findings are robust, have no side effects, and are useful in applied settings to ameliorate human suffering. However, it is dangerous if such findings are much more limited in their application than advertised. More disturbing is the fact that more than altruistic policy makers and practitioners believe in the tabula rasa dogma. Others with less pure motives operate on this conviction. Sensitizing, conditioning, and training are relatively convenient and economical methods for altering human behavior (if only temporarily and often with great difficulty) for selfish or antisocial reasons—certainly much easier than genetic engineering. Although such methods are engaged in daily by well-meaning parents, educators, counselors, and clinicians, there are many others more interested in controlling purchasing and consuming behavior. The tobacco, alcohol, and useless food and toy industries apply well-tested CL methods as do ideologues, propagandists, hate mongers, and security forces. All operate on the conviction that controlling CL processes is the most rapid means of altering human behavior. Learning from STE sources that humans frequently operate on the basis of evolutionarily predetermined directions and hard-wired preferences only adds to the problem of the misuse of CL methods. This whole issue is obviously complicated and implicates the whole nature/nurture spectrum. Having a society that knows about both genotypes and environments and their interaction can help clarify it. Cultivating a climate of awareness of "pop environmentalism" along with that of pop Darwinism should help balance out this situation.

Before proceeding further, it should be noted that upgrading attitudes also applies to genetic or neural determinists who tend to downplay the role cultural factors play in shaping human behavior. Such determinists should recognize that culture, as the major causal environmental determinant of human behavior is a powerful, ubiquitous human adaptation that has played a very significant evolutionary role in making humans what they are. The biological triumphalism that is currently sweeping large segments of the scientific academy today is refreshing in view of the long dominance of environmental dogma in Western thought, but we will only repeat past errors if we fail to recognize that culture made possible by human genes and brains has emergent influences on human behavior that cannot be solely accounted for or predicted by knowledge of DNA and neurochemistry.

Altering and Prioritizing Research

Concrete ways to link CL research to problems of human adaptation already exist. It is has generally been recognized in psychology that human adaptation is the instrumental expression of needs, motivations, and desires (for better or worse) in terms of the various socialization and educational modes of a particular culture. The need for empirical research into this area has already been well-recognized. In 1967, for example, Spence and Spence published the first volume of the now well-known series *The psychology of learning and motivation*. Their aim was to bring together research in complex learning, memory, and problem solving with "motivational" research including "acquired complex forms as well as simple primary ones" (p. viii). Up until 1993, 211 papers have appeared (see Nakamura, Medin, & Taraban, 1993). In a rough content analysis of these papers, I discovered that over 90% of them deal exclusively with cognitive processes, less than 10% with motivational and cognitive. I used a broad definition of motivation—papers on food preferences, emotional processing, fear, Type A motivation, hippocampal processes, anxiety, early isolation effects on activity, learned helplessness, imprinting, self-punitive behavior, frustration escape, avoidance, curiosity, and biological constructs. I list these because STE theorists may find them very useful to study because they bear directly upon evolved, brain mediated need mechanisms and stimulus preferences that are served (and misserved) by CL processes. It is most likely that needs and motivations appeared very early in evolution, possibly several million years before complex CL processes. When the latter appeared on the scene they rapidly evolved (became more complex and numerous) because they presumably were able to satisfy such needs under increasingly more complex and competitive conditions. For example, insect behaviors are driven by internal need mechanisms to forage, feed, mate, and reproduce as well as by the motivating effects of various external stimuli. Although some learning may take place in their relatively small nervous systems, their behavior is pretty much a function of DNA preprogrammed behavior mechanisms that respond to vital need states and need-reducing external stimuli. No higher cognitive processes are present or necessary. Early human ancestors with much smaller brains than today's humans had to perform generically similar behaviors without the help of complex CL processes. CL processes, most probably, also complicated, as well as enriched, the lives of the species that evolved them, accelerating, the need for even more complex CL processes.

The rationale for linking current motivational and CL processes is obvious. It is the needs, motivations and attitudes of people—not climate, positrons, mountain ranges, animals, plant life—that are endangering our planet. Instructing people in the most productive (or at least less destructive) way to meet their needs is the most crucial task we can engage in. Knowledge of the CL processes and how they interact with needs and motivations to affect our environment and others is currently more crucial than more knowledge of the physical world. Even demographic factors such as fertility, mortality, and migration are ultimately influenced by CL processes. Researchers interesting in ameliorating the human condition can not ignore them. Of course, nonhuman factors (sun spots, tectonic plates, nearby asteroids) also endanger human populations, but the best step toward minimizing their effect is to educate humans to behave rationally toward them. Effective education requires, among other things, basic knowledge of CL processes.

CONCLUSION

Evolutionary theory can enrich our understanding of learning, cognition, and development, if not in terms of proximate mechanisms, which existing models deal with best, at least in terms of the adaptive functions associated with CL processes and their significance for the greater picture of human behavior and its origins. Drawing on evolutionary theory will allow CL researchers to identify some of the empirical and interpretive limitations of traditional theories of cognition, learning, and development as well as encourage researchers to take a broad, cross-disciplinary and functional view of these significant processes of behavioral change.

However, despite benefits from strengthening the link between evolutionary theory and CL research, the link by itself cannot do the kind of comprehensive job that needs to be done to account for the origins and functions of CL phenomena within the full range of the human condition. Humans operate unceasingly and expansively within complex contingencies generated by interactions between their genetic dispositions and their own individual conscious choices, life histories, social/cultural backgrounds, and physical ecologies. To deal with such complexities, research models based on a more comprehensive approach will have to be taken more seriously. Traditional causal models are no longer adequate. A broader, multivariate, (and perforce probabilistic) and on-line view of this complex picture is necessary to produce satisfactory coverage of variables relevant for a general theory of CL and the developmental processes which constitute its temporal context. Such a view is imperative if CL researchers wish to make informed contributions to solving major social problems. This is where the synoptiscope can be useful.

In taking this approach, we should keep in mind that no matter how infinitely generative and ingenious CL processes are in producing cultural products such processes still serve as major tools (for better or worse) for satisfying a relatively few basic human biological needs. Because CL processes are located in evolved brain mechanisms, which in turn are grounded in DNA, as well as conditioned by proximate environments over developmental time, researchers will have to establish firmer, more compatible connections with the neurosciences, genetics, and developmental psychology. Evolutionary theory makes this task much easier.

As social accountability of human research increases, CL researchers will eventually be pressed to deal more vigorously with the various roles CL processes play in everyday adaptational problems and the cultural, economic, and physical environmental factors surrounding them. There is no doubt that CL processes are greatly responsible for the current status of human adaptation as well as maladaptation. Such processes are also directly responsible for the unpredictable future of the human condition. Given the urgency of this state of affairs, limiting research solely to describing such processes psychometrically or explaining them at a molecular causal level is no longer defensible. CL processes operative at the macro level of everyday adaptation are necessary to identify and to understand because it is these processes that society can access and regulate for meliorative purposes. Also, it is these CL processes and their associated behaviors upon which natural selection operates and hence ultimately affects subsequent generations.

A more synoptic view of human adaptation will reveal that there is more to CL phenomena than revealed in most traditional research and that there is much more to come in the evolution of human affairs as a result of CL processes. We are not sure what will come: Human behavior and its products are constantly generating novel selection pressures. Although we may not be able to explain fully what does come, we will at least be able to describe CL phenomena more comprehensively than we ever had in the past and that will be a good first step toward understanding them.

REFERENCES

Alcock, J. (1975). *Animal behavior: An evolutionary approach*. Sunderland, MA: Sinauer.

Alexander, R. D. (1987). *The biology of moral systems*. New York: Aldine de Gruyter.

Alexander, R. D. (1990). Epigenetic rules and Darwinian algorithms: The adaptive study of learning and development. *Ethology and Sociobiology*, *11*, 241–303.

Baldwin, J. M. (1902). *Development and evolution*. New York: Macmillan.

Barkow, J. H. (1989). *Darwin, sex and status: Biological approaches to mind and culture*. Toronto: University of Toronto Press.

Barkow, J. H., Cosmides, L., & Tooby, J. (1992). *The adapted mind: Evolutionary psychology and the generation of culture*. New York: Oxford University Press.

Bekoff, M., & Byers, J. A. (1985). The development of behavior from evolutionary and ecological perspectives in mammals and birds. *Evolutionary Biology, 19*, 215–286.

Blanshard, B. (1940). *The nature of thought*. London: George Allen & Unwin.

Blanshard, B. (1962). *Reason and analysis*. LaSalle, IL: Open Court.

Blanshard, B. (1965). Autobiography. In E. Nagel & R. B. Brandt (Eds.), *Memory and knowledge: Systematic readings in epistemology* (pp. 139–152). New York: Harcourt, Brace & World.

Bogdan, R. J. (1994). *Grounds for cognition: How goal-directed behavior shapes the mind*. Hillsdale, NJ: Lawrence Erlbaum Associates.

Bolles, R. C., & Beecher, M. D. (Eds.). (1988). *Evolution and learning*. Hillsdale, NJ: Lawrence Erlbaum Associates.

Bonner, J. T. (1958). *The evolution of development*. Cambridge, England: Cambridge University Press.

Bonner, J. T. (1980). *The evolution of culture in animals*. Princeton, NJ: Princeton University Press.

Bonner, J. T. (1993). *Life cycles: Reflections of an evolutionary biologist*. Princeton, NJ: Princeton University Press.

Bowler, P. J. (1992). *The environmental sciences*. New York: Norton.

Boyd, R., & Richerson, P. J. (1985). *Culture and the evolutionary process*. Chicago: University of Chicago Press.

Breland, K., & Breland, M. (1961). The misbehavior of organisms. *American Psychologist, 16*, 681–684.

Cary, S., & Gelman, R. (Eds.). (1991). *The epigenesis of mind: Essays on biology and cognition*. Hillsdale, NJ: Lawrence Erlbaum Associates.

Charlesworth, W. R. (1979). Ethology: Understanding the other half of intelligence. In M. von Cranach, K. Foppa, W. Lepenies, & D. Ploog (Eds.), *Human ethology: Claims and limits of a new discipline* (pp. 491–519). Cambridge, England: Cambridge University Press.

Charlesworth, W. R. (1992). Darwin and developmental psychology: Past and present. *Developmental Psychology, 28*, 5–16.

Charlesworth, W. R. (1994). *Human ethology: A good idea for the behavioral sciences and society*. Address given to the 12th Congress of the International Society for Human Ethology, August 6, Toronto, Canada.

Cohen, J., & Cohen, P. (1975). *Applied multiple regression/correlations analysis for the behavioral sciences*. Hillsdale, NJ: Lawrence Erlbaum Associates.

Cosmides, L. (1989). The logic of social exchange: Has natural selection shaped how humans reason? Studies with the Wason selection task. *Cognition, 31*, 187–276.

Costall, A. (1986). Evolutionary gradualism and the study of development. *Human Development, 29*, 4–11.

Cronbach, L. J., & Meehl, P. E. (1955). Construct validity in psychological tests. *Psychological Bulletin, 52*, 281–302.

Crook, J. H. (1980). *The evolution of human consciousness*. Oxford: Clarendon Press.

Daly, M., & Wilson, M. I. (1978). *Sex, evolution and behavior*. North Scituate, MA: Duxbury.

Darwin, C. (1877). A biographical sketch of an infant. *Mind: Quarterly review of psychology and philosophy, 2*, 285–294.

Darwin, C. (1890). *The formation of vegetable mould, through the action of worms, with observations on their habits*. New York: D. Appleton.

Dawkins, R. (1976). *The selfish gene*. Oxford: Oxford University Press.

Degler, C. N. (1991). *In search of human nature*. New York: Oxford University Press.

Dobzhansky, T. (1963). Cultural direction of human evolution. *Human Biology, 35*, 311–316.

Donald, M. (1991). *Origins of the modern mind: Three stages in the evolution of culture and cognition*. Cambridge, MA: Harvard University Press.

Eibl-Eibesfeldt, I. (1989). *Human ethology*. New York: Aldine de Gruyter.

Feyerabend, P. (1975). *Against method: Outline of an anarchistic theory of knowledge*. London: NLB.

Flavell, J., Miller, P. H., & Miller, S. A. (1993). *Cognitive development*. Englewood Cliffs, NJ: Prentice-Hall.

Galton, F. (1907). *Inquiries into human faculty and its development*. London: Macmillan.

Garcia, J., McGowan, B. K., & Green, K. F. (1972). Biological constraints on conditioning. In A. H. Black & W. F. Prokasy (Eds.), *Classical conditioning II: Current research and theory*. New York: Appleton-Century-Crofts.

Ghiselin, M. (1969). *The triumph of the Darwinian method*. Berkeley, CA: University of California Press.

Gigerenzer, G., & Hug, K. (1992). Domain-specific reasoning: Social contracts, cheating, and perspective change. *Cognition, 43*, 127–171.

Gleick, J. (1987). *Chaos: Making a new science*. New York: Penguin.

Goodall, J. (1986). *The chimpanzees of Gombe: Patterns of behavior*. Cambridge, MA: The Belknap Press of Harvard University Press.

Gottlieb, G. (1991). Experiential canalization of behavioral development: Theory. *Developmental Psychology, 27*, 4–13.

Gould, S. J. (1977). *Ontogeny and phylogeny*. Cambridge, MA: The Belknap Press of Harvard University Press.

Gould, S. J., & Vrba, E. S. (1982). "Exaption"-a missing term in the science of form. *Paleobiology, 8*, 4–15.

Griffin, D. R. (1976). *The question of animal awareness: Evolutionary continuity of mental experience*. New York: Rockefeller University Press.

Griffin, D. R. (1992). *Animal minds*. Chicago: University of Chicago Press.

Gruneberg, M. M., Morris, P. E., & Sykes, R. N. (Eds.). (1988). *Practical aspects of memory: Current research and issues*. New York: Wiley.

Hamilton, W. D. (1964). The genetical theory of social behavior. I and II. *Journal of Theoretical Biology, 7*, 1–52.

Harlow, H. F. (1958). The evolution of learning. In A. Roe & G. G. Simpson (Eds.), *Behavior and evolution* (pp. 269–290). New Haven, CT: Yale University Press.

Hinde, R. A. (1982). *Ethology: Its nature and relations with other sciences*. New York: Oxford University Press.

Hodos, W., & Campbell, C. B. G. (1969). Scala naturae: Why there is no theory in comparative psychology. *Psychological Review, 76*, 337–350.

Humphrey, N. K. (1976). The social function of intellect. In P. P. G. Bateson & R. A. Hinde (Eds.), *Growing points in ethology* (pp. 303–317). Cambridge, England: Cambridge University Press.

Jenkins, J. J. (1974). Remember that old theory of memory? Well forget it! *American Psychologist, 29*, 785–795.

Johnston, J. M. (1979). On the relation between generalization and generality. *The Behavior Analyst, 2*, 1–6.

Kitcher, P. (1985). *Vaulting ambition: Sociobiology and the quest for human nature*. Cambridge, MA: MIT Press.

Kuhn, T. S. (1970). *The structure of scientific revolutions* (2nd ed.). Chicago: University of Chicago Press.

Lehner, P. N. (1979). *Handbook of ethological methods*. New York: Garland STPM Press.

Lockard, R. B. (1971). Reflections on the fall of comparative psychology: Is there a message for us all? *American Psychologist, 26*, 168–179.

Lorenz, K. (1965). *Evolution and modification of behavior*. Chicago: University of Chicago Press.
Lykken, D. T. (1968). Statistical significance in psychological research. *Psychological Bulletin, 70*, 151–159.
Lykken, D. T. (1991). What's wrong with psychology anyway? In D. Cicchetti & W. M. Grove (Eds.). *Thinking clearly about psychology: Matters of public interest* (Vol. 1, pp. 3–39). Minneapolis: University of Minnesota Press.
MacDonald, K. B. (1988). *Social and personality development: An evolutionary synthesis*. New York: Plenum.
Malthus, T. R. (1978/1826). *An essay on the principles of population, as it affects the future*. London: J. Johnson (according to Mayr, 1982, Darwin read the 6th edition published in 1826 by London: Murray).
Maynard Smith, J. (1982). *Evolution and the theory of games*. Cambridge, England: Cambridge University Press.
Mayr, E. (1974). Behavior programs and evolutionary strategies. *American Scientist, 62*, 650–659.
Mayr, E. (1982). *The growth of biological thought: Diversity, evolution, and inheritance*. Cambridge, MA: The Belknap Press of Harvard University Press.
McQuire, M., & Troisi, A. (in press). *Evolutionary Psychiatry*.
Meehl, P. E. (1978). Theoretical risks and tabular asterisks: Sir Karl, Sir Ronald, and the slow progress of soft psychology. *Journal of Consulting and Clinical Psychology, 46*, 806–834.
Meehl, P. E. (1990). Why summaries of research on psychological theories are often uninterpretable. *Psychological Reports Monograph, 66* (Suppl. 1), 195–244.
Mendel, G. (1866). Versuche ueber Pflanzenhybriden. *Verhandlungen des Naturforschenden Vereines in Bruenn, 4*, 3–47. (Also available in E. W. Sinnett, L. C. Dunn, & T. Dobzhansky (1950), *Principles of genetics*. New York: McGraw-Hill.)
Morgan, C. L. (1895). *Animal life and intelligence*. Boston: Ginn.
Morss, J. R. (1990). *The biologizing of childhood: Developmental psychology and the Darwinian myth*. Hillsdale, NJ: Lawrence Erlbaum Associates.
Nagel, E., & Brandt, R. B. (Eds.). (1965). *Meaning and knowledge: Systematic readings in epistemology*. New York: Harcourt & Brace (excerpts from Blanshard, 1939, op. cit.)
Nakamura, G. V., Medin, D. L., & Taraban, R. (1993). *The psychology of learning and motivation* (Vol. 29). San Diego, CA: Academic Press.
Neisser, U. (1982). *Memory observed: Remembering in natural contexts*. San Francisco: W. H. Freeman.
Nesse, R., & Williams, G. C. (1994). *The dawn of Darwinian medicine*. New York: Random House.
Parke, R. D., Ornstein, P. A., & Rieser, J. J., & Zahn-Waxler, C. (Eds.). (1994). *A century of developmental psychology*. Washington, DC: American Psychological Association.
Petrinovich, L. (1981). A method for the study of development. In K. Immelmann, G. W. Barlow, L. Petrinovich, & M. Main (Eds.), *Behavioral development: The Bielefeld Interdisciplinary Project* (pp. 90–130). Cambridge, England: Cambridge University Press.
Plotkin, H. C. (1988). Learning and evolution. In H. C. Plotkin (Ed.), *The role of behavior in evolution* (pp. 133–164). Cambridge, MA: The MIT Press.
Plotkin, H. C. (1993). *Darwin machines and the nature of knowledge*. Cambridge, MA: Harvard University Press.
Reichenbach, H. (1932/1933, 1949). The logical foundations of the concept of porbability. In H. Feigl & W. Sellars (Eds.), *Readings in philosophical analysis* (pp. 305–323). New York: Appleton-Century-Crofts.
Richards, R. (1987). *Darwin and the emergence of evolutionary theories of mind and behavior*. Chicago: The University of Chicago Press.
Riedl, R. (1979). *Biologie der Erkenntnis: die stammesgeschichtlichen Grundlagen der Vernunft*. Berlin: Verlag Paul Parey.

Ristau, C. A. (Ed.). (1991). *Cognitive ethology: The minds of other animals*. Hillsdale, NJ: Lawrence Erlbaum Associates.

Rogoff, B., & Lave, J. (1984). *Everyday cognition: Its development in social context*. Cambridge, MA: Harvard University Press.

Romanes, G. (1898). *Mental evolution in man: Origin of human faculty*. New York: O. Appleton.

Rue, L. (1994). *By the grace of guile: The role of deception in natural history and human affairs*. Oxford: Oxford University Press.

Runes, D. D. (Ed.). (1958). *Dictionary of philosophy*. Ames, IA: Littlefield and Adams.

Sackett, G. P. (Ed.). (1978). *Observing behavior: Theory and applications in mental retardation* (Vol. 1). Baltimore, MD: University Park Press.

Scarr, S. (1983). An evolutionary perspective on infant intelligence: Species patterns and individual variations. In M. Lewis (Ed.), *Origins of intelligence: Infancy and early childhood* (3rd ed.). New York: Plenum Press.

Seligman, M. E. P., & Hager, J. L. (1972). *Biological boundaries of learning*. New York: Appleton-Century-Crofts.

Skinner, B. F. (1950). Are theories of learning necessary? *Psychological Review, 57*, 193–216.

Spence, K. W., & Spence, J. T. (1967). *The psychology of learning and motivation* (Vol. 1). New York: Academic Press.

Stenhouse, D. (1974). *The evolution of intelligence: A general theory and its implication*. London: Allen & Unwin.

Thorpe, W. H. (1956). *Learning and instincts in animals*. Cambridge, MA: Harvard University Press.

Tinbergen, N. (1963). On aims and methods of ethology. *Zeitschrift für Tierpsychologie, 20*, 410–433.

Tooby, J., & Cosmides, L. (1989). Evolutionary psychology and the generation of culture. *Ethology and sociobiology, 10*, 29–49.

Trivers, R. L. (1971). The evolution of reciprocal altruism. *Quarterly Review of Biology, 46*, 35–57.

Wallace, A. R. (1891). *Natural selection and tropical nature: Essays on dscriptive and theoretical biology*. London: Macmillan.

Weiner, J. (1994). *The beak of the finch: A story of evolution in our time*. New York: Alfred A. Knopf.

White, M. S. (1985). On the status of cognitive psychology. *American Psychologist, 40*, 117–119.

Wilson, E. O. (1975). *Sociobiology: The new synthesis*. Cambridge, MA: The Belknap Press of Harvard University Press.

Wittgenstein, L. (1922). *Tractatus Logico-Philosophius*. London: Routledge & Kegan Paul.

9 The Evolution of Mind and Culture: A Commentary on Charlesworth

James E. Turnure
University of Minnesota

I gather firewood
As if I had been at it
For a million years
—Charlesworth (1978)

Child Development, as a field, may well have had its origin in the seminal work of Charles Darwin, who provided a basis for studying the whole range of psychological characteristics of infants and children (Kessen, 1965). Charlesworth (this volume; see also 1976) has focused on the role of evolution in the expression of learning, cognition, and intelligence in humans. This contemporary array of interests leads him to grapple with the most complex of human concerns; the nature of the human mind and its place in nature. In discussing this facet of human characteristics, he extends prior, recent evolutionary and genetic reviews by himself (Charlesworth, 1978, 1986, 1992) and others (e.g., Jerison, 1982; Scarr & Carter-Saltzman, 1982), but this is a more personal statement, a kind of magisterial summing up of 3 decades of research and thought. Going beyond a delineation of possible effects of surviving genetic programs on behavioral patterns or propensities, Charlesworth presents an analysis and critique of contemporary cognitive theorizing, and proposes a conceptual scheme to enliven research, which leads, finally, to recommendations for basic and applied research, and even approaches to public policy. Only a basic belief in individual differences and intraspecies variation could motivate an expression of some differential points and positions regarding all of this. Fortunately, as Charlesworth points out, following Mayr (1974), we can expect "closed" genetic programs, involving an array of standard social signals and species relevant cooperating behaviors, to meliorate any tendency toward extreme reactions that might exceed even "open" programs, involving "idiosyncratic learning or cognitive novelties" (p. 181) that we might expect to have developed due to the reactor living in an esoteric, "ivory tower" environment. It turns out I am in sympathy with Charlesworth's general purpose and most main points, but I do view various aspects of his presentation and his interpretation differently than he; thus, cultural evolution proceeds.

Charlesworth continues his historical analyses of evolution and development (Charlesworth, 1986, 1992) in his first main section, integrating a more detailed depiction of the waxing and waning influence of cognitive concepts of the "mind" in evolutionary theorizing. His presentation is densely and tightly packed conceptually, and is a plausible, if abstract, *tour-de-force* presentation of his basic hypothesis that modern evolutionary thinking (the Synthetic Theory of Evolution, or STE) is the most satisfactory framework for establishing coherence in the fractured and fragmented field of psychology (and all its subdivisions), integrating it with not only the neighboring and essential biological sciences, but with the social sciences, which are now re-recognized as equally essential for a complete understanding of the evolution of Homo sapiens (which may be termed the Super Synthetic Theory of Evolution, or SSTE). SSTE then, is not only required to integrate "genes, brains, behavior and CL" (cognitive and learning processes; which are identified as habit; problem solving; abstract reasoning; counting ability; and language), but to further integrate these with environmental challenges, such as, physical, economic, and social forces in a "dynamic view of (human) life" (paren. added). It is a tribute to Charlesworth's wisdom and rhetorical skills that he is able to produce a compelling picture of all this (complete with embellishments) as succinctly as he does.

A few "embellishments" must be mentioned. Among them are: A welcome emphasis on "resource economics," or the cost of traits in terms of risks to survival and energy expenditures; distinctions made between learning, development, and adaptation; and the identification of "culture" as (following Dawkins, 1976), "the other source (besides DNA in the human gene pool) of inherited information passed from one generation to another," by means of communication.

With this broad intellectual landscape in mind, one can say, "Well, yes; all this can and should be conceptually integratable, but I wonder . . . ?" What about the resource economics, just on the biological level, of keeping species members alive long after their reproductive lives end, often (especially for women) for a period as long as their basic reproductive lives (see, Minsky, 1994)? Also, if brains (and "big brains" especially) are the mechanisms of adaptivity, as in LC, why has development (and dependency) been extended so far into the reproductive years so that brains can be "fully developed" (see, for instance, Huttenlocher, 1994)? And, why, after achieving "independence" do many highly learned, and, presumably, greatly adapted individuals further delay reproduction until they are in high risk periods of fertility? Charlesworth contends that "STE presents us with a dynamic view of life, . . . with instincts as well as habits and thinking as modes of adaptation" (p. 183). The general question may be "Do these modes always work in concert"; or as clinicians often ask, "What's wrong with this picture?" Further consideration of these, and other issues of cultural adaptation, I defer for now.

In his second section, Charlesworth presents his view of how early and then recent ethologists, comparative and general experimental psychologists, and most recently sociobiologists and "evolutionary psychologists," have worked mostly in isolation from each other, and occasionally in conflict, but, perhaps, at present may be converging on mutually supportive research questions. He presents an interesting perspective on the benefit and limitations of each approach. While lauding a variety of conceptual and empirical innovations emerging in recent approaches of the ethologists, sociologists, and evolutionary psychologists, Charlesworth finds problems apparent at each point. He applauds these researchers consistent emphasis on broad observational data bases, for instance, while noting their delay and reluctance toward using experimentation as a means to delimit and test their *theories, hypotheses,* and *conjectures* as he terms many of their proposals. Perhaps the major issue that emerges from a close reading of his presentation involves their basic premise that contemporary cognitive systems and mechanisms are continuous extensions of our prehistoric ancestors mental systems. Given this, a standard procedure is to create plausible scenarios regarding ancient survival problems and the mechanisms involved in how they were solved, *ipso facto* (since we are here now), and to argue that present day problem solving in analogous circumstances reflects the continuous operation of the mechanisms postulated. Two problems with this approach need solving, it appears to me. The first, primarily methodological problem centers on finding valid means of establishing homologous relationships among species cognitive systems (cf. for instance, Reynolds, 1981; Stebbins, 1982). *The Naked Ape* (Morris, 1967) *may* evoke a valid analogy, but the actual biological continuities underlying characteristic performances have not, as far as I know, been established. The second, related problem is more conceptual, and is illustrated by Gould's (1994) observation that "the standard misapplication of evolutionary theory assumes that biological explanation may be equated with devising accounts, often speculative and conjectural in practice, about the adaptive value of any given feature in its original environment (human aggression as good for hunting, music and religion as good for tribal cohesion, for example)" (p. 85). As Stebbins (1982) has noted, "Since behavior patterns are not preserved in the fossil record, we will never be able to trace the origin of such complex behavior patterns with any certainty" (p. 328). The hypothetical "architecture" of the human mind must have evolved, and we probably have a lot in common with our ancestors, as we do with many other species (and indeed, as "we" do with "other" societal groupings), but to say what the equivalencies are among these arrays of entities seems to require more than an exceptionally strong commitment to "family resemblances" (Wittgenstein, 1953) as the linchpin of comprehension and explanation. Therefore, just as there are paradoxes evident in applying the basic biological principles of evolutionary theory to contemporary human behavior, there are vexing imponderables at the level of comparative biopsychological analyses.

As regards comparisons of evolutionary research with general experimental psychology, Charlesworth extols the empirical, methodological rigor found there, but decries the narrow focus of its application. In this he is quite in harmony with others, for instance, Jerison (1982, esp. pp. 749–752). Both Charlesworth and Jerison also present views of evolution that substantively integrate cognitive phenomena and theorizing with their attempts to salvage much of the traditional learning phenomena, and they each provide either more implicit (Charlesworth) or explicit depictions of the integral role of language in CL processes than I have found elsewhere (cf. Turnure, 1985). Nevertheless, Charlesworth, and Jerison, recognize that traditional CL research has not been the locus of much information pertaining to STE to date, and vice versa.

Charlesworth then proceeds to offer an analysis of the obstacles that have impeded any coordination, much less integration, of CL research and STE conceptualizations. The major problems he identifies are not unfamiliar, for the most part: Limited, and limiting, theoretical concepts; inappropriate assumptions (e.g., the *scala naturae*); dichotomous thinking and typologing (see, most recently, Herrnstein & Murray, 1994); methodological reductionism, which might better be labeled *methodological imperialism*; and, finally here, the combined problems of the complexity and "infinite capacity" of CL processes, which almost necessarily lead to the fragmentation of theories of these processes. Most of us have our own version of these or related problems and concerns, and each of us may find Charlesworth's critical "shoe," pinching one or another of our personal conceptual or methodological "toes," so these words to the wise may help us achieve better research "fitness." I would point to Charlesworth's emphasis on the presumed infinite capacity of our species' cognitive and learning processes, because it at least alludes to a continually vexing issue; the controversy over the nature of intelligence. I wonder if the sense of "unlimited modifiability" and generativity he presents is not actually the general intuition that supports the basic idea of Spearman's "g," the hypothetical mental "capacity" or "power" that theoretically underlies the distribution of IQ scores? Such a unitary conception of intelligence is at variance with concepts of a partitionable mind, say in terms of mental abilities (Thurstone, 1938) "multiple intelligences" (Gardner, 1983), or "mental modules" (cf. Minsky, 1994); even sociobiologists posit "a large number of complex, content-dependent computational mechanisms that are specialized for solving the adaptive problems that our hunter-gatherer ancestors faced" (Citation, 1994, p. 270). Charlesworth's presentation suggests that human "minds" may be infinitely adaptable (see Minsky, 1994, for a contrary view), but, given that there is supposed to be some range of variability on every characteristic, what are the dimensions of variability? I assume'no one'human mind can know and do everything, but that some one of all the minds, over time, could do any one of all things to be done: The question then becomes, can any one mind do anything (perhaps given that it has enough "g")? If not, why not? If so, could we say that Charlesworth is cognitivism's J. B. Watson!? This issue is related to Charlesworth's reservation regarding psychological theories based on "constraints," but I think some such concept is fundamental and essential (see Holland, Holyoak, Nisbett, & Thagard, 1986, pp. 4–5), and I don't see how he can theorize about the "unlimited modifiability" and "unrestrainable ability" (p. 196) of the infinitely adaptable human nervous system without some such concept to account for individual differences and species variability. The variation in our species CL capabilities that exists and continues to emerge in response to today's tumultuous cultural changes seems to overwhelm understanding such matters even by the application of basic evolutionary concepts such as natural selection and inclusive fitness, which require environmental stability to function strongly (Stebbins, 1982). Thus, profound ambiguity reigns at the biocultural level of analysis.

At any rate, Charlesworth's creative contribution to resolving some of the existing difficulties he has identified is a "conceptual tool" labeled the *synoptiscope*. This tool, and the five steps required to use it, appear rather like a heuristic to me, although Charlesworth contends it is not. Given the probability that anything that encourages us to look at the forest is going to be of benefit, at least in the long run, this tool is a useful prod. Examples of the synoptiscope are presented by Charlesworth, but none of them is worked through in any detail. I am loath to try and characterize the four figures presented as examples, but a basic depiction involves a central construct or phenomenon (P's, which involve, The *common cold, Sex, Memory*, and *Sources of synoptiscopic information*), surrounded by boxes labeled with words of a wide variety; concrete and abstract nouns, descriptive phrases and phrase stems (e.g., *costs of, heritability of*) which constitute relevant variables (V's). These are not fixed or ordered in any obvious way, but, as I understand it, can be rearranged or considered in a variety of ways, at least until the empirical investigations they are designed to stimulate provide data to establish "weights" and, presumably, orderings of the "V's" in relation to a "P." Charlesworth provides brief commentaries for each example.

I found the "V's" that Charlesworth identified in each case interesting and stimulating, and, as he would expect and encourage, thought of some "V's" of my own. However, I do not know if he would expect that I could consider many of the "V's" for any one "P" interchangeable with or additive to any one or all of the other "P's." This experience reminded me of Kurt Lewin's Field Theory, which included the idea of a "permeability of the boundaries" of segments of the life space. This may not be all bad, or bad at all, but I believe the system needs more explication and/or context to be used as a particular kind of tool (and no "tool" is an all purpose tool, any more than, as I argued earlier, any "mind" is an all purpose mind). It appears to me that Charlesworth is here (and elsewhere) operating in the spirit of one or another of what are called Tinbergen's "four questions" (cf. Papaj, 1993), but that the application of the questions is not uniform or complete in regard to various of the questions or problems identified. Charlesworth describes the questions as relating to proximate causation, adaptive function, phylogenetic status, and development (or, according to Papaj, 1993, questions of causation, function, evolution, and ontogeny). The special qualities of behavior, especially LC directed behavior, have produced recommendations for tightening theoretical questions by researchers such as Gould (1993, 1994) and Papaj (1993), who appear to be at least as, if not more concerned with the problem of how to structure rich but rigorous research than Charlesworth.

Besides my differences with Charlesworth over the meanings of *heuristic,* and *constraint,* in this instance I am obliged to insert a demurrer over the rather short shift he gives here to the idea of contextualism. I don't at all agree that contextualism leads to deconstructionism, as he asserts, although I agree that deconstructionism often, if not usually, leads to loss of meaning. In fact, I see the synoptiscope as a particular version of contextualistic analysis (although, of course, I may simply be assimilating here). Consider this quote from Jenkins (1974; a paper Charlesworth cites elsewhere rather approvingly), regarding a contextualist's analysis of all the processes that contribute to memory: The contextualist, Jenkins says, "avoids despair at this point, not by predicting success for a global assault on all higher mental processes simultaneously but by asking again,

> What kind of an analysis of memory will be useful to use in the kinds of problems you are facing? What kinds of events concern you? If you limit the events for some purpose, he will lead you into an analysis of context, textures that support experiences, strands that interrelate aspects of experiences, etc.
>
> You should notice that methodological issues and the choices of experimental paradigms become crucial when you take the contextualist view. It is *not* true in this view that one can study any part of the "cosmic machine" to just as good an effect as any other part. The important thing is to pick the right kinds of events for your purposes . . . In short, contextualism stresses relating one's laboratory problems to the ecologically valid problems of everyday life. (p. 794)

Note the emphasis placed on limiting "events for some purpose." Identifying the purpose for choosing some event to study, or just talk about, almost inherently involves meaning. And choosing parts of the "cosmic machine" to study in context at least prioritizes relative assessments of value or worth. And I believe Charlesworth must applaud the stress Jenkins puts on ecological validity and problems of everyday life.

Asserting the congruence or complementary of contextualism and the snyoptiscope does not diminish the particular value of Charlesworth's contribution, nor does it imply that contextualism would lead to the sorts of research issues that he is advancing, especially as regards to STE. It is more the case, I think, that as a long-time contextualist (cf. Turnure, 1975) I am quite sympathetic to Charlesworth's wide ranging analyses of the contemporary research scene, even though I have never tried to relate CL research to STE, and remain fascinated by, but unconvinced of the present acceptability of accounts of human functioning based on STE theorizing, primarily for the reasons noted earlier. Charlesworth presents a sophisticated rationale for the ultimate acceptance of the kind of research and theory development he is recommending, but he provides no example of a final product for our consideration.

Charlesworth completes his presentation with a plea and proposal for socially relevant research with an emphasis on research on learning and cognition, couched in terms of evolutionary theory but not limited by existing formulations.

In striving to establish a balanced vision of the interaction of biological and environmental processes in his final section, Charlesworth notes that the extraordinary and perhaps potentially explosive expansion of the human species and its culture has produced "the major threat to human existence." At the biological level, this observation could be seen as simply a continuation of the evolutionary process, that is, successful adaptations increase reproductive success producing population pressures which cause the population numbers to collapse, providing for the survival of selected covariants of the species, which increases until it reaches the limits of resources in the particular niche available, and so on (see, for instance, Gribben & Gribben, 1993; Kates, 1994).

But the human species has produced a major new factor in this pattern, called culture, which seems to require drastic reconceptualizations, some presented here by Charlesworth. He has produced an eminently fair array of general recommendations for progressive research, as well as for reasonable attitudes regarding the interplay of biological and cultural evolution. But, they are, necessarily, summary abstractions, and appear to leave a number of issues and problems in their wake. Not the least of these pertain to professional and disciplinary matters, such as the nature and scope of training programs for both basic and applied researchers, and division of labor and specialization requirements.

More basic issues inspired by Charlesworth's analyses and admonitions might include an even greater emphasis on the implications of earthly history having reached a point of radical cultural, especially technological, evolution, and how this issue interacts with the population explosion. He notes, rightly, that "there is no satisfactory technological fix to solving the problems facing our planet today," but technology has been the major impetus to recent cultural change and will undoubtedly continue to provide opportunities and threats to some or all segments of humanity, in various scenarios throughout our existence. Charlesworth appears all too sanguine that such change can be managed by "humans who are mindful, playful, predictable as well as very unpredictable." With even greater reservations about the benign CL capabilities of humans (cf. Langer, 1989), and the unintended as well as dubious intended impacts of cultural innovation, one has to wonder, "How much more can we take?" This question obviously pertains as well to the issue of population growth, which, according to news reports from the United Nations Conference on World Population, in Cairo, estimates that the present population of 5.7 billion will be added to at a rate of approximately 2 billion people every quarter century, until it "stabilizes" at around 11 1/2 to 12 billion people over the next 150–200 years (see Kates, 1994; Salk & Salk, 1981 for details). The interanimation of biology and culture, recently termed *gene-culture coevolution* (Lumsden & Wilson, 1983), a concept that serves rather well to coalesce the problem, is clearly among the most complex issues in the life-and social sciences, as well as being among the most emotionally inflammatory of social issues (the release of Herrnstein & Murray's *The Bell Curve,* 1994 occurred during the writing of this reaction). While others (see especially, Degler, 1991; Edelman, 1992; Gould, 1987; Kitcher, 1985) have developed an array of arguments against certain of the positions that (I assume) Charlesworth is referring generally to as "genetic determinists" (as is almost traditional in this literature) I am most concerned with the inability of theoreticians to establish the reasonable boundaries of scope and speculation. In this I sense agreement with Charlesworth in striving to find a middle ground that will encourage appreciation of the indivisible interplay of the basic genetic (DNA) operations and the immediate physical influences of non DNA factors. Neuroscientists have advanced detailed depictions of the influence of the immediate surround on the genes and the genes operations in the individual cells. The basic principles were worked out decades ago (cf. Moore, 1963) and are presented in extraordinary detail at present (see Edelman, 1992).

Many knowledgeable psychologists have contributed data, theory, and advice regarding the fundamental interpenetration of the genetic material and the physical substances and energizing forces that are operative in embryological development and subsequently in physical maturation, as well as in a number of specific cases of psychological phenomena (see for instance, Jerison, 1982; Plomin, 1989; Scarr & Carter-Saltzman, 1982). Establishing the proper conceptualization of the fundamental processes, and even the appropriate terminology to characterize and communicate the concepts in question seems to me to have been elusive (recall my differences with Charlesworth over *heuristic, constraint,* and *contextualism*). For instance, I have just used the terms *interanimation, interplay,* and *interpenetration* to convey the close and inseparable mutual influence of DNA and the substances surrounding it; I used to simply say they *interact*. But, a number of colleagues have a very restricted sense of that term, usually based in statistics, which actually seems to reinforce a sense of the general separateness or independence of the partners in the process (Edelman, 1992, appears to use the term *interaction* with the same intent I have had). Essentially, the problem probably rests in dichotomous thinking, as Charlesworth implied earlier on, and, as Gould (1987, 1993) has argued in attempting to establish a clearer process-oriented view of human evolution. Indeed, Gould (1987) has presented possibly the most straightforward analysis of the potential misunderstanding emerging from the general use of interaction, particularly as it is implicated in some formulations of gene-culture coevolution. Gould recommends the adoption of dialectical thinking to properly capture the basic process of gene-environment operation. The result would be a more holistic view that sees "change as interaction among components of complete systems, and sees the components themselves not as a priori entities but as both products of and inputs to the system" (Gould, 1987, p. 154). Once the complete melding of gene-context embryological development is discerned, implications that congenital = heredity are basically dispelled, and postnatal development is rather readily perceived as a continuation of maturation and experience, incorporating genetic (growth, mylenation, etc.), physical (nutrition, health, etc.), sociopsychological (parenting, stimulation, etc.), and cultural (language, toys, etc.) factors.

The result of a resolution of the nature–nurture controversy that would be more penetrating and precise than the rather general or confusing reliance on interactionism would appear to lead to a more complete acceptance of individual differences as representative of population thinking, in contrast to typologies, and so would be more in accord with the position advanced by Charlesworth, and others (see especially, Plomin, 1989; Scarr & Carter-Saltzman, 1982). But few, if any scientific disciplines are well prepared presently to articulate the conceptual basis for linking genetic variation, child development, and evolution with culture, much less with cultural change. I am not even sure that a coordinated attack based on Tinbergen's "four questions," as Charlesworth, and others (cf. Papaj, 1993), have urged could handle the problems that have emerged as representatives of Homo sapiens have learned to control and exploit sources of energy, from coal to oil and from electricity to atomic, in the past several centuries (creating what Stebbins calls "The Age of Harnessed Energy," p. 432), and now combine that energy with incredible advances in how to organize and transmit information (see Donald, 1991). How could any species be genetically predisposed to function comfortably in the past hundred years, or worse, the next hundred? Charlesworth notes this issue, and proposes that major resources be applied to the human sciences. The question that would arise were this unlikely, if rational, event to occur is, "What would we do with them and how much good would it do?"

Charlesworth proposes much more research on (evolutionary guided) CL processes, and a great expansion of education, primarily to remedy problems and threats that exist now. I would agree with the general principle, but I wonder where the cultural changes to allow this will occur. The need for all of this work will require resources, but, among other problems inherent in attempting such changes, the need for resources to provide a reasonable existence for the doubling or tripling of the species in the next hundred years or so seems preclude any such focused allocation. Salk and Salk (1981) provide a sobering view of the probable reproductive success of Homo sapiens into the next century, with population increases building on the sixfold rise in population over the 200 years from 1800–2000. They also recommend and, indeed, assume that increased availability of education and economic development will decrease birth rates, so as to eventually produce a stabilization of population at around 12 billion people. They also optimistically foresee a change in values and attitudes such that these huge numbers of people will live in harmony, but only after a long period of tension and conflict, just the period when Charlesworth proposes his urgent program of research and education. Thus, we have a marginally optimistic scenario of a race to survival between forces of rationality (Charlesworth's "mindful, planful, predictable" humans) and other forces forged in our earlier, primitive epoch (cf. Salk & Salk, 1981), which is probably still in progress.

The problem evident for sometime (cf. Comfort, 1966), is that the subcultures that developed and control the energy and material resources of the planet, many of which are nonrenewable and so not unlimited, have evolved into "lifestyles" that presently utilize 75% of the earth's resources despite constituting only 25% of the world's population, and these ratios are still diverging as far as I can see. In effect, it is too expensive, indeed, probably impossible, to have cultural (or western or northern hemisphere environmental) evolution continue to be the coevolutionary counterpart of our present state of biological evolution (see Kates, 1994). That is, the costs of doing it our, western or developed way are prohibitive. To be precise, the investments made in fully developing the "minds" of many of our recent progeny which appears inherent in reducing and limiting (or even in some cases eliminating) reproduction to replacement rates (or below) cannot be a general survival strategy, unless individual intellectual development can be made radically more efficient, say by a factor of 10 over the next hundred years. The way developed nations stabilize their populations is by investing in prolonged education and providing desirable alternatives to childbearing, leading to what is known as "demographic transition." But as indicated, this investment is incredibly expensive, and furthermore, because of this, tends to impact affluent, well educated women and families first (Herrnstein & Murray, 1994; Stebbins, 1982), leading to differential reproductive rates across social classes. This sort of imbalance has occasionally given rise to social concerns revolving around claims of a dysgenic effect, or a reduction in "national intelligence" occurring (Herrnstein & Murray, 1994; Stebbins, 1982). Such controversies appear misguided (see Beardsley, 1995; Stebbins, 1982, p. 441), but important, because they influence public policy. Nevertheless, such controversies are secondary to the basic issue of controlling mass population increases presumably via the same practices. However, given the basic thrust of Charlesworth's paper, and the basic premise of gene-culture coevolution, it seems that the nature of the problem can be seen differently than in the past.

The first consideration is to fully understand (see Minsky, 1994) that it is Homo sapiens unique place in the biosphere that is central to every aspect of the "threats" that Charlesworth emphasizes. Homo sapiens are the only creatures aware of the threats, and Homo sapiens are the creators of the most of the threats, both to the species itself and, perhaps, to life in general (see, Calvin, 1994; Gould, 1994; Kates, 1994; Minsky, 1994). It appears most important, furthermore, to realize that nature, and evolution, doesn't care one iota about any aspect of these matters. If Homo sapiens become extinct, one way or the other, some form of life would probably "fill our niche." It seems apparent that evolutionary principles mandate maximum population expansion, until "fate" intervenes to constrain it, fate in human terms being identified with famine, pestilence, natural disasters and war, the mythic "Four horsemen of the apocalypse." This seems important, because most responses to the threat to the species argue that cultural development, usually identified with a subset of human characteristics (e.g., specifically, intelligence, consciousness, etc., or generally, fitness, adaptability, etc.), be rapidly expanded to nondeveloped areas of the world, to reduce population expansion. It does appear an ultimate irony that intelligence somehow might get established as the "fifth horseman," at least in terms of functional equivalence. But the problems of cost in resource allocation identified earlier are unsolvable now, and into the foreseeable future. Because I am an optimist (see the Calvin, Gould, Kates, & Minsky references), I am in favor and hopeful of the survival of the species; but this stance requires reconsidering what the "fittest" means in cultural terms. Thus the need to consider not just gene/culture coevolution, but genetic variation, child development, culture(s), and cultural change in relation to evolution. The daunting dimensions of this perspective appear awesome, but so does life. The magnitude of the task overshadows the incredible, if costly, cultural achievements of the species so far, and induces a sense of humility akin to that which Gould (1994) admonishes us to adopt. It is at this point that Charlesworth's proposals regarding large investments in relevant research and radical rethinking of cognitive theories is encouraging and stimulating, and that "there is much more to come in the evolution of human affairs" (p. 213). He also warns us not to accept simplistic solutions, or even complicated theories that lead to simple solutions.

I would conclude by citing the endings of three articles referred to earlier, which, along with Gould (1994), all are written in the spirit of Charlesworth's call to take evolution seriously and substantively into account. Calvin (1994) concludes his article by quoting Gould, regarding what is needed for longer-term survival: "We have become by the power of a glorious evolutionary accident called intelligence, the stewards of life's continuity on earth. We did not ask for this role, but we cannot abjure it. We may not be suited for it, but here we are" (p. 107). Minsky (1994) sums up his position by asserting, "We owe our minds to the deaths and lives of all the creatures that were ever engaged in the struggle called evolution. Our job is to see that all this work shall not end up in meaningless waste" (p. 113). Kates (1994) proposes an "evolutionary tilt toward optimism," because, he says "hope is simply a necessity if we as a species, now conscious of the improbable and extraordinary journey taken by life in the universe, are to survive" (p. 122). Work such as Charlesworth's contributes to our sense of hope.

REFERENCES

Beardsley, T. (1995). For whom the bell curve really tolls. *Scientific American, 272,* 14–17.

Buss, D. M. (1994). The strategies of human mating. *American Scientist, 82,* 238–249.

Calvin, W. H. (1994). The emergence of intelligence. *Scientific American, 271,* 100–107.

Charlesworth, W. R. (1976). Human intelligence as adaptation: An ethological approach. In L. B. Resnick (Ed.), *The nature of intelligence.* Hillsdale, NJ: Lawrence Erlbaum Associates.

Charlesworth, W. (1978). *One year of haiku.* Minneapolis: Nodin Press.

Charlesworth, W. R. (1986). Darwin and developmental psychology: 100 years later. *Human Development, 29,* 1–35.

Charlesworth, W. R. (1992). Darwin and developmental psychology: Past and present. *Developmental Psychology, 28,* 5–16.

Citation. (1994). Leda Cosmides. *American Psychologist,* 269–271.

Comfort, A. (1966). *The nature of human nature.* New York: Harper and Row.

Dawkins, R. (1976). *The selfish game.* Oxford: Oxford University Press.

Degler, C. N. (1991). *In search of human nature.* New York: Oxford University Press.

Donald, M. (1991). *Origins of the modern mind: Three stages in the evolution of culture and cognition.* Cambridge, MA: Harvard University Press.

Edelman, G. M. (1992). *Bright air, brilliant fire.* New York: Basic Books.

Gardner, H. (1983). *Frames of mind: The theory of multiple intelligences.* New York: Basic Books.

Gould, S. J. (1987). *An urchin in the storm.* New York: Norton.

Gould, S. J. (1993). *Eight little piggies.* New York: Norton.

Gould, S. J. (1994). The evolution of life on the earth. *Scientific American, 271,* 84–91.

Gribbin, M., & Gribben, J. (1993). *Being human.* London: J. M. Dent.

Herrnstein, R. J., & Murray, C. (1994). *The bell curve.* New York: The Free Press.

Holland, J. H., Holyoak, K. J., Nisbett, R. E., & Thagard, P. R. (1986). *Induction.* Cambridge, MA: MIT Press.

Huttenlocher, P. R. (1994). Synaptogenesis, synapse elimination, and neural plasticity in human cerebral cortex. In C. A. Nelson (Ed.), *Threats to optimal development: Integrating biological, psychological, and social risk factors.* Minnesota Symposium on Child Development (pp. 35–54). Hillsdale, NJ: Lawrence Erlbaum Associates.

Jenkins, J. J. (1974). Remember that old theory of memory? Well forget it! *American Psychologist, 29,* 785–795.

Jerison, H. J. (1982). The evolution of biological intelligence. In R. J. Sternberg (Ed.), *Handbook of human intelligence.* Cambridge, England: Cambridge University Press.

Kates, R. W. (1994). Sustaining life on the earth. *Scientific American, 271,* 114–121.

Kessen, W. (1965). *The child.* New York: Wiley.

Kitcher, P. (1985). *Vaulting ambition: Sociobiology and the quest for human nature.* Cambridge, MA: MIT Press.

Langer, E. J. (1989). *Mindfulness.* Reading, MA: Addison Wesley.

Lumsden, C. J., & Wilson, E. O. (1983). *Promethean fire.* Cambridge, MA: Harvard University Press.

Mayr, E. (1974). Behavior programs and evolutionary strategies. *American Scientist, 62,* 650–659.

Minsky, M. (1994). Will robots inherit the earth? *Scientific American, 272,* 108–113.

Moore, J. A. (1963). *Heredity and development.* New York: Oxford University Press.

Morris, D. (1967). *The naked ape*. New York: McGraw Hill.

Papaj, D. R. (1993). Review of the Tinbergen legacy. *American Scientist, 81,* 390–391.

Plomin, R. (1989). Environmental genes: Determinants of behavior. *American Scientist, 44,* 105–111.

Reynolds, P. C. (1981). *On the evolution of human behavior.* Berkeley: University of California Press.

Salk, J., & Salk, J. (1981). *World population and human values.* New York: Harper & Row.

Scarr, S., & Carter-Saltzman, L. (1982). Genetics and intelligence. In R. J. Sternberg (Ed.), *Handbook of human intelligence.* Cambridge, England: Cambridge University Press.

Stebbins, G. L. (1982). *Darwin to DNA, molecules to humanity.* San Francisco: Freeman.

Thurstone, L. L. (1938). *Primary and mental abilities.* Psychometric Monographs 1. Chicago: University of Chicago Press.

Turnure, J. E. (1975, March). *A description and analysis of contextualism in mental retardation R & D.* Invited symposium paper. Gatlinburg Conference on Research in Mental Retardation, Gatlinburg, TN.

Turnure, J. E. (1985). Communication and cues in the functional cognition of the mentally retarded. In N. R. Ellis & N. W. Bray (Eds.), *International review of research in mental retardation.* New York: Academic Press.

Wittgenstein, L. (1953). *Philosophical investigations.* New York: Macmillan.

Author Index

A

Alberts, J. R., 28, 29
Alcock, J., 180, 213
Alexander, R. D., 183, 189, 213
Allport, A., 20, 29
Altom, M. W., 20, 31
Anderson, J., 34, 35, 43, 53, 55, 60, 73
Anglin, J. M., 5, 29
Applegate, B., 163, 172
Aslin, R., 70, 72 Au, T. K., 23, 29, 67, 72
Azuma, H., 142, 149

B

Baillargeon, R., 65, 72
Baker, C. L., 47, 53
Baker, E., 2, 30
Baldwin, D. A., 25, 29
Baldwin, J. M., 177, 213
Banigan, R. L., 67, 72
Barkow, J. H., 183, 188, 190, 214
Bateman, B., 162, 170
Bates, E., 27, 29, 43, 49, 51, 53, 55, 60, 73
Bauer, P. J., 66, 72, 73
Bavin, E. L., 27, 29
Beardsley, T., 228, 230
Beecher, M. D., 186, 214
Behrend, D. A., 63, 66, 72
Bekoff, M., 179, 214
Bempechat, J., 157, 170
Bertanfly, L. von, 27, 30
Bertrand, J., 67, 74
Bever, T. G., 34, 54
Biddle, B., 103, 130
Biederman, I., 6, 30
Bill, V. L., 82, 88, 99, 100
Blanshard, B., 207, 214
Blass, E. M., 28, 31
Bloom, L., 6, 30
Bloom, P., 63, 72
Bogdan, R. J., 177, 189, 214
Bolles, R. C., 186, 214
Bonner, J. T., 179, 182, 214
Bowerman, M., 5, 30, 48, 53
Bowler, P. J., 178, 214
Bowman, L. L., 4, 31
Boyd, R., 182, 214
Boyes-Braem, P., 65, 75
Brandt, R. B., 207, 216
Breland, K., 186, 192, 214
Breland, M., 186, 192, 214
Brennan, S. E., 86, 100
Brimmell, T., 27, 29
Brooks-Gunn, J., 164, 170
Brophy, J., 103, 130
Broughton, J., 6, 30
Brown, J. S., 79, 96, 99, 100, 154, 170
Bruner, J. S., 65, 74, 90, 101
Bullinaria, J., 40, 53
Burgess, N., 47, 53

Burr, D. J., 49, 54
Butterworth, G., 65, 72
Byers, J. A., 179, 214

C

Calvin, W. H., 229, 230
Campbell, A., 153, 171
Campbell, C. B. G., 186, 193, 215
Campbell, J. R., 151, 152, 172
Carey, S., 22, 23, 32, 162, 170
Carpenter, T. P., 103, 130
Carraher, D. W., 75, 76, 79, 100
Carraher, T. N., 75, 76, 78, 100
Carter-Saltzman, L., 219, 226, 227, 231
Cary, S., 192, 214
Case, R., 95, 100, 162, 171
Cauzinille-Marmeche, E., 81, 86, 100, 101
Ceci, S. J., 162, 171
Chalkley, M., 39, 55
Charles, R. I., 76, 100
Charlesworth, W. R., 178, 182, 190, 199, 209, 214, 219, 220, 221, 224, 230
Chen, C., 139, 141, 149, 152, 154, 173
Chi, M. T. H., 162, 171
Choi, S., 27, 30
Churchland, P. S., 60, 72
Clark, E. B., 5, 30
Clark, H. H., 86, 100
Cobb, P., 93, 101
Cohen, J., 207, 214
Cohen, M., 47, 53
Cohen, P., 207, 214
Cole, E., 26, 31
Comfort, A., 228, 230
Cooney, T. J., 131, 149, 151, 171, 172
Cosmides, L., 182, 183, 188, 189, 190, 214, 217
Costall, A., 190, 214
Cottrell, G., 35, 36, 43, 53
Coulthard, R. M., 88, 101
Cronbach, L. J., 205, 214
Crook, J. H., 177, 214
Crosswhite, F. J., 131, 149, 151, 171, 172
Cuban, L., 156, 171
Culicover, P., 47, 57

D

Daelemanns, W., 39, 54
Daly, M., 183, 204, 214
Darwin, C., 176, 214
Davidson, D., 108, 130
Dawkins, R., 220, 230
Deak, G., 67, 72
Decsy, G. J., 29
Degler, C. N., 210, 214, 226, 230
deKleer, J., 96, 100
Dell, G., 35, 43, 54, 60, 72
Devescovi, A., 51, 53
Dobzhansky, T., 182, 214
Donald, M., 177, 215, 227, 230
Donaldson, M., 93, 100
Dornbusch, S. M., 165, 173
Dossey, J. A., 131, 149, 151, 152, 171, 172
Dromi, E., 6, 8, 30, 65, 72
Duff, M. A., 28, 32
Dunkin, M., 103, 130
Durieux, G., 39, 54
Dweck, C. S., 157, 158, 170, 171
Dyer, M., 44, 50, 56

E

Ebmeier, M., 120, 130
Edelman, G. M., 226, 230

Edelson, S. M., 20, 31
Eibl-Eibesfeldt, I., 184, 215
Eilers, R. E., 46, 56
Elman, J. L., 36, 46, 49, 54, 56, 61, 72

F

Fantz, R. L., 14, 30
Fegley, S., 165, 173
Fentress, J. C., 28, 30
Fernandez, C., 119, 121, 127, 130
Feyerabend, P., 205, 215
Finn, C. E., Jr., 151, 169, 171
Fischer, K. W., 95, 100
Flavell, J., 190, 215
Fodor, J. A., 3, 4, 26, 30, 34, 54
Forbus, K. D., 96, 100
Francis, W., 37, 54
Frazier, L., 49, 54
Freeman, K. E., 66, 72
Freko, D., 20, 31
Fuligni, A. J., 143, 149
Furstenberg, F. F., Jr., 164, 170
Fuson, K. C., 93, 100

G

Gabriel, B., 27, 29
Gallistel, C. R., 71, 73, 81, 100, 161, 171
Galton, F., 176, 215
Garcia, J., 192, 215
Gardner, H., 222, 230
Garrett, M. F., 34, 54
Gasser, M., 11, 30, 65, 73
Gelman, R., 2, 14, 24, 30, 31, 71 73, 81, 100, 161, 171, 192, 214
Gelman, S. A., 22, 30, 32, 161, 172, 173
Gentile, C. A., 151, 152, 172
Gentner, D., 6, 30
Gershkoff-Stowe, L., 6, 8, 16, 21, 26, 30, 31, 32
Ghiselin, M., 183, 215
Gibson, E. J., 27, 30
Gigerenzer, G., 190, 215
Gilbert, J. H. V., 46, 57
Gillis, S., 39, 54
Ginsburg, H. A., 103, 130
Gleick, J., 206, 215
Gleitman, H., 47, 54
Gleitman, L. R., 47, 54
Glusman, M., 67, 72
Goldfield, B. A., 6, 30
Goldsmith, J., 36, 54
Golinkoff, R. M., 67, 74
Good, T. L., 103, 120, 130
Goodall, J., 187, 215
Goodman, N., 3, 30
Gopnik, A., 8, 27, 30, 65, 73
Gottlieb, G., 28, 30, 66, 73, 183, 215
Gould, S. J., 179, 193, 215, 224, 226, 227, 229, 230
Graham, P. A., 105, 130
Graham, T., 144, 149
Gray, W. D., 65, 74
Green, K. F., 192, 215
Greeno, J. G., 79, 85, 91, 101, 155, 172
Greenough, W. T., 66, 73
Gresham, F. M., 167, 171
Gribbin, J., 225, 230
Gribbin, M., 225, 230
Griffin, D. R., 187, 215
Griffin, P., 88, 100
Grossberg, S., 34, 47, 53, 54
Grouws, D., 120, 130
Guo, G., 164, 170
Gupta, P., 35, 44, 54

H-I

Hagar, J. L., 192, 217
Hall, J., 93, 100
Hamilton, M. A., 165, 171
Hamilton, S. F., 165, 171
Hamilton, W. D., 188, 215
Hanson, S. J., 49, 54
Harkness, S., 158, 173
Harley, T., 35, 54
Harlow, H. F., 177, 215
Harris, C. A., 163, 172
Hatch, T., 67, 74
Herrnstein, R. J., 222, 226, 228, 230
Hertz, J., 35, 54
Hess, R., 142, 149
Hill, T., 20, 31
Hinde, R. A., 192, 215
Hinton, G., 35, 37, 54, 56
Hirsh-Pasek, K., 27, 32
Hitch, G., 47, 53
Hodos, W., 186, 193, 215
Hoeffner, J., 43, 54
Holland, J. H., 223, 230
Holyoak, K. J., 223, 230
Hopfield, J. J., 34, 54
Houghton, G., 46, 49, 54
Hsu, C. C., 138, 139, 144, 149
Hug, K., 190, 215
Humphrey, F., 88, 100
Humphrey, K., 46, 57
Humphrey, N. K., 177, 215
Hutchinson, N. L., 183, 171
Huttenlocher, P. R., 220, 230
Imai, M., 6, 30

J

Jaeger, J. J., 34, 54
James, W., 20, 30
Jarrett, N., 65, 72
Jenkins, J. J., 198, 215, 224, 230
Jenkins, L., 152, 171
Jerison, H. J., 219, 222, 226, 230
Johnson, D. M., 65, 74
Johnston, J. M., 206, 215
Johnston, T. D., 66, 73
Jones, L. V., 151, 171
Jones, S. S., 2, 5, 6, 8, 9, 14, 15, 16, 17, 18, 19, 21, 22, 30, 31, 32, 67, 73
Jungeblut, A., 152, 153, 171

K

Kalish, C. W., 161, 172
Kariya, T., 165, 172
Kashiwagi, K., 142, 149
Kates, R. W., 225, 226, 228, 229, 230
Katims, N., 151, 171
Katz, N., 2, 30
Kawamoto, A., 35, 43, 49, 55, 56
Keil, F. C., 63, 66, 73, 161, 173
Kessen, W., 219, 230
Kifer, E., 131, 149, 151, 171, 172
Kim, J., 42, 55
King, A. P., 28, 32
Kirsch, I. S., 152, 153, 171
Kitamura, S., 138, 139, 144, 149
Kitcher, P., 210, 215, 226, 230
Klahr, D., 34, 55
Kohn, A. S., 77, 101
Kohonen, T., 34, 44, 55
Kolstad, A., 152, 171
Kopcke, K. -M., 39, 55, 57
Kosowski, T. D., 2, 32
Kotovsky, K., 34, 55
Kozol, J., 159, 171
Krogh, A., 35, 54
Kucera, H., 37, 54
Kuczaj, S. A., 4, 31, 63, 73
Kuhl, P., 46, 55

Kuhn, T. S., 200, 215
Kwon, Y., 93, 100

L

Laframboise, D. E., 23, 29
Lamb, S., 35, 55
Lampert, M., 99, 100, 151, 171
Landau, B., 2, 5, 6, 8, 9, 16, 17, 19, 21, 22, 30, 31, 32, 67, 73
Langer, E. J., 225, 230
Lapointe, A. E., 160, 171
Latham, A. S., 151, 152, 172
Lave, J., 75, 100, 191, 217
Lee, S. Y., 104, 130, 138, 139, 141, 144, 149, 152, 154, 159, 173
Leer, M. N., 88, 99
Leggett, E. L., 157, 158, 171
Lehner, P. N., 199, 215
Lehrman, D. S., 28, 31
Leinbach, J., 35, 36, 39, 44, 55, 60, 61, 62, 73
Lesgold, S., 82, 100
Lewicki, P., 20, 31
Lickliter, R., 66, 73
Lifter, K., 6, 30
Liitschwager, J. C., 67, 73
Linell, P., 34, 55
Ling, C., 38, 40, 55
Lockard, R. B., 185, 215
London, P., 157, 170
Lorenz, K., 177, 184, 216
Lucker, G. W., 144, 138, 149
Lumsden, C. J., 226, 230
Lykken, D. T., 197, 207, 216
Lynn, R., 137, 149
Lyons, B., 93, 100

M

MacAndrew, S., 35, 54
MacDonald, K. B., 183, 216
Macnamara, J., 2, 30
MacWhinney, B.,4, 31, 33, 35, 36, 38, 39, 43, 44,47, 49, 51, 53, 54, 55, 56, 60, 61, 62, 63, 73
Malthus, T. R., 178, 216
Mandler, J. M., 66, 73
Maratsos, M., 39, 55, 63, 67, 72, 73
Marchman, V., 35, 55
Marcus, M., 49, 56
Marinov, M., 38, 55
Markman, E. M., 2, 3, 4, 6, 22, 23, 25, 29, 30, 31, 32, 63, 65, 66, 67, 73, 74, 93, 100
Marler, P., 28, 31
Marsh, H. W., 165, 171
Marslen-Wilson, W. D., 35, 56
Massey, C., 14, 31
Mathieu, J., 81, 86, 100, 101
Maynard Smith, J., 188, 216
Mayr, E., 190, 194, 216, 219, 230
McCarthy, J. J., 47, 53
McClelland, J., 34, 35, 36, 43, 46, 49, 56, 57, 60, 63, 74
McCormick, M., 161, 172
McDonald, J., 35, 36, 39, 44, 49, 51, 52, 55, 56, 60, 61, 62,73
McDonough, L., 66, 73
McGowan, B. K., 192, 215
McKnight, C. C., 131, 149, 151, 171, 172
McNew, S., 51, 53
McQuire, M., 183, 197, 216
Mead, N. A., 160, 71
Meck, B., 161, 162, 171
Medin, D. L., 20, 31, 211, 216
Meehl, P. E., 197, 205, 207, 216, 219
Mehan, H., 88, 100
Meltzoff, A. N., 8, 30, 65, 73
Mendel, G., 17, 216
Mercer, C. D., 163, 172
Merriman, W. E., 4, 31, 63, 74

Mervis, C. B., 65, 67, 72, 74
Messer, D. J., 65, 74
Miikkulainen, R., 44, 50, 56
Miller, J., 46, 55
Miller, P. H., 190, 215
Miller, S. A., 190, 215
Miller, S. P., 163, 172
Mills, A. E., 39, 56
Minsky, M., 221, 222, 228, 229, 230
Montague, M., 163, 172
Moore, J. A., 226, 230
Morgan, C. L., 177, 216
Morgan, J., 47, 56
Morris, D., 221, 231
Morss, J. R., 190, 216
Moser, J. M., 103, 130
Mozer, M. C., 35, 54
Muchisky, M., 26, 31
Mullis, I. V. S., 151, 152, 160, 172
Murphy, C. M., 65, 74
Murphy, J., 151, 172
Murray, C., 222, 226, 228, 230
Murray, F. B., 156, 172

N

Nagel, E., 207, 216
Nakamura, G. V., 211, 216
Nash, P., 151, 171
Neisser, U., 191, 216
Nelson, K., 4, 31, 63, 74
Nespor, M., 36, 56
Nesse, R., 201, 216
Newell, A., 34, 56
Newport, E. L., 47, 54
Ng, B. C., 27, 29
Nisbett, R. E., 223, 230
Norman, D., 46, 57
Nosofsky, R. M., 20, 31
Nunes, T., 75, 79, 100

O

O'Sullivan, C., 151, 152, 172
Ogbu, J. U., 166, 172
Ohala, J., 34, 56
Okazaki, S., 166, 173
Oller, D. K., 46, 56
Omanson, S. F., 79, 81, 101
Ornstein, P. A., 197, 216
Osherson, D. N., 3, 31
Owen, E. H., 152, 172
Oyama, S., 27, 31, 66, 74

P

Palmer, R., 35, 54
Papaj, D. R., 224, 227, 231
Parke, R. D., 197, 216
Pedersen, P. E., 28, 31
Pellegrini, A. D., 158, 172
Pergament, G., 93, 100
Perry, M., 106, 117, 120, 130
Petrinovich, L., 207, 216
Phillips, G. W., 152, 160, 171, 172
Piaget, J., 27, 31
Piatelli-Palmarini, M., 3, 26, 31
Pinker, S., 42, 47, 55, 56, 71, 74
Plaut, D., 43, 56
Plomin, R., 226, 227, 231
Plotkin, H. C., 177, 187, 190, 216
Plunkett, K., 35, 36, 43, 53
Poole, D., 88, 100
Prasada, S., 42, 55
Prince, A., 42, 55, 71, 74

Q-R

Quine, W. V., 2, 31
Reams, L. E., 88, 99
Rebarber, T., 151, 169, 171
Reber, A., 20, 32

Reichenbach, H., 208, 216
Resnick, D. P., 168, 172
Resnick, J. S., 6, 30
Resnick, L. B., 77, 79, 81, 82, 85, 86, 88, 91, 99, 100, 101, 151, 154, 161, 168, 172, 173
Reynolds, P. C., 221, 231
Ricco, G., 78, 101
Richards, J., 93, 101
Richards, R., 176, 216
Richerson, P. J., 182, 214
Riedl, R., 177, 216
Rieser, J. J., 197, 216
Riley, M. S., 155, 172
Ristau, C. A., 188, 217
Rogoff, B., 191, 217
Romberg, T. A., 103, 130
Rosch, E., 6, 32, 65, 74
Rosenbaum, J. E., 165, 172
Rosengren, K. S., 161, 172
Ross, G., 90, 101
Rue, L., 196, 217
Rumelhart, D., 34, 36, 37, 46, 56, 57, 60, 63, 74
Runes, D. D., 207, 216

S

Salk, J., 226, 227, 228, 231
Salk, J., 226, 227, 228, 231
Sameroff, A. J., 163, 172, 173
Sasak, I., 20, 31
Saxe, G. B., 75, 101
Scaife, M., 65, 74
Scarr, S., 190, 217, 219, 226, 227, 231
Schaffer, M., 20, 31
Schliemann, A. D., 75, 76, 79, 100
Schoenfeld, A. H., 76, 99, 101
Schwartz, J. L., 96, 101
Scribner, S., 75, 101
Seidenberg, M., 43, 57
Seligman, M. E. P., 192, 217
Sera, M., 81, 101
Shallice, T., 35, 54
Siebert, J., 93, 100
Siegler, R. S., 4, 27, 32
Silver, E. A., 76, 100
Simmons, W., 151, 173
Simon, H., 34, 56
Sinclair, J. M., 88, 101
Singer, J. A., 77, 101
Skinner, B. F., 198, 217
Smith, L. B., 2, 5, 6, 8, 9, 11, 14, 15, 16, 17, 18, 19, 20, 21, 22, 30, 31, 32, 65, 67, 73, 81, 101
Smith, S., 51, 53
Smolensky, P., 60, 74
Soja, N., 6, 22, 23, 24, 32
Spelke, E. S., 22, 23, 32, 65, 72, 74, 161, 171
Springer, K., 161, 173
Squire, L., 34, 57
St. John, M., 35, 57
Stanic, G. M. A., 158, 172
Stebbins, G. L., 221, 223, 227, 228, 231
Steffe, L. P., 93, 101
Steinberg, L., 165, 173
Stemberger, J., 35, 43, 57, 60, 74
Stenhouse, D., 177, 217
Sternberg, R. J., 162, 173
Stevenson, H. W., 104, 105, 107, 108, 109, 110, 128, 130, 138, 139, 141, 143, 144, 149, 151, 152, 154, 157, 168, 169, 173
Stigler, J. W., 104, 106, 117, 119, 120, 127, 130, 138, 139, 144, 149, 154, 157, 168, 173
Stob, M., 3, 31
Stone, G., 47, 54
Strauss, S., 47, 57

Styfco, S. J., 156, 173
Sue, S., 166, 173
Super, C. M., 158, 173
Swafford, J. O., 131, 149, 151, 171, 172

T

Taraban, R., 35, 36, 39, 44, 55, 60, 61, 62, 73, 211, 216
Taylor, M., 22, 32
Tees, R. C., 46, 57
Templin, M. C., 27, 32
Thagard, P. R., 223, 230
Tharp, R. G., 166, 173
Thelen, E., 26, 27, 31, 32
Thorpe, W. H., 184, 217
Thurstone, L. L., 222, 231
Tinbergen, N., 198, 217
Tobin, J., 108, 130
Tobin, K., 167, 173
Tocci, C. M., 151, 171
Tooby, J., 182, 183, 188, 189, 190, 214, 217
Touretzky, D., 35, 57
Trammell, R., 34, 57
Travers, K. J., 131, 149, 151, 171, 172
Travis, L., 47, 56
Trivers, R. L., 188, 217
Troisi, A., 183, 197, 216
Troyer, D., 81, 101
Tucker, M., 27, 32
Turnure, J. E., 222, 225, 231
Twain, M.,38, 57

U

Uchida, N., 6, 30

V

VanLehn, K., 79, 99, 101, 154, 170
Vergnaud, G., 77, 101
Vogel, I., 36, 56
von Glasersfeld, E., 93, 101
von Neumann, J., 34, 57
Vrba, E. S., 193, 215

W

Wachtel, G. F., 63, 67, 74
Waddington, C. H., 25, 26, 32
Wallace, A. R., 176, 217
Wasserman, S., 65, 72
Waxman, S. R., 2, 32, 67, 74
Weiner, J., 202, 217
Weinstein, S., 3, 31
Wellman, H. M., 161, 171, 173
Werker, J. F., 46, 57
Werner, H., 27, 32
West, M. J., 28, 32
Wexler, K., 47, 57
White, M. S., 197, 217
Williams, G. C., 201, 216
Williams, R., 37, 56
Wilson, E. O., 184, 217, 226, 230
Wilson, M. I., 183, 204, 214
Wittgenstein, L., 201, 202, 203, 204, 217, 222, 231
Wood, D., 90, 101
Woodward, A. L., 3, 4, 32, 63, 66, 74
Wu, D. Y., 108, 130

Y-Z

Yoshida, M., 119, 127, 130
Younger, B., 20, 32
Zahn-Waxler, C., 197, 216
Zigler, E., 156, 173
Zubin, D., 39, 55, 57

Subject Index

A

Attention, 20-25(fs)
  as an open process, 20
  children's, 21
  nonlinear, 21-22
  self-adjusting learning biases, 25
Artificial Intelligence (AI) 33, 34
  see also, Von Neumann serial computer

B

Biased learning
  constraints, 3-4
  developmental view, 4
  induction problems, 3
Big Mean Rules, MacWhinney's, 33-34
  explained, 33
  weaknesses, 33-34

C

Cognition
  among primitive peoples, 196
  covert quality of, 196
  generative capacity of processes, 196
Cognition and learning processes (CL)
  abandoning reductionism, 19
  and behavior, 180
  and comparative psychology, 183-187
  and development, 178-180
  and sociobiology, 188
  chimp research, limitations of, 193
  CL research and STE, integration problems, 222
  conceptual labels, limitations of, 192-194
  dangers in interpreting findings, 210
  evolution of, 182-184
  fragmented field of knowledge, 176, 193, 197, 107
  future links with STE, 198, 209
  heredity, role of, 177
  methodological reductionism, dangers in, 195
  research and human adaptation, 211
Comparative psychology, in evolutionary thought and proximate mechanisms, 185
  limitations, 185-186
Complexity theory (Chaos theory), 106
  coherence theory, 207-208
  concatenation, 208
  Meehl's "crud" factor, 207

Computational skills
additive composition, 77(f), 80(f)
buggy algorithms, 79, 154
equivalence classes of differences, 86
proratio reasoning, 78-79(f) (t)
street math vs. school math vs. math math, 76
see also, School math
Connectionist theory, in language acquisition
first language vs. second language, 62
learning musical notes, 60
subsymbolic learning vs. "top-down" learning, 62
see also, Hand-wiring, in connectionist models, Language acquisition

D

Development constrained, examples of, 28

E

Ethology, research methods
see, Synoptigram, Synoptiscope
Ethology and evolution
current thought, 187-191
Darwin's impact, 190
early approaches, 184-185
early limitations, 185
new research, 190-191
shortcomings in thinking, 189
Evolution
19th-century theorists, 176-177
cultural, future of, 227-228
Darwin's theory, 177, 198
development, role in, 178
endogenous change, 179
environment, effect on, 178
exogenous change, 178-179
Galapagos finches, synoptigram, 202(f)
heredity, effect on, 177
memory, synoptigram, 240(f)
population, future trends, 228
resource economics, effect on, 178
sex and reproduction, synoptigram, 203(f)
see also, Comparative psychology in evolutionary thought, Evolution, human, Synoptic approach to evolution, Synthetic Theory of Evolution
Evolution, human
culture, role of, 182
memes, 182
overview, 181-182
see also, Evolution, Evolution and development
Evolution and development
closed vs. open brain programs, 181
cognition and learning, as evolutionary adaptations, 179
development, as evolutionary adaptation, 179
genetic determinism, 183
organism/environmental interac tion, 182-183
see also, Cognition and learning processes, Evolution, Evolution, human, Synthetic theory of evolution
Evolutionary psychology
behavioral variation, 189
proposed and explained, 188
see also, Sociobiology
Exaptation, 193

F-G

Facultative traits, in evolution, 184
Gene-culture coevaluation, 226

H

Hand-wiring, in connectionist models
arguments against, 60
computer vs. human, 61
defined, 62

I

Infant intelligence, as species adaptation, 190
Interaction, term use and misuse, 227

L

Language acquisition
auditory-articulatory correspondence, 46-47
buffering and segmentation, 47
competition model, 49-52(f)
first words, 65
implicit vs. explicit processes, 70-71
output form vs. residual auditory form, 70-71
overgeneralization, 47
second language learning, 51-52
Language acquisition, models of
connectionist models, 36-40(fs)
connectionist models, constraints, 35-36
connectionist models, weaknesses, 41-43
lexicalist connectionism, 43-46(f)
symbol passing and self organization, 35
symbolic systems, 33
Learning constraints
incompatible with STE, 192
vs. evolved capacities, 192

M

Math, developmental roots
numbers, 94
operators, 95
Piaget's theory, differences, 91
protoquantities, 93
quantities, 93
representational structures, 93-95(t)
thinking levels, coherence across, 96-97(f)
thinking levels, coexistence of, 95-96
Math, learning from instruction
characteristics of lesson, 119
empirical studies, 120-128(fs)
goals and expectations, 120
on-line recognition measure and sense-making orientation, 124(f)
relevant prior knowledge, 120
Math, teaching in school
accelerated introduction of concepts, 83-84
as socialization, 99
discussion-based learning, 86, 88-91(f)
equations at an early age, 86
linking representations, 90-91, 92(f)
math practice, and cognitive competence, 98
math practice, and social competence, 98

principles of, 82-88(f)
reconnecting to street math, 82-83
revoicing, 88-90(f)
Math education, cross-cultural comparison
allocation of time, 142-144
changes in instructional methods, effects questioned, 160
conceptual information, 147(f), 154
contrasting attitudes and beliefs, 163-164
cultural patterns, effects questioned, 158
effort vs. ability of students, 107(f)
individual differences vs. similarity in students, 106-110
low motivation, indices of, 140
motivations compared, 138
performance differences, causal factors, 158
procedural information, 147, 154
research approaches characterized, 155-156
satisfaction levels, compared, 138-139(f)
standards of education, 140-141
student academic achievement compared, 134-137
student effort and ability, 141-142
student intelligence compared, 137-138(fs)
study sampling, 132-133
teachers and daily schedules, 144-145
teachers and lesson types, 145
teachers, as obstacles in American classrooms, 148
test materials, 133
testing instruments, 133-134
understanding how children learn, problems with, 103-104
whole class instruction, 145-147(fs)
why compare, 104
Math education, in Japan
class discrimination, effect of, 166
discourse, questions, 114-116(t) (f)
lesson structure, 110-114(t)
pace of instruction, 116-118
sense making, 118
teacher's role, 110(f), 116-117
test results vs. American, 105
whole class vs. individual, 109-110
Math education, in United States
ability grouping, 108
any job prospects, 164
changing goals, 105
cyclic nature of reform, 156
discourse, questions, 114-116(t)(f)
family factors, 164
individualization of instruction, 108, 109
lesson structure, 110-113(t)
National Assessment of Educational Progress (NAEP) scores, 152
pace of instruction, 116-118
poor teaching methods, 154-155
recommendations for instructional improvements, 155
reform, barriers to, 167-169
remedies attempted, 151
research cutbacks, 156
research, need for additional, 157-160
signs of progress, 152

small classes, emphasis on, 108(f)
social factors, minority, 166-167
social factors, whole society, 164-166
special education, 108
student employment, effect of, 165
students not reaching potential, 153-154
teacher's role, 110(f), 116-117
teaching methods and the learning disabled, 162-163
teaching methods, applications to other domains, 160-162
teaching methods, expanding to new populations, 162-163
tracking, 107
unique obstacles, 164
see also, Math, learning from instruction, Math education, in Japan

O-P

Obligative traits, in evolution, 184
Preadaptation, 193
Prepared learning, 192
Privileged learning, 192

Q

Quantitative literacy, 152-153
and poor adult performance, 152
and poor youth performance, 153

R

reductionism
see, Cognition and learning processes
Resource economics, 220

S

Scala naturae, 185-186, 193
School math
cognitive disconnect, 81
explained, 81
motivational disconnect, 82
vs. street math vs. math math, 76, 81
see also, Math, teaching in school, Street math
Shape bias, in word learning
basic level vs. superordinate level, 65-66
context, importance of, 67-69
developmental origins of, 6-10
early learning, 5-6
experimental models of learning, 10-13(f)
illustrative experiments, 5-6(f), 7-8(f), 8-9(f)
innate vs. learned, 66-67
Sociobiology
cognitive and learning processes, importance of, 188
focus on cognitive architecture of behavior, 189
shortcomings in evolutionary thinking, 189
see also, Evolutionary psychology
Spearman's "g", 222
Street math
explained, 75-76
studies of, 75-76
vs. school math vs. math math, 76
Super synthetic theory of evolution (SSTE), 220
Synoptic approach to evolution, 200-205
Feyerabend, Paul, 205

pluralistic methodology, 205
Synoptigram, 202-205(fs)
Synoptiscope, 199-207
applications, 206-207
as contextualist analysis, 224
as heuristic?, 223-224
proposed and explained, 199, 205
weaknesses, 224
Synthetic theory of evolution (STE)
conceptual problem with theory, 221-222
culture, 182
development, 179
explained, 175
future of, 198
genetic determinism, 183
methodological problem with theory, 221
vs. cognition and learning, 179-180, 192

T-V

Tinbergen, Niko
advice to ethologists, 198
Von Neumann serial computer, 34
flaws in computational architecture, 34
importance in AI systems, 34
vs. neural nets, 34
see also, Language acquisition, models of

W

Word learning
adaptive learning biases, 19(f)
attentional learning, 20-21
constraints, defined, 63
constraints theory, weaknesses, 67
content dependency, 18
count and mass nouns, 23-24(fs)
developmental instabilities, 18-19(f)
eyes, importance in naming, 14(f)
naming explosion, 8
nouns vs. adjectives, 22-23
regularity, importance in naming, 15(f)
spontaneous naming, 8-10
syntactic frame, 16-17(f)
see also, Attention
Word learning, biased
context and learning, 24-25
in children, 2
indeterminacy of translation, 2
Waddington's epigenetic landscape, 25-27
see also, Word learning

www.ingramcontent.com/pod-product-compliance
Ingram Content Group UK Ltd.
Pitfield, Milton Keynes, MK11 3LW, UK
UKHW011000180926
475701UK00004B/485
* 9 7 8 1 1 3 8 9 8 1 1 6 4 *